# The Soul of Athens

# The Soul of Athens

*Shakespeare's*
A Midsummer Night's Dream

Jan H. Blits

LEXINGTON BOOKS
*Lanham • Boulder • New York • Oxford*

LEXINGTON BOOKS

Published in the United States of America
by Lexington Books
A Member of the Rowman & Littlefield Publishing Group
4501 Forbes Boulevard, Suite 200, Lanham, Maryland 20706

PO Box 317
Oxford
OX2 9RU, UK

British Library Cataloguing in Publication Information Available

**Library of Congress Cataloging-in-Publication Data**

Blits, Jan H.
    The soul of athens : Shakespeare's A midsummer night's dream / Jan H.
    Blits.
        p. cm.
    Includes index.
    ISBN 0-7391-0653-8 (pbk. : alk. paper) — ISBN 0-7391-0652-X (cloth :
    alk. paper)
    1. Shakespeare, William, 1564–1616. Midsummer night's dream  2.
    Shakespeare, William, 1564–1616—Knowledge—Athens (Greece) 3.  Athens
    (Greece)—In Literature. 4. Comedy. I. Title.

    PR2827 .B65 2003
    822.3'3—dc21
                                                                    2003005437

Printed in the United States of America

♾ ™ The paper used in this publication meets the minimum requirements of
American National Standard for Information Sciences—Permanence of Paper for
Printed Library Materials, ANSI/NISO Z39.48-1992.

To the memory of S. M. E., who introduced me,
at a young age, to Shakespeare

# Contents

# Preface

The seriousness of tragedies seems self-evident. The seriousness of comedies is not so apparent. Not surprisingly, while the early development of tragedy is known, "comedy," Aristotle writes, "because it was not treated seriously from the beginning went unnoticed" (Aristotle, *Poetics*, 1449a38–b1). Indeed, according to Plutarch, "the Athenians considered the writing of comedy so undignified and vulgar a business that there was a law forbidding a member of the Areopagus to write comedies."[1] A serious book on a comedy thus runs at least two risks. It may seem to take the comedy more seriously than the comedy warrants or its author intends, making the study's author at least as laughable as his subject—and humorless to boot. And it may make unfunny the work whose humor it is discussing. Explained jokes are, after all, no longer funny jokes.

Despite the risks, this book, like my previous books on *Macbeth* and *Hamlet*, proceeds scene-by-scene, line-by-line, through *A Midsummer Night's Dream*, reaching its conclusions by closely examining Shakespeare's text—his plot, characters, language, allusions, puzzles, and other devices. Shakespeare's play, like any great work of art, is a whole. And, as with any great work of art, none of its parts can be properly understood in isolation from the whole, nor can the whole be understood apart from all of its parts. As each presupposes the other, the two must be seen together. The details must be carefully related to the major themes, while the themes must be grounded in and supported by the details. Fittingly enough, the needed double perspective in poetry and the relation of whole to parts—both of which the artisans fail to grasp—are explicit themes of *A Midsummer Night's Dream*.

I owe special thanks to Kathleen Blits, Harvey Flaumenhaft, Mera Flaumenhaft, and Linda Gottfredson for helping me think through many of the issues presented in the play, both in conversation and by reading all or part of earlier versions of the manuscript.

## Note

1. Plutarch, *Whether the Athenians Were More Famous in War or in Wisdom*, 348b.

~

# Introduction

A *Midsummer Night's Dream* portrays the foundation of Athens. Yet, Athens
itself and the political world as a whole seem largely absent from the play.
Notwithstanding Pericles' claim that the Athenians regard the man who
takes no part in public affairs, not as one who meddles in nothing, but as one
who is good for nothing,[1] no one in *A Midsummer Night's Dream* seems to
show the slightest interest in public affairs. All the characters are absorbed,
instead, in their private lives. Not only do Lysander and Demetrius flee
Athens for love without giving a moment's thought to their obligations to
their city. Even Theseus, Athens's ruler and legendary founder, confesses
that, "being over-full of self-affairs" (1.1.113),[2] he has been diverted from his
public duties by his private love.

   While Shakespeare traces the founding of the Roman republic to the estab-
lishment of the tribunate and the city's mixed regime,[3] he depicts the founding
of Athens without mentioning any Athenian political office or institution, or,
indeed, without even mentioning Theseus's unification of the villages of Attica, traditionally considered his founding act.[4] Shakespeare gives Theseus the
title of duke, a title which is neither Greek in origin nor definite in meaning.[5]
Apart from Theseus, the only Athenian who might be thought to have a public office or function is Philostrate. But although his Greek name means "lover
of battle," Philostrate's sole duty is to be Theseus's "manager of mirth" (5.1.35).
All the Athenian noblemen in the play—Theseus, Egeus, Lysander,
Demetrius, and Philostrate—have the names of famous, formidable warriors or
the name "lover of battle" itself. But all are either lovers, the angry father of a

lover, or the provider of private pleasures.⁶ Even Shakespeare's title points away from politics to a purely private realm.⁷

The difference between Shakespeare's presentations of the founding of Athens and of Rome reflects the essential difference between the two cities themselves. Republican Rome is a thoroughly political world. To the Romans, no good stands higher than political honor and glory. The private realm is thus largely suppressed or subordinated to the public realm, though the two realms remain in an irresolvable tension with each other. The city of citizen soldiers is also the city of godlike ambition on the one hand and filial piety on the other. Rome is thus the stuff of tragedy. As we see in *Coriolanus*, the hero who prides himself above all on his godlike self-sufficiency ultimately has no place in the city he saves or in the family he reveres.⁸ In Athens, by contrast, despite the city's imperial greatness and glory, politics is not the highest, let alone the only, human activity. The Athenians are lovers of beauty and of the mind. Athena is the goddess of wisdom as well as of war. The highest and most distinctive Athenian activities are thus private, not public.⁹ Where love and art enter Rome only late and only as forms of Greek corruption,¹⁰ the love of the beautiful and the triumph of art are of the essence of Athens at its peak.

Love and art, and their close connections, constitute the core of *A Midsummer Night's Dream*. In addition to Theseus's associating lovers, lunatics, and poets (5.1.4–17), there are young lovers who think of their own love as literature and of their beloveds as works of art (e.g., 1.1.132–55, 235–39; 2.1.230–31; 2.2.121), and whose lovesick entanglements in the woods Oberon and Puck regard as a play ("Shall we their fond pageant see?" [3.2.114; also 3.2.118–19, 353]). There are also artisans who, though literal-minded and unerotic themselves, prepare and perform a play about love (1.2.11–91; 3.1.8–98; 5.1.56–57, 108–338); and the king of the fairies who, among other things, imitates a poetic imitation of a lover (Corin), who is himself a poetic imitator ("Playing on pipes of corn, and versing love"), pursuing a poetic imitation of a beloved (Phillida) (2.1.65–68). Throughout the play, not only does love inspire poetry and poetry express love, but each also imitates the other. As "imitation" means both emulation and simulation,¹¹ love imitates poetry by beautifying its object, while poetry imitates love by representing it. Love and poetry—the passion and its speech—illustrate each other, the one by emulating poetry, the other by portraying love.

Shakespeare shows that poetry and love are linked largely by the imagination. As Theseus disparagingly observes, both poetry and love involve seeing or imagining what is absent (5.1.4–22). Art, particularly dramatic poetry, involves impersonation ("[T]ell them that I, Pyramus, am not Pyramus, but Bottom the weaver" [3.1.19–20]), while love involves idealization ("[T]he lover . . . / Sees Helen's beauty in a brow of Egypt" [5.1.10–11]). Both involve seeing something as something else. The double vision of imagination is especially clear in art, where, contrary to what the artisans fear, imitations announce their simultaneous reality and unreality.[12] They are what they are not and are not what they are: Bottom is and is not Pyramus. And we, as spectators, naturally distinguish between the image and the reality, the imitation and the imitated. The double vision that is obvious in drama is, furthermore, characteristic of human thinking as a whole. Human beings naturally see double:

> Methinks I see these things with parted eye,
> When everything seems double.

> (4.1.188–89)

We see what is before us with our body's eye and see what it means with our mind's eye. Able to separate the significance of a sight from the sight itself, we are able to see or to imagine what is absent and therefore to generalize ("The course of true love never did run smooth" [1.1.134]); to speak in metaphors ("When we have laugh'd to see the sails conceive / And grow big-bellied with the wanton wind" [2.1.128–29]); to utter aphorisms ("Love looks not with the eyes, but with the mind" [1.1.234]); to play on words ("And here I am, and wood within this wood" [2.1.192]); to substitute a part for the whole, a particular for the general ("Jack shall have Jill, / Nought shall go ill" [3.2.461–62]); to name one thing by another ("I woo'd thee with my sword" [1.1.16]), to make vows ("And then end life when I end loyalty" [2.2.62]); to pretend or suspect others of pretending ("Fie, fie, you counterfeit! You puppet you" [3.2.288]); to offer tokens ("thou hast . . . / . . . interchange'd love-tokens with my child" [1.1.28–29]); to put together lists ("And stol'n the impression of her fantasy / With bracelets . . . , rings, gauds, conceits, / Knacks, trifles, nosegays, sweetmeats" [1.1.32–34]); to idealize or beautify; and to make poems and plays. Dreams and literalness are both opposite our natural double vision. Instead of recognizing an image as an image, when we dream or are literal-minded, we take a likeness for the thing itself. Rather than distinguishing the image from the reality, we believe the reality of the image: "What a dream was here! / . . . . / Methought a serpent ate my heart away" (2.2.148). The distinction between the likeness and that of which it is a likeness vanishes. The natural doubleness of human thinking collapses into one.

Love, paradoxically, resembles both drama and dreams. Like art or drama, love beautifies or idealizes its object. It naturally projects an imaginary form upon what it sees:

> Things base and vile, holding no quantity,
> Love can transpose to form and dignity.

> (1.1.232–33)

But love also tends to deny that it embellishes. Owing precisely to the strength of its spell, it claims that it does not adorn or transform but simply sees:

> So is mine eye enthralled to thy shape;
> And thy fair virtue's force perforce doth move me
> On the first view to say, to swear, I love thee.

> (3.1.134–36)

A combination of idealization and literalness, love first beautifies its object but then takes its own idealization literally. Notwithstanding that the one depends upon the imagination while the other shows no trace of imagination at all, in the end the lover's view of his beloved at least partly matches the players' view of their art.

The close connections between art and love, reason and passion, are central not only to Athens, but to the premodern conception of the human soul. Since early modernity, philosophers have tended to separate and even to oppose reason and passion. Reason is often thought to be loveless calculation and passion to be irrational feeling, with nothing joining them from within to make man whole. According to the premodern view, however, the soul brings together reason and desire, thinking and life. As man is seen as a rational animal, both parts of his composite nature are thought to have a common source—namely, the soul. The soul is the cause of thinking and hence of human cognition in all of its forms, including art. The soul is also the cause of life and hence of animal motion of every kind, including desire. Awareness is of the essence of desire, while desire is of the essence of thought. The soul—"an union in partition" (3.2.210)—is naturally drawn both to beauty and to wisdom. Shakespeare's study of Athens is thus a study not only of a particular city, but of the doubleness of the human soul. Coupling the triumph of art and the love of the beautiful, Athens, we might say, is a Shakespearean metonymy for the soul's dual nature, putting forth the effect for the cause.

Nearly everything in A Midsummer Night's Dream has a dual character or is double. Theseus, who has won Hippolyta with his sword, promises to marry her in "another key" (1.1.18). Hermia's father demands her "consent" to his choice of a husband (1.1.40). Theseus tells Hermia that her eyes must look with her father's judgment (1.1.57). Hermia and Lysander meet in the woods where they met once before on another May Day morning and where Hermia and Helena used to meet when they were young girls (1.1.166–67, 214–17). Helena wishes to be Hermia "translated" (1.1.191). Bottom, who is "translated" or "trans-formed" (3.1.113–14; 4.1.63), becomes half man, half ass, while Hercules, who is himself half human, half divine, once fought a creature that was half man and half beast (5.1.44–47). Oberon and Titania quarrel over a "changeling" boy (2.1.120). Oberon's love juice duplicates Cupid's fiery arrow (2.1.155–72). Lysander and Demetrius are "two . . . rival enemies" (4.1.141). Puck mistakes the one for the other, turning a true love false rather than a false love true (3.2.88–91). The fairies and the actors are "shadows" (3.2.347; 5.1.208, 409). The artisans, who in addition to doubling or dividing themselves as actors, all practice trades which join things together. Hermia and Lysander are "two bos-oms and a single troth" (2.2.49), while Hermia and Helena were once

> Like to a double cherry, seeming parted,
> But yet an union in partition,
> Two lovely berries moulded on one stem.

> (3.2.209–11)

Lysander makes vows to both women, "truth kill[ing] truth" (3.2.129). Puck, who initially finds the greatest amusement in "two at once woo[ing] one" (3.2.118), finally welcomes that "[t]wo of both kinds makes up four" (3.2.438). The moon, whose own light is a reflection, is at once passionless and passion-ate,[13] new and full.[14] And whereas the play begins with lovers either sundered or threatened with separation, it ends with the "couples . . . eternally . . . knit" (4.1.180).

More particularly, doubles frequently take the form of imitation, both ex-plicitly and implicitly. Just as "imitation" has the twin meanings of emulation and simulation, acting and play acting, the artisans, combining both senses, emulate actors performing a drama—a drama which is itself based on a tra-ditional love story (Ovid, *Metamorphoses*, 4.55–166). And while it is an im-itation of an imitation, the artisans' play also mirrors a principal part of Shakespeare's own plot—the plight and the plan of Hermia and Lysander. The play and the play within the play reflect each other, the one as comedy, the other as tragedy. Indeed, while *Pyramus and Thisbe* is played twice, once in rehearsal and once in performance, it proves to be both tragedy and com-edy when performed. The actors' incompetence transforms the one into the other. The tragedy becomes a comic parody of itself (5.1.66–70). Besides Oberon imitating an imitation of an imitative lover, pursuing an imitation of a beloved (2.1.65–68), an Indian woman "imitate[s]" ships imitating her (2.1.128–34); Helena, reversing the myth, imitates Daphne chasing Apollo (2.1.230–31); Egeus accuses Lysander of "feigning love" (1.1.31); and Helena accuses the other young lovers of "counterfeit[ing] sad looks" to mock her (3.2.237). Moreover, the lovers are to think the events in the woods were a dream (3.2.370–71; 4.1.67–68). Bottom thinks they were and would have Quince write a ballad of the dream, which he would sing at the end of the artisans' play (4.1.203–17). Puck, who mimics the shape and sound of anything (e.g., 2.1.44–57; 3.1.101–6), regards the lovers' imbroglio as a play, in which he is playwright and stage manager as well as actor and audience. And, while Puck is both "an auditor" and "[a]n actor too" in the artisans' rehearsal (3.1.75–76), he is also both character and actor in the epilogue (5.1.409–24) and the onstage narrator of events which we have already seen for ourselves (3.2.6–34). Throughout Shakespeare's play, art imitates life imitating art. The image and the reality are not so much opposed as brought ambiguously together.

Shakespeare presents the relation of image and reality, art and life, with deliberate ambiguity throughout A Midsummer Night's Dream. Implicit in the title, the ambiguity is especially present in the woods and largely characterizes the fairies. As already suggested, Puck, in particular, makes no distinction between theater and life. He turns the lovers' actions into a stage play on the one hand and the artisans' rehearsal into action on the other. Further, while the fairies tend not merely to speak but to recite narratives, their narratives often prove to be fictitious even within the fiction of Shakespeare's play. In the longest fairy narrative, Titania, for example, describes vast floods and a great disorder in the seasons, which she says her quarrel with Oberon has caused (2.1.82–117). Yet, nothing else in the play suggests or even permits the floods or disorder. Indeed, not only does the rest of the plot plainly contradict what Titania says, her narrative contradicts itself. Titania's titanic narrative proves mythical in matter as well as in manner.

While the play's action contradicts Titania's narrative, more surprisingly, the words of another character, Philostrate, contradict her action, even though, paradoxically enough, we see the action for ourselves. Bottom is the only human to see any of the fairies. Yet, he cannot recall what he saw, except to suppose that it was a dream, as Oberon wished him to think (4.1.63–68). And when Bottom decides to have Quince write a ballad of the dream, he names the ballad for what he says the dream lacks: "[I]t shall be called 'Bottom's Dream,' because it hath no bottom" (4.1.214–15). The literal-minded

Bottom may speak truer than he knows. What he saw may indeed have no foundation, no bottom. It may be merely a dream. In a play in which there are many strange twists, none appears more curious—and more needless—than Philostrate's thrice-uttered insistence that he saw the entire *Pyramus and Thisbe* play rehearsed, even though we saw Puck interrupt it after just ten lines (3.1.73ff.): "[I]n all the play, / There is not one word apt, one player fitted"; "For Pyramus therein doth kill himself, / Which when I saw rehearsed"; "It is not for you; I have heard it over" (5.1.64–65, 67–68, 77). Philostrate's repeated claim, which seems wholly unnecessary to the plot in any ordinary sense, implicitly denies that the episode between Bottom and Titania ever actually took place. Despite what we have seen, the episode may have been as purely imaginary as Oberon courting Phillida in the guise of Corin, Titania's narrative of the upheaval in nature, and many other episodes and narratives involving the fairies.

Now, because love is closely joined to the imagination, for the young lovers it is primarily looking at rather than being with the beloved. Love is connected more to sight than to touch. Oberon's love juice is only a comic exaggeration of the intimate tie. Hermia, who wishes her father "look'd but with [her] eyes" and curses "choos[ing] love by another's eyes," traces falling in love with Lysander to "the time [she] did Lysander see" (1.1.57, 140, 204). And while Hermia says that she and Lysander must "starve [their] sight / From lovers' food" until they meet in the woods, Helena will tell Demetrius where they have gone so that she can "have his sight thither and back again" (1.1.222–23, 251). In fact, for Lysander and Demetrius, eyes are not only the organ of love's sight but its object as well: "To what, my love, shall I compare thine eyne?" (3.2.138). If love is the sight of beauty in the beloved, for the two young men it is the sight of beauty especially in the beloved's eyes: "as he errs, doting on Hermia's eyes" (1.1.230; also 1.1.183, 188; 2.2.90–92, 120–21; 3.2.450–57).

Theseus, by contrast, decries love's close connection to sight. To him, lovers, like lunatics, claim to see what exists merely in their imagination. "Lovers and madmen have such seething brains," he says with a telling pun,

> Such shaping fantasies, that apprehend
> More than cool reason ever comprehends.
>
> (5.1.4–6)

As fear leads the lunatic to see more devils than vast hell could hold, love leads the lover to see great beauty even in an ugly face: "[T]he lover, all as frantic, / Sees Helen's beauty in a brow of Egypt" (5.1.10–11). So, too, with the poet, whose "imagination bodies forth / The forms of things unknown," giving bodily shape to "airy nothing" (5.1.14–16). For Theseus, the heroic warrior, that which can be touched is real and that which exists in the imagination is illusory. Accordingly, just as the young lovers tend to confuse love and letters, so, too, does Theseus, but with the opposite import. For him, the resemblance among "[t]he lover, the lunatic, and the poet," who "[a]re of imagination all compact" (5.1.7–8), lowers the lover and the poet to the level of the lunatic. Ironically, the founder of the city renowned for the love of beauty and the highest accomplishments in art, disparages both love and art. In a most important way, Athens's founder does not fit into the city that he founds. If heroic ambition places Coriolanus outside of Rome, heroic taste places Theseus outside of Athens. The hero who is himself an "antique fable" (5.1.3), and who has emulated another antique fable (5.1.44–47), has no taste for such tales.

Shakespeare presents Theseus as a lover, but his presentation, like so much else, is ambiguous. Theseus begins and ends the play expressing his impatient desire. Whether four days or three hours, waiting for his desire's satisfaction is "the anguish of a torturing hour" (1.1.1–6; 5.1.32–37). That Theseus waits at all, however, is surprising. Theseus was notorious for ravishing and abandoning women, as Oberon, echoing Plutarch,[15] recounts:

> Didst not thou [Titania] lead him through the glimmering night,
> From Perigouna, whom he ravished;
> And make him with fair Aegles break his faith,
> With Ariadne and Antiopa?
>
> (2.1.77–80)

Yet, notwithstanding his incontinent and even brutal past, Shakespeare's Theseus is an eager bridegroom who, despite his torturing desire and having won his bride through conquest, awaits his wedding day. The play ends with the lawful fulfillment of his desire as well as that of the young lovers. Shakespeare's portrayal shows a change in Theseus from heroic virtue to moral virtue, from heroic immoderation to civic moderation in sexual desire.[16] Erotic desire is civilized or tamed in Theseus and, by implication, in Athens as well.

Love is not only moderated in Theseus's Athens. It is also liberated. Despite the general suppression of politics in the play, Theseus performs one political act. He overthrows the authority of fathers and hence of the ancestral gods ("To you your father should be as a god" [1.1.47]). And he does so in the name of freedom or "consent" in marriage (1.1.40, 82; cf. 1.1.25; 4.1.157–58).[17]

Whereas his ancient sources place Athens's founding in Theseus's unification of the demes of Attica, Shakespeare locates it in Theseus's liberating love from patriarchal authority. Love is linked to marriage on the one hand and freed from patriarchal authority on the other:

> Egeus, I will overbear your will;
> For in the temple, by and by, with us,
> These couples shall eternally be knit.

> (4.1.178–80)

The claims of erotic love defeat those of generation; the love of the beautiful replaces the love of one's own ("[W]hat is mine my love shall render him; / And she is mine" [1.1.96–97]). It surely is no accident that Shakespeare (changing only a diphthong for a long vowel) gives Hermia's father the name which Plutarch gives to Theseus's own father (Aegeus), for whose death Theseus was at least indirectly responsible.[18] Whereas *A Midsummer Night's Dream* begins with a father invoking "the ancient privilege of Athens" (1.1.41) to marry his daughter to the man he wishes, it ends with the father absent from his daughter's wedding. Once Theseus "overbear[s]" (4.1.178) his will, Egeus—the only father in *A Midsummer Night's Dream*[19]—says not another word and disappears from the play with hardly a trace. And just as no father is present during the wedding celebration, so, too, even the parents originally included in *Pyramus and Thisbe* (1.2.56–59) are missing from the play. Shakespeare seems to understand Theseus's overthrow of patriarchal authority as tantamount to his unification of the villages. The former points up the significance of the latter, for it turns Athens from a collection of sovereign fathers who, as in Rome, have absolute power over their family members to a union of families or households in which the city's power can reach family members.[20] The political counterpart of the union of reason and passion, love and art, Theseus's action democratizes Athens by replacing fathers with families as the fundamental component of the city.

Though the ancestral gods are deposed, they are not simply replaced by the Olympian gods or gods of the city. In contrast to Rome, where the Romans think of the gods in everything they do and thank them for everything they gain, the gods seem largely absent or irrelevant in Shakespeare's Athens.[21] Theseus does not speak of any god when overruling Egeus's will, and his only hint of the gods in connection with the marriages is his saying that the weddings will take place "in the temple" (4.1.179; also 4.1.196; 4.2.15). Theseus, in fact, never mentions a god in his own name after the opening scene, when he admonishes Hermia to think of her father as one and then threatens to punish her with a celibate life in the worship of Diana if she defies him (1.1.89). His only reference to an Olympian thus expressly associates piety and punishment, holiness and unhappiness (1.1.65–78). As one might expect, Cupid is mentioned far more frequently than any other god (1.1.169, 235; 2.1.157, 161, 165; 3.2.102, 440; 4.1.72). Venus comes second (1.1.171; 3.2.61, 107). The two gods most often mentioned correspond directly to an experience of the human soul. Still, not even these gods are mentioned by anyone after Theseus overturns Egeus's authority. Once Theseus acts, humans speak of Greek gods only in the titles or the dialogue of the artisans' poetry or in profane, mock oaths (5.1.48, 52, 176, 273–74, 307–8, 323–28). The gods, now existing chiefly in fiction, seem to be expelled from Athens by love and replaced by art. Accordingly, while the virgin Athena is never mentioned, the only religious practice in the play appears to be that of young lovers going into the woods early on a May morning "to observe / The rite of May" (4.1.131–32; also 1.1.167).[22] At least after Theseus deposes the ancestral gods, a holiday is not a holy day in Athens. Only fairies are now said to follow a god ("[W]e fairies, that do run / By the triple Hecate's team" [5.1.369–70]).

Shakespeare's depiction of Athens is also equivocal. The Athens we see in the play, although ostensibly Athens at its foundation, reflects Athens at its peak as well as its beginning—its flourishing as well as its founding. Unlike Shakespeare's Roman plays, which depict specific moments in Roman history, *A Midsummer Night's Dream* is entirely synchronic. The shifts from Theseus's brutal record of rape to his lawful marriage, and from his threat to enforce Athens's ancestral law to his overturning that law, are perhaps the most obvious examples of Shakespeare's bringing together different and even contradictory times. But they are not the only ones. Throughout the play, Shakespeare portrays—or parodies—the peak of Athens as present at its founding. Notwithstanding the artisans' efforts, tragedy, for example, did not appear in Athens until the time of Solon,[23] who lived a long time after Theseus and an even longer time after Cadmus, with whom Hippolyta says she once hunted in Crete (4.1.111–13). Nor is it much less anachronistic that the productive arts—weaving, carpentry, bellows-mending, tailoring, wood-joining, and tinkering—appear to be thriving. And while Athenian farmers (originally Athens's second largest class[24]) are never mentioned,[25] the artisans—"Hard-handed men that work in Athens here, / Which never labour'd in their minds till now" (5.1.72–73)—seek to trade their manual arts for arts of the mind.[26] In Shakespeare's presentation, Thesean Athens is already a city of artisans and of high art. Right from the start, leisure seems to have supplanted necessity. Exempt from the imperfections of the beginnings of civic life, leisure-rich Athens goes beyond the needs of the body and pursues the accomplishments of the mind.

Shakespeare, in fact, treats thematically Athens's transformation from barbaric to civilized, through a series of substitutions, immediately following the young lovers' night in the woods. Beginning with Theseus's appearance with his hunting party in the morning (4.1.102ff.), he compresses developments into a few key steps. First, Hippolyta, recounting the time when she, Hercules, and Cadmus bayed bears with Spartan hounds in Crete, replaces the hunt itself with the "musical . . . discord" (4.1.117) of the hounds' gallant cry, which she acclaims as unequaled. Theseus, then, replaces the Spartan hounds' discordant sound with what he describes as the melodious ("tuneable" [4.1.123]) sound of his own hounds. Although his hounds are "bred out of the Spartan kind" (4.1.118), he praises them as superior to Spartan hounds. Where Spartan hounds are renowned for their savagery and speed, Theseus says that his are slow and extols them for their musical sound. The slow and musical replace the fast and fierce. And although Hippolyta praised the Spartan hounds in Crete for their "mutual cry" (4.1.116), Theseus lauds his for the harmony of their individual sounds ("match'd in mouth like bells, / Each under each" [4.1.122–23]). The individual replaces the chorus, as the Athenian exceeds the Spartan. Furthermore, owing to an art—the art of breeding—descendants exceed their ancestors. In Athens, the new surpasses the old. The excellence of art replaces the authority of age. Crete and Sparta, the oldest and most venerable cities of Greece, whose fundamental principle, moreover, is reverence for age, and whose laws are traceable to Zeus and Apollo,[27] are surpassed by Athens, whose principle is freedom and art. Accordingly, Theseus, next, hearing that the young women whom they have come upon are Egeus's daughter and "old Nedar's Helena" (4.1.129), orders that the four sleepers be awakened by the sound of horns: the music of human art replaces the musical sound of beasts. Then, learning that Demetrius once again loves Helena, Theseus summarily deposes the ancient authority of Athenian fathers, allowing the lovers to marry as they choose (4.1.178–80). Finally, "the morning . . . now something worn" (4.1.181), Theseus expressly "sets aside" the "purpos'd hunting" (4.1.182), so that the three couples can return to Athens for "a feast in great solemnity" (4.1.184)—a wedding celebration that takes the form of a dramatic presentation. Act 4, scene 1— Theseus's central scene—links the ferocity of ancient heroism on the one end and the civility of Athenian intellectual and democratic life on the other. The barbaric passes into the civilized. Fittingly, Theseus's presence in the scene is followed immediately by the lovers' discussion of thinking's natural double vision (4.1.186–98).

Shakespeare's historical compression goes still further. Not only does Hippolyta tell of hunting with Cadmus and Hercules in Crete, both of whose ancestors include Olympian gods.[28] Theseus mentions a song describing the battle in which his "kinsman" Hercules fought and defeated the centaurs (5.1.44–47).[29] Within the lifetime of the Duke and Duchess of Athens, Athens faced half-human, half-bestial foes, which are now present only in song. Shakespeare similarly brings together the autochthonous beginning and the fratricidal culmination of Thebes. While Hippolyta recounts her hunting with Cadmus, who founded Thebes by sowing the teeth of a dragon sacred to Mars in the earth, from which sprang fully armed warriors who immediately began killing one another,[30] Theseus tells, again in the context of art, of his ending the Theban civil war in which Oedipus's sons slaughtered each other (5.1.48–51).[31] Between them, Hippolyta and Theseus span the five generations of Theban history from Cadmus to his fratricidal descendants.[32]

A *Midsummer Night's Dream* points also to the end as well as to the beginning of Athens. If Theseus, Egeus, and Hippolyta represent Athens's beginning, Lysander and Demetrius represent its end. Shakespeare gives the two young lovers the names of two principal enemies of Athens, both of whom defeated Athens by imitating it. The Spartan Lysander defeated Athens at sea in the last battle of the Peloponnesian War, while the Macedonian Demetrius, son of Antigonus, conquered Athens in the guise of saving it following Alexander's death, much as Athens had done with its allies a century and a half earlier in establishing its own empire.[33]

Despite all this, commentators often doubt that A *Midsummer Night's Dream* is really about Athens at all.[34] The characters, they say, have mixed origins or attributes. Theseus may have a classical hero's name; may refer to his kinsman Hercules; may have ravished Perigouna, Aegles, Ariadne, and Antiopa; may have ended the Thebean civil war; and may have defeated the Amazon queen, "[y]et to the Elizabethan audience he cannot have been far removed from a nobleman—perhaps a duke—of their own times." Hippolyta may be called a warrior queen and have hunted with Hercules and Cadmus in Crete, yet she lacks "many of the characteristics of a Queen of the Amazons." Oberon and Titania may be "strongly reminiscent of classical deities," yet Oberon "smacks of medieval romance," and he and Titania are "more than once associated with India." Even less Athenian, commentators say, are the fairies and the artisans. While Puck is "a well-known figure in [British] folk-lore," "Shakespeare makes no attempt to portray [the artisans] as Athenians." On the contrary, "the 'hard-handed' men of Athens are countrymen of England, through and through."[35]

It is certainly true that while no one should mistake Shakespeare's Romans for Englishmen in togas, it seems possible to take his Athenians for Englishmen in "Athenian garments" (2.1.264; 2.2.70; 3.2.349). But, far from detracting from Shakespeare's portrayal of what is essential to Athens, the universality of the characters seems to point it up. Unlike Rome, which is roofed and walled (*Coriolanus*, 1.1.217; 2.1.208; 3.1.203, 5.3.1), and whose eventual universality took the form of conquest and rule (*Julius Caesar*, 1.1.44, 122, 129, 133–34; 4.1.14), Athens is universal not only in its openness to foreign customs and ways,[36] but more fundamentally in its central concern for the love of the beautiful and the achievements of art. Though a particular city, Athens represents something that is universal or transpolitical in principle. Athens's particularity is thus ultimately self-canceling. Its universality effaces its particularity. More precisely, its particularity and universality remain together, but only with great ambiguity. Athens is always pointing away from itself to the human as such; yet, in so doing, it is always pointing back to itself as a particular city—the first universal city.

To the extent to which Athens stands for something universal, it ceases to be Athens. But to the extent to which it "stands for" rather than is something, it is at a still further remove from the particular. To bring out what is most distinctly Athenian, Shakespeare centers *A Midsummer Night's Dream* on questions concerning poetry and love, and hence on the ambiguous relation of image and reality. Just as that relation involves simultaneously being and not being something, however, so too does "standing for" something. Athens stands for something that essentially involves what it means to stand for something else. Shakespeare, unlike his artisans, certainly does not reduce his characters to stock characters. Lysander and Hermia are not Pyramus and Thisbe, let alone Corin and Phillida, Limander and Helen, or Shafalus and Procus. They are not merely representative figures, like Moonshine or Wall. They are full characters, though, as commentators often note, at least somewhat slightly drawn. Shakespeare's deliberately slight characterization of all the young lovers may serve to heighten the puzzle and absurdity of love's choices by making the lovers exchangeable.[37] But, along with the fairies themselves and the many discrepancies between what we see and what is described, the lovers' characterization also serves ironically to represent the nature of the city that they leave and to which they finally return. The curious combination of the characters' apparent universality on the one hand and incompleteness on the other reflects the genuine universality of Athens itself. As what it stands for, Athens is and is not what it is.

## Notes

1. Thucydides, *The Peloponnesian War*, 2.40.2.

2. All references are to the Arden edition, ed. Harold F. Brooks (1979; reprint, London: Routledge, 1994). I have occasionally revised quotations, based on the New Variorum Edition, ed. Horace Howard Furness Jr. (1895; New York: Dover Publications, 1963).

3. *Coriolanus*, 1.1.203–20, the Arden edition, ed. Philip Brockbank (London: Methuen, 1976).

4. Plutarch, *Theseus*, 24–25; also Thucydides, 2.15; Machiavelli, *The Prince*, 6, 16; *Discourses on Livy*, 1.1.2.

5. "Duke," from the Latin *dux*, means "commander," "guide," or "leader," particularly of an army. Dante, Boccaccio, and Chaucer also give Theseus that title: Dante, *Inferno*, 12.17; Boccaccio, *Teseida delle Nozze d'Emilia*, 1.13; Chaucer, *The Knight's Tale*, 860. In Plutarch, Theseus's title is king: Plutarch, *Theseus*, 24.2; *Comparison of Theseus and Romulus*, 2.1. Historically, Athens did not have a leader with the title of duke until nearly the end of the Crusades, in 1280 A.D.; see *The Cambridge Medieval History*, ed. J. M. Hussey, 8 vols. (Cambridge: Cambridge University Press, 1966), 4.1:409–10.

6. The words "act" and "deed" never appear in *A Midsummer Night's Dream*. "Action" occurs twice, once meaning a full rehearsal of the artisans' play (3.1.5) and once referring to Cobweb bringing Bottom a honey-bag (4.1.14). By contrast, "play" and its variants appear forty-two times (all but once in the theatrical sense) and "actor(s)" five times (always in the theatrical sense).

7. Richard H. Cox, "Shakespeare: Poetic Understanding and Comic Action (A Weaver's Dream)," in *The Artist and Political Vision*, ed. Benjamin R. Barber and Michael J. Gargas McGrath (New Brunswick, N.J.: Transaction Books, 1982), 167.

8. *Coriolanus*, 3.3.120–35; 5.3.22ff.

9. Whereas the words "city" and "country" occur forty times each in *Coriolanus* and always in a political sense, "city" is mentioned only twice in *A Midsummer Night's Dream* and only in a nonpolitical sense (1.2.96; 2.1.215) while "country" is mentioned just once and also in a nonpolitical sense (3.2.458). Likewise, in *Coriolanus*, apart from stage-headings and -directions, "the people" (etc.) appears seventy-seven times, "tribunes" and "consul" (etc.) thirty-five times each, "senate" (etc.) twenty-five times, "nobles" and "nobility" (the class) and "citizens" thirteen times each, "commons" (etc.) and "patricians" twelve times each, and "commonwealth" once. Besides the absence of an Athenian political title other than "Duke," in *A Midsummer Night's Dream* the commoners are never explicitly identified as a political class, but rather as practitioners of manual arts or trades (2.2.9–10; 4.1.9–10; 4.2.7–10; 5.1.72–73), and "civil" never means civic, but always calm or courteous (2.1.152; 3.2.147).

10. Horace, *Letters*, 2.1.156–57; Plutarch, *Marcellus*, 21; *Cato the Elder*, 22–23. While the people's specific trades are emphasized right at the beginning of *Julius Caesar*, none is ever specified in *Coriolanus*. In addition, in *Caesar* we see foreigners and poets, neither of which appear in *Coriolanus*; we also see that the republican leaders are inclined to Greek philosophical teachings and away from the gods of Rome. See, further, Jan H. Blits, *The End of the Ancient Republic* (Lanham, Md.: Rowman & Littlefield, 1993), 21–61.

11. Aristotle, *Poetics*, 1448b4–19.

12. Michael Davis, *Aristotle's Poetics* (Lanham, Md.: Rowman & Littlefield, 1992), 39.

13. For example, 1.1.3–6, 9–11, 30, 73, 89–90; 2.1.141, 156, 162; 4.1.72; 5.1.135–37.

14. For example, 1.1.2–11, 209–10; 1.2.95; 2.1.60; 2.2.85; 3.1.48–54; 3.2.177–82.

15. Plutarch, *Theseus*, 8.2–3; 19.1–3; 20.1–2; 26.1–2; 29.1–2, 31; *Comparison of Theseus and Romulus*, 6.1; see also Ovid, *Metamorphoses*, 8.174ff.; *The Heroides*, 10; Chaucer, *The Legend of Good Women*, 6.

16. Aristotle, *Nicomachean Ethics*, 1145a15–33.

17. Howard B. White, *Copp'd Hills Towards Heaven: Shakespeare and the Classical Polity* (The Hague: Martinus Nijhoff, 1970), 49; David Lowenthal, "The Portrait of Athens in *A Midsummer Night's Dream*," in *Shakespeare's Political Pageant: Essays in Literature and Politics*, ed. Joseph Alulis and Vickie Sullivan (Lanham, Md.: Rowman & Littlefield, 1996), 79.

18. Plutarch, *Theseus*, 22.1; *Comparison of Theseus and Romulus*, 5.2; Ovid, *Metamorphoses*, 7.404ff.; Apollodorus, *Library*, 3.16.1.

19. Helena's father "old Nedar" is mentioned twice (1.1.107; 4.1.129) but is never seen or heard from.

20. Thucydides, 2.15–16; Plutarch, *Theseus*, 24.1. See also Plato, *Laws*, 680b ff.; Aristotle, *Politics*, 1252b15–16, 23–24, 27–29; 1280b33–35. On the contrast between Roman and Greek fathers, see Dionysius of Halicarnassus, *Roman Antiquities*, 2.26–27.

21. Cf. Aristotle, *Politics*, 1328b11–12.

22. Lowenthal, 80.

23. Plutarch, *Solon*, 29.4–5.

24. Plutarch, *Theseus*, 25.1–2.

25. Titania and Puck mention "the ploughman," but only in contexts not specific to Athens (2.1.94; 5.1.359).

26. For the link between agriculture and the rise of civilized life, see Homer, *The Odyssey*, 9.118–35; in connection with Theseus, see Euripides, *The Suppliant Women*, 201–7; in regard to Athens, see Isocrates, *Panegyricus*, 28.

27. See, for example, Plato, *Laws*, 624a1–6, 634a1–2, 662c7, d7–e7; *Minos*, 318c1–3.

28. Hesiod, *The Shield of Heracles*, 1–56; Apollodorus, *Library*, 2.4.8, 3.1.1.

29. Diodorus Siculus, *Library* 4.12.1–6; Apollodorus, *Library*, 2.5.4; Virgil, *Aeneid*, 8.293–95.

30. Ovid, *Metamorphoses*, 3.1–130.

31. Aeschylus, *Seven against Thebes*; Sophocles, *Antigone*; Euripides, *The Suppliant Women*; Apollodorus, *Library*, 3.4–7; Plutarch, *Theseus*, 29.4–5; Statius, *Thebaid*, 112.464–809.

32. Sophocles, *Oedipus Tyrannus*, 266–68; Herodotus, *The Persian Wars*, 5.59.

33. On Lysander, see Plutarch, *Lysander*, 11; also Xenophon, *Hellenica*, 2.1.1–29; Diodorus Siculus, 13.104–6. On Demetrius, see Plutarch, *Demetrius*, 8.3–9.1, 10; 23.1–2; 30.2–4; 33–34, and cf. Thucydides, 1.97–99; Diodorus, 12.1–2; Plutarch, *Themistocles*, 4.4; 7.2–3: *Pericles*, 12.

34. Notable exceptions are White, 43–64; Cox, 165–92; Lowenthal, 77–88.

35. *A Midsummer Night's Dream*, ed. Stanley Wells, The New Penguin Shakespeare (London: Penguin Books, 1995), 17–20.

36. Plato, *The Republic*, 327a–28a, 354a; Xenophon, *The Athenian Constitution*, 2.7–8; Strabo, *Geography*, 10.3.18. Neither the Duke nor the Duchess of Athens—Theseus or Hippolyta—was born there (Plutarch, *Theseus*, 3–4; 13.1; 27.4).

37. See, for example, H. B. Charlton, *Shakespearian Comedy* (London: Methuen, 1949), 115; C. L. Barber, *Shakespeare's Festive Comedy* (Princeton, N.J.: Princeton University Press, 1959), 128; Jan Kott, *Shakespeare Our Contemporary* (Garden City, N.J.: Doubleday, 1964), 212; R. W. Dent, "Imagination in *A Midsummer Night's Dream*," *Shakespeare Quarterly* (1964), 116; Brooks, cx–cxi; *A Midsummer Night's Dream*, The New Folger Library Shakespeare, ed. Barbara A. Mowat and Paul Werstine, (New York: Washington Square Press, 1993), xii; Stuart M. Tave, *Lovers, Clowns, and Fairies: An Essay on Comedies* (Chicago: University of Chicago Press, 1993), 9.

# ACT ONE

~

## Act One, Scene One

### 1. The Martial and the Marital

Theseus, impatiently awaiting his wedding to Hippolyta, his captured Amazon queen, at first suggests that the four days of waiting will quickly pass:

> Now, fair Hippolyta, our nuptial hour
> Draws on apace; four happy days bring in
> Another moon.
>
> (1.1.1–3)

But Theseus no sooner says this than he abruptly reverses himself and—with an adversative "but" and a string of long vowels mimicking the time's sluggish pace[1]—plaintively exclaims how slow the time will be: "[B]ut, O, methinks, how slow / This old moon wanes!" (1.1.3–4). Theseus connects desire and time, as he will do again, with even greater impatience, as his wedding nears: "this long age of three hours" (5.1.33; also 5.1.39–41). Desire involves a gap between longing and fulfillment. We desire something that we lack, something that is absent in reality and present only in our perception or imagination. Desire thus orients us toward the future. As its object is absent, its aim is to turn the future into the present—the "not yet" into the "now."[2] Theseus thus describes not only his desire but its satisfaction in temporal terms. Just as his wait is to be "four . . . days," so his wedding is to be

17

his "nuptial hour." The "long age" of waiting—"the anguish of a torturing hour"—is to end at "bed-time" (5.1.33, 34, 37).

The arrival of that hour depends on the arrival of the new moon. "[T]his old moon" must pass and be replaced by "[a]nother moon." Theseus, speaking here as people ordinarily do, suggests that the beginning of a new month entails the replacement of one moon by another, distinct moon, rather than the completion of the cycle of the moon's phases. Another month means "another" moon—a "new moon" (1.1.83). Seeming to take the moon's appearance at face value, Theseus speaks as though there is no continuity behind or beyond the moon's ever-changing appearance. The appearance is the reality.

The moon is mentioned often in A Midsummer Night's Dream, as commentators frequently point out.[3] And much like the moon itself (and Theseus's patience in the first three lines), what is said about it changes completely from time to time. At times, the moon is closely associated with chastity, piety, and even perpetual celibacy. Oberon, for example, will speak of "the cold moon" and its "chaste beams" (2.1.156, 162), and Theseus will soon warn Hermia of a life devoted to "[c]hanting faint hymns to the cold fruitless moon" (1.1.73). At other times, however, the moon is just as closely associated with love, festivities, and the escape from patriarchal authority. Egeus, for example, will accuse Lysander of singing love songs at Hermia's window "by moonlight" (1.1.30), Titania will speak of "our moonlight revels" (2.1.141), Lysander and Hermia will flee Athens "when Phoebe doth behold / Her silver visage in the wat'ry glass" (1.1.209–10), and Pyramus and Thisbe will elope "[b]y moonlight" (5.1.136). If Diana is identified with the moon (1.1.89, 209; 4.1.72), Cupid is no less at home in its light (2.1.155–68). Here, the first time it is mentioned, the moon points directly to the tension between piety and love, the authority of age and the enjoyment of pleasure. Theseus likens the old moon to a stepmother or widow, who, while remaining alive, spends the money her stepson or son could otherwise enjoy:

> She lingers my desires,
> Like to a step-dame or dowager
> Long withering out a young man's revenue.

> (1.1.4–6)

Theseus will, later, overrule a father's authority in the name of a young daughter's love (4.1.178–80). Here, thinking of his own love, he attacks a father's wife in the name of a young son's desire. In his very first speech, Theseus impugns age in the name of youth, piety in the name of pleasure.

Theseus's first simile reminds us that his stepmother was Medea, who, according to ancient legend, sought not merely to wither out his revenue, but to kill him during a celebration in his honor, fearing that he rather than her own son would become Athens's king. In Shakespeare's happy play, erotic love, ending in marriage, replaces attempted murder, ending in banishment.[4] Comedy replaces tragedy; a young man's unsatisfied erotic desire replaces a stepmother's treacherous murder plot. While there are no living mothers in A Midsummer Night's Dream, Medea is the first of four stepmothers. As we shall see, she is paired with the last, Phaedra (5.1.387–400), whose presence Shakespeare also leaves only implicit.

Hippolyta stresses how fast, not how slow, the time will pass. Twice using the word "quickly," she answers Theseus's complaint, "Four days will quickly steep themselves in night; / Four nights will quickly dream away the time" (1.1.7–8). This is the play's first mention of dreams or dreaming. Hippolyta means the word in its usual and literal sense: dreams are the visions that appear in one's mind during sleep. As days will quickly pass into night, nights will quickly pass away in dreams. "And then the moon," Hippolyta continues,

> like to a silver bow
> New bent in heaven, shall behold the night
> Of our solemnities.
>
> (1.1.9–11)

"[A] silver bow" is a fitting simile for Hippolyta, the first of only two that she ever uses (cf. 5.1.122–23). The bow was once her weapon. As a simile is meant to explain the less well known by the better known, the bow is what she knows best (cf. 4.1.111–17). Yet, Hippolyta's simile seems askew in two respects. Both concern sight. First, as Hippolyta describes it, the moon does not light the night of their celebration, but rather "beholds" it. What itself is to be seen, or what illuminates other things, is, instead, what sees. Seer and seen are reversed. Hippolyta's "behold" is the first verb of seeing in the play. Second, contrary to what she plainly intends, there will be no moon on the night in question. Unlike a crescent or even a waning moon, a new moon is invisible; it gives no light. It neither can be seen nor does it illuminate other things. Both of Hippolyta's confusions will be repeated by others.

It is hard to judge how happy Hippolyta is at the prospect of marrying Theseus. Throughout the play, Theseus calls her "my love" (1.1.84, 122; 4.1.105; 5.1.46), "sweet" and "gentle sweet" (5.1.87, 99), "my Hippolyta" (1.1.122), and "fair Hippolyta" (1.1.1). But Hippolyta only once uses a term of endearment for him ("my Theseus" [5.1.1]) and only after they are married. That is also the only time she ever mentions him by name. Theseus will soon say that he "won [her] love" (1.1.17), but Hippolyta never says that she loves him or (apart from that single phrase) anything like it. While she speaks here entirely in a flat future tense, without any use of the optative,[5] her concluding phrase "our solemnities" is also her only reference to their wedding.

Not satisfied with Hippolyta's reassurance, Theseus looks for another way to hasten the lingering time. "Go, Philostrate," he orders;

> Stir up the Athenian youth to merriments;
> Awake the pert and nimble spirit of mirth;
> Turn melancholy forth to funerals;
> The pale companion is not for our pomp.
>
> (1.1.11–15)

The pleasures of youth are to remedy the delays of old age. Wakefulness and merriments, not sleep and dreams, will fill and shorten the time. Theseus speaks of his "pomp"—literally, his splendid procession. According to Shakespeare's sources, Theseus, after marrying in Scythia, returns with his bride to Athens from the Amazon war at the head of a triumphant procession. His "solemnities" ("solempntee") are not his wedding, but his military triumph.[6] Shakespeare, altering his sources' account, shifts Theseus's "solemnity" from his heroic triumph to his wedding celebration.[7] Putting off their wedding until after Theseus and Hippolyta have returned to Athens, he substitutes the marital for the martial. Theseus calls upon Philostrate. Philostrate is Theseus's only officer. Despite his name ("lover of battle"), Philostrate is Theseus's "usual manager of mirth" (5.1.35). His only duties are to arouse the Athenian youth to merriment and mirth, and, when the day arrives, to provide Theseus with some diversionary delight "[t]o ease the anguish of a torturing hour" between dinner and bed-time on his wedding night (5.1.37). The only battle he fights is against a lover's impatience.

Later, we will hear of Theseus's notorious exploits with women—his ravishing of Perigouna and his abandoning Aegles, Ariadne, and Antiopa (2.1.78–80).[8] Although able to brave pain and death, Theseus was unable to face pleasure and desire. But despite his eager desire, and despite having won Hippolyta through conquest, Theseus now awaits his wedding day. In place of rape, he settles for merriment and mirth. Distractions mitigate his desire. His sexual desire has become civilized or tamed. In sharp contrast to what we hear of Theseus's heroic, warrior past, brute force has now given way to love and law.

Theseus, turning again to Hippolyta, expressly but equivocally addresses the question of why she may be less than happy at the prospect of marrying him:

> Hippolyta, I woo'd thee with my sword,
> And won thy love doing thee injuries.
> But I will wed thee in another key,
> With pomp, with triumph, and with revelling.

(1.1.16–19)

Theseus, contrasting his wooing and his winning with his wedding, stresses the shift from heroic to civil life. He says that he "woo'd" Hippolyta with his valor and "won" her love vanquishing her, but he will marry her in a different key. What he means by "won" is unclear. The battle against the Amazons was the Athenians' first valorous deed against a foreign foe.[9] Hippolyta, who could be "woo'd" by heroic prowess, may have fallen in love with Theseus because of his victory over her, not in spite of it. He may have won the warrior queen's love precisely *by* doing her injuries, by displaying his heroic virtue. On the other hand, Theseus may be speaking hopefully, proleptically, or even euphemistically and apologetically. Hippolyta may be his war prize, whose love he hopes yet to win *despite* his having done her injuries. Whatever the case, Theseus, using a musical metaphor (and delivering some of his most poetic lines), promises to marry her "in another key." Merry festivities will replace martial victory. Theseus again uses "pomp" to refer to his wedding celebration rather than to his military triumph. In fact, in addition to "pomp," he (redundantly) uses the word "triumph," with its strong implications of the solemn procession of a victorious Roman general and his army,[10] to refer to what he explicitly declares will stand in contrast to a military victory. But Hippolyta, who never speaks with such passion or at such length as when recounting the time she bayed the bear with Hercules and Cadmus in Crete, will later say that the music that most fills her heart is the "cry"—the "sweet thunder"—of the Spartan hounds on that hunt (4.1.111–17). It is the music of the heroic hunt, not the music of revelling festivals. It is in the same, not a different, key from the one in which Theseus claims to have "won" Hippolyta's love. Paradoxically, if Theseus has, indeed, already won her love, Hippolyta may not welcome his promise to wed her in another key. She may still prefer the heroic to the civil. Hunting and war may still be this "warrior love['s]" (2.1.71) deepest passion.

## 2. Desire and Duty

Egeus enters with his daughter, Hermia, and her two suitors, Lysander and Demetrius. Egeus, the first to mention Theseus's name, describes him as "our renowned Duke" (1.1.20). Egeus's appreciative description points to the apparent absence of conflict in the play between Theseus and the Athenian nobles. According to Plutarch, while the "poor people and private men" were "ready to obey and follow [Theseus's] will" in unifying Attica, "the rich and such as had authority in every village [were] all against it." To mollify them, Theseus promised to share power with them, reserving to himself the command of the army and "the preservation of the laws."[11] It is in Theseus's capacity as preserver of the laws that Egeus has come to him.

In Shakespeare's sources (and *The Two Noble Kinsmen*), Theseus's "solemnities" are interrupted by something else. Theseus's triumphant entry into Athens after the Amazon war is interrupted by grieving Argive women who beseech him to make war on Creon, the Theban king. Following the civil war between Oedipus's sons, Creon, having taken the throne after each brother killed the other for the crown, refused to permit the corpses of his dead enemies, including the suppliants' husbands, to be buried. Theseus, always generous in granting help when implored, immediately took his army to Thebes, defeated and killed Creon, and allowed all the dead to be buried.[12] In *A Midsummer Night's Dream*, the fratricidal war in Thebes is replaced by a dispute about marriage in Athens. Where Thebes, at once autochthonic and fratricidal, epitomizes the love of one's own that ultimately destroys one's own, Theseus will moderate that love by overturning patriarchal authority in Athens.

Egeus says that he brings a "complaint / Against my child, my daughter Hermia" (1.1.22–23). His real anger and indignation seem directed not against her, however, but against Lysander, whom he accuses of having "bewitch'd the bosom of my child" (1.1.27). Egeus must proceed against his daughter rather than her lover, for he has authority as a father over her but not over him. His authority is limited to what is his own. Proceeding as in a courtroom, Egeus delivers a forensic speech, claiming the support of "the ancient privilege" and "law" of Athens (1.1.41, 44). His speech, using classical rhetoric to appeal, anachronistically, to pre-Thesean law,[13] contains the four principal parts of a classical forensic speech: (1) an introduction (*prooimiom*) (1.1.22–23), (2) a narration (*diêgêsis*) (1.1.24–27), (3) a proof (*pistis*) (1.1.28–38), and (4) a conclusion (*epilogos*) (1.1.38–45). An introduction aims to gain the judge's interest and good will; the narration briefly describes the facts of the case; the proof supplies the argument in support of the speaker's position; and the conclusion sums up, while exciting indignation or ill-will against the opponent.[14] After delivering his brief introduction ("Full of vexation come I, with complaint / Against my child, my daughter Hermia" [1.1.22–23]), Egeus calls forth Hermia's two suitors and states his position: "This man hath my consent to marry her. . . / . . . . / This hath bewitch'd the bosom of my child" (1.1.25–27). Then, turning to his proof, he enumerates "cunning" ways in which Lysander has "filch'd my daughter's heart" (1.1.36). The list—the first of many long lists in the play[15]—contains two general sorts of seductive tricks: "rhymes" (1.1.28) or words, including poems and songs, and material "love-tokens" (1.1.29), including "bracelets of [his] hair, rings, gauds, conceits, / Knacks, trifles, nosegays, [and] sweetmeats" (1.1.33–34). Egeus seems to consider the latter even more dangerous than the former, for while the poems and songs speak directly of love ("With faining voice verses of feigning love" [1.1.31]), the "love-tokens" are mere "messengers" (1.1.34). Standing at least at one remove from what they are meant or thought to express, they work entirely upon the imagination ("And stol'n the impression of her fantasy" [1.1.32]). They could be taken to mean anything the recipient wants them to. Egeus's proof is the first time that imagination is said to cause love or to steal someone's heart and the first time that something is said not to be what it seems. It is also the only time that moonlight ("Thou hast by moonlight at her window sung" [1.1.30]) is associated with causing the lunacy of love.[16]

Finishing his proof, Egeus charges Lysander:

> With cunning hast thou filch'd my daughter's heart,
> Turn'd her obedience (which is due to me)
> To stubborn harshness.
>
> (1.1.36–38)

Egeus's charge is twofold. Lysander has stolen Hermia's heart and, thereby, robbed Egeus of her obedience. The theft is double. In robbing the daughter of her heart, Lysander has robbed the father of his due. Indeed, in Egeus's eyes, the latter seems the more serious loss. As he repeatedly insists, Hermia is "my child" (1.1.23, 27, 29), "my daughter" (1.1.23, 36); and "[a]s she is mine, I may dispose of her" (1.1.42; also 1.1.96–97). Egeus may really believe that Lysander has deceived Hermia, but the charge of deceit seems largely beside the point. Whether or not Lysander has "feign[ed] love" (1.1.31), Egeus's complaint would be the same. What matters most to him is his authority as a father, something that Hermia has evidently never challenged before (cf. 1.1.204–5). And Lysander's true love would rob him of that as much as his false love. The question, for Egeus, concerns not love, but obedience or consent.

Beginning his conclusion, Egeus emphasizes Hermia's refusal to give her consent to his consent. She will not "consent" to marry the man who has her father's "[c]onsent" to marry her (1.1.25, 40). As Egeus's charge is twofold, so, too, is his underlying complaint. Consent is itself double. Literally, "feeling, judging, thinking together," it implies agreement or concurrence. In this case, it is doubly double, for it involves one person's consent to another's consent—a daughter's to a father's. In Egeus's view, a daughter must acquiesce to her father's choice. Her consent must echo his. It thus seems no accident that Egeus frequently speaks in doubles in presenting his case. But even as duplication—indeed redundancy—characterizes his speech, the basis of his complaint rests on his collapsing two into one: to Egeus, Hermia is simply "my child," "my daughter," "mine." She is simply his own. Egeus's doubleness of speech expresses his singleness of thought. Not surprisingly, "my" is, by far, his favorite word.[17]

Egeus, continuing his conclusion, appeals specifically to the ancient law of Athens. If Hermia will not now, before Theseus,

> Consent to marry with Demetrius,
> I beg the ancient privilege of Athens:
> As she is mine, I may dispose of her;
> Which shall be either to this gentleman,
> Or to her death, according to our law
> Immediately provided in that case.

> (1.1.40–45)

The old law of Athens allows a father to marry his daughter to whom he sees fit and, if she refuses, expressly allows him to put her to death. The fathers' "ancient privilege" crystallizes the state of affairs before Theseus's unification of Athens. Before then, every family in Attica occupied a village and lived in absolute independence, each worshiping its own ancestors, and each governed by a sovereign father.[18] With the unification, the preservation of the law passed to Theseus (or to the city), and Athens became—or began to become—a union of families under civic law. Although Theseus does not overthrow the patriarchal law until much later, here we can see the initial effect of his promising to look after "the preservation of the laws." On the one hand, Egeus appeals explicitly both to the "ancient privilege" and to the principle of privacy upon which it rests: "As she is mine, I may dispose of her." But, on the other hand, even as Egeus asserts his ancient privilege, he must now come to Theseus to petition ("beg" [1.1.41]) for it. His patriarchal power is no longer absolute. If his daughter must still give her consent to his consent, he nevertheless cannot punish her disobedience without Theseus's consent. The private is now at least partly subject to the public.

Theseus, who does not speak to Egeus again in this scene except to order him and Demetrius, in the same breath, to leave with him (1.1.114–16, 123–26), now turns to Hermia. As if explaining and supporting Egeus's premise, he admonishes her that "[t]o you your father should be as a god" (1.1.47). Hermia should regard her father as a god, not only because he has "compos'd [her] beauties" (1.1.48), but, even more so, as Theseus stresses with an amplifying "yea" (1.1.48), because he has given her her life or her being. To her, he says, her father should be one to whom she is

> but as a form in wax,
> By him imprinted, and within his power
> To leave the figure, or disfigure it.
>
> (1.1.49–51)

Begetting implies absolute power over one's offspring and absolute obedience to one's begetter. A father may either sustain or destroy the life he has formed. But having stated Egeus's premise in the starkest possible terms, Theseus suddenly, if implicitly, abandons it: "Demetrius is a worthy gentleman" (1.1.52). The issue is no longer Egeus's arbitrary power, but rather his good judgment. It is an issue that permits a reply.

Hermia speaks for the first time. Unlike her father, she uses no formal term of address (cf. 1.1.20, 24, 26, 38, 39) and, responding only to the question of worthiness, goes so far as to challenge Theseus: "So is Lysander" (1.1.53). Hermia's curt retort forces Theseus to backtrack and partly reassert a father's authority. Just as he told Hermia how to think of her father, Theseus now tells her how to think of her suitors. Distinguishing between someone "[i]n himself" and someone as he must be "held" to be, he acknowledges that Lysander is a worthy gentleman "[i]n himself":

> But in this kind, wanting your father's voice,
> The other must be held the worthier.
>
> (1.1.53–55)

In regard to marriage at least, a father's approval adds to a young man's worthiness and makes all the difference. The father's choice must be "held" to be the worthier, regardless of the inherent worthiness of the man himself. Hermia, again terse, and again refraining from a formal term of address, half shifts the issue: "I would my father look'd but with my eyes" (1.1.56). Introducing the theme of judgment and sight, Hermia places the former in the latter. To see as she sees would mean to judge as she judges. Theseus, however, reasserting a father's authority, corrects her: "Rather your eyes must with his judgement look" (1.1.57). Rather than Egeus looking with her eyes, Hermia's eyes must look with his judgment. She must see as he judges or wishes.

Perhaps surprisingly, Hermia asks what is the worst that may happen to her if she refuses to marry Demetrius. She apologizes for asking the question, saying she does not know what "power" (1.1.59) makes her so bold or how her pleading her thoughts in such noble company may affect her "modesty" (1.1.60). But she makes no apology for doubting that Egeus has the "power" (1.1.50) which he has just claimed and which Theseus seems to have confirmed. Twice now using a formal term of address (1.1.58, 62), she apologizes to Theseus for her boldness in submitting her thoughts to him, but not for doubting her father's authority. Hermia's modesty, which will keep her and Lysander apart when they are sleeping in the woods (2.2.55–59), does not keep her from publicly challenging her father's authority as a father.

Theseus alters what Egeus said. He adds a second possible punishment: "Either to die the death, or to abjure / For ever the society of men" (1.1.65–66). But although having softened her possible punishment, Theseus immediately warns Hermia against its severity. Hermia, he says, should question her own "desires" (1.1.67), consult her "youth" (1.1.68), examine well her passions ("blood" [1.1.68]), whether she could "endure" (1.1.70) the barren, cloistered life of perpetual celibacy, "[c]hanting faint hymns to the cold fruitless moon" (1.1.73). The pious devotion to Diana is punishment for the impious disobedience to her father. Theseus grants that some people might consider such a life blessed and voluntarily choose it. "Thrice blessed they that master so their blood / To undergo such maiden pilgrimage" (1.1.74–75). But blessedness is not the same as earthly happiness:

> But earthlier happy is the rose distill'd
> Than that which, withering on the virgin thorn,
> Grows, lives, and dies in single blessedness.

> (1.1.76–78)

Life's sweetness is Theseus's standard. As a single life resembles a rose that withers unplucked, a married life is like a rose that is plucked so its fragrance can be distilled in perfume. Marriage—or love—sweetens human life. Nowhere in the speech does Theseus suggest that Hermia should think of her father as a god. On the contrary, he urges her to consult her own desires in deciding what to do. Her youth and passions, not her father's age and au-

2

1

1

2

1

1

thority, are to determine whether or not she will "yield to [her] father's choice" (1.1.69). Desire is to decide whether or not she will do her daughterly duty.

Hermia does not hesitate. Evidently taking for granted that her punishment would be enforced celibacy rather than death, and closely echoing Theseus's words, she decides on the spot not to marry a man she does not want:

> So will I grow, so live, so die, my lord,
> Ere I will yield my virgin patent up
> Unto his lordship whose unwished yoke
> My soul consents not to give sovereignty.
>
> (1.1.79–82)

Hermia, describing marriage as a form of rule, speaks of a husband as a "lordship" possessing "sovereignty" (1.1.81, 82). The husband rules the wife. But, contrary to the authority that her father claims, a husband's sovereignty over his wife is—or at least, in Hermia's view, ought to be—voluntary. It is based not on authority or command but on choice or "consent" (1.1.82). The sovereignty of the husband rests on the wishes of the wife. It is hierarchical rule based on a democratic foundation. In keeping with her political description of marriage, Hermia uses a strictly legal term for the right or privilege to her virginity: "my virgin patent" (1.1.80). As legitimate sovereignty rests on consent, Hermia has title to the possession and disposal of her virginity. No where else does Hermia ever talk in political or legal terms.

Theseus, urging Hermia to take time to reconsider, gives her until the next new moon—his wedding day—to decide. Like Hermia, he emphasizes marriage's legal aspect ("the sealing day" [1.1.84]). And, despite what ancient legends describe as his own "marriages,"[19] he characterizes marriage as an "everlasting bond of fellowship" (1.1.85). Much as Hermia suggested, it is a permanent union between equals. But Theseus also reaffirms what lies ahead for Hermia. On the next new moon, she is either to die for disobedience to her father's will, to wed Demetrius, as her father wishes, or "on Diana's alter" to vow ("protest") forever ("For aye") "austerity and single life" (1.1.89–90). This is the play's first explicit mention of an Olympian deity and Theseus's only one in his own name (cf. 5.1.48, 52). While Theseus mentions the word "god" only when reminding Hermia that she should consider her father as one (1.1.47), he mentions an Olympian when threatening her with punishment. In his mouth, the divine appears as tyrannical authority, on the one hand, and, along with death, its punishment, on the other.

The two young men, who have been silent so far, now speak. Demetrius asks Hermia to relent and Lysander to yield his flawed "title" to Demetrius's "certain right" (1.1.92, 93). Basing his claim on Egeus's, he claims the support of law. Lysander, in contrast, speaks of love. On the tacit but taunting premise that one should marry someone who loves one, Lysander suggests that he should marry Hermia (who loves him) and Demetrius should marry Egeus (who loves him): "You have her father's love, Demetrius: / Let me have Hermia's; do you marry him" (1.1.93–94).

Egeus does not deny that he loves Demetrius. Accepting half of Lysander's premise while scolding him for impudence, he argues that one should give one's own to one's love. Hermia is his, he says, and he will give her to whom he loves:

> Scornful Lysander, true, he hath my love;
> And what is mine my love shall render him;
> And she is mine, and all my right of her
> I do estate unto Demetrius.

> (1.1.95–98)

If, earlier, Egeus employed forensic rhetoric to accuse Lysander, now he answers him in the form of a full syllogism, while emphasizing legal terminology. Reason and law, in his view, go together:

Major premise: My love shall give what is mine;
Minor Premise: She is mine;
Conclusion: Therefore, I will give all my right of her to Demetrius, whom I love.

As before, Egeus stresses what is his, referring to himself or to what is his six times in four lines (and repeating his earlier "she is mine" [cf. 1.1.42]). He twice mentions his love, but neither here nor anywhere else does he ever mention his love for Hermia.

Lysander, in defense, pleads for himself, answering both Demetrius's and Egeus's claims of "right." Like Egeus, he offers a list, as he will often do.[20] He is, he says, as well born and as wealthy as Demetrius; his love for Hermia is greater; his standing is esteemed as highly if not more so than Demetrius's; "[a]nd, which is more than all these boasts can be, / I am belov'd of beauteous Hermia" (1.1.103–4). Given all his merit and especially Hermia's love for him, why then, Lysander asks rhetorically, should he not "prosecute [his] right?" (1.1.105; cf. 1.1.92, 97). Where Egeus's right rests on ancient law and fatherhood, and Demetrius's rests on Egeus's patriarchal right and his love for Demetrius, Lysander's alone rests on Hermia's love. Rather than being in conflict with right, reciprocal love is a basis for right. Unlike a father's consent (about which Lysander says nothing), it is necessary to a marital right.

The rivals' claims mirror what Plutarch tells of their namesakes. Describing how the Macedonian Demetrius came to be so great, Plutarch says:

> Demetrius's power and greatness fell unto him by inheritance from his father, Antigonus, who became the greatest and mightiest prince of all the successors of Alexander and had won the most part of Asia before Demetrius came of full age. (Plutarch, *Comparison of Demetrius with Mark Antony*, 1.1; North, 6:89)[21]

Lysander, by contrast, who "grew to be [a] great m[a]n, rising of [himself] through [his] own virtue," tried to overthrow the exclusive claim of two families to the Spartan throne,

> which [attempt] . . . , according to nature, doubtless seemed very just: that he which was the best among good men should be chosen king of that city, which was the chief over all Greece, not for her nobility, but for her virtue only. (Plutarch, *Comparison of Sulla with Lysander*, 1; 2.1; North, 3:320, 321)[22]

The one owes his greatness to birth; the other, to virtue or nature.

Lysander, having set forth his own claims, states why Demetrius is unworthy of Hermia. With a solemn declaration that he will prove it to his face ("I'll avouch it to his head"), he charges that Demetrius wooed Helena ("Made love to Nedar's daughter, Helena"), became engaged to her ("And won her soul"), and then left her to pursue Hermia;

> and she, sweet lady, dotes,
> Devoutly dotes, dotes in idolatry,
> Upon this spotted and inconstant man.

> (1.1.106–10)

Demetrius's treacherous treatment of Helena proves that he is unworthy of Hermia. Egeus had accused Lysander of bewitching Hermia with false love. Lysander turns the charge back against the man Egeus favors for his daughter. Not only was Demetrius's love false or fickle, its effect, as Lysander underscores with lavish alliteration and repetition, was to make Helena madly love the wrong man. What happened to "Nedar's daughter" is just what a father should fear. Interestingly, Demetrius does not attempt to defend himself.

While Demetrius remains silent, Theseus confirms Lysander's charge, adding that he had intended to speak to Demetrius about the matter, but, distracted by his own personal affairs, forgot to: "[B]eing over-full of self-affairs / My mind did lose it" (1.1.113). Theseus's private affairs got the better of his public duties. His own love overcame his governance or guidance of young Athenian lovers. As though correcting his lapse, Theseus calls upon both Demetrius and Egeus to go with him: "I have some private schooling for you both" (1.1.116). Where originally he had intended to teach the young man, now he wants to teach the father, too. We cannot be sure, however, what Theseus's lesson is, or whether he ever delivers it. After this speech, we never hear another word about it. Nor will Demetrius or Egeus seem changed the next time either appears. Demetrius will still be pursuing Hermia and despising Helena (2.1.188ff.), and Egeus will still be demanding his due as a father under Athenian law (4.1.153–58).

Turning to Hermia, Theseus admonishes her to prepare herself to fit her thoughts of love ("fancies" [1.1.118]) to her father's will or else face death or a vow of single life, as prescribed by "the law of Athens" (1.1.119). Theseus adds parenthetically that "by no means we may extenuate" the law (1.1.120). Although he uses the royal pronoun here for the first time, he suggests that his power is limited, that he must fully preserve and not in any way mitigate the ancient privilege of Athenian fathers. He appears determined to live up to his promise to the nobles to see to "the preservation of the laws."

Hippolyta, who has not said a word since replying to Theseus's opening speech, has listened to Hermia's travail in silence. Theseus, evidently thinking that she is downcast, asks, "[W]hat cheer, my love?" (1.1.122), and she does not answer. We might wonder whether Hippolyta's look and silence do not reflect the disquiet of a matriarchal Amazon queen viewing Athenian patriarchy. Be that as it may, while the Athenian patriarchy is the mirror image of the Amazon matriarchy, Theseus, having already defeated the latter abroad, will soon defeat the former at home.

Theseus, concluding his speech, calls again upon Egeus and Demetrius to go with him. This time, he gives two reasons. Besides repeating that he wants to confer with them about something that closely "concerns yourselves" (1.1.126), he says that he needs their service "in some business" pertaining to his own wedding (1.1.124). As with his lesson, we never again hear of their service. Egeus will be with Theseus and Hippolyta when they go hunting on the morning of their wedding day (4.1.102ff.). One might think that Egeus has something to do with arranging the hunt, but that is never said and, apart from his being with them, there is no reason to suppose that he does. A trace of Demetrius's service seems even slighter. Neither Theseus nor anyone else will ever mention the service again, and while Demetrius soon flees Athens, Theseus never comments on his absence.

Egeus, speaking for Demetrius and himself, answers, "With duty and desire we follow you" (1.1.127). Egeus's obeisant response is unwittingly ironic. The tension between duty and desire is just what marks his conflict with Hermia. Hermia can follow him only in duty and not with desire. Indeed, the gravamen of Egeus's complaint against her is that a daughter's desire should submit to her duty.

## 3. Love and Letters

Theseus's order to Egeus and Demetrius to go with him has the effect of leaving Hermia and Lysander alone to plan their escape. If the effect is inadvertent (as seems most likely), the order is the first in a long series of errors and happenstance that will determine the action of the play. The exchange between Lysander and Hermia is one of only two occasions when they are alone on stage. Where the first shows Lysander and Hermia planning to flee Athens, the second (2.2.34–64) will show them losing their way in the woods. The latter occasion marks not only the farthest from Athens the lovers ever manage to reach, it is also a crucial turning point in the play. Lysander's confusion, combined with Hermia's modesty, leads directly to Puck's mistaken application of his love juice to Lysander's eyes (2.2.65–82) and to all that follows from that error.

Lysander begins the exchange by asking Hermia a question about herself. His concern is not surprising, but his question surely is: "How now, my love? Why is your cheek so pale?/ How chance the roses there do fade so fast?" (1.1.128–29). Lysander seems oblivious to the obvious. How does it happen ("chance"), he asks, that Hermia's cheeks have lost their color? Lysander evidently sees no connection between Hermia's miserable choice and her ashen face. Hermia, for her part, latches onto Lysander's metaphor and answers entirely figuratively: "Belike for want of rain, of which I could well / Beteem them from the tempest of my eyes" (1.1.130–31). As the double meaning of "[b]elike" suggests, Hermia's answer is both likely and a likeness. While what it suggests is most likely, it is an image or resemblance of the truth.

Lysander, who can understand Hermia's metaphorical answer but not read her face, corroborates her suggestion by telling what he has learned from books and tales:

> Ay me! For aught that I could ever read,
> Could ever hear by tale or history,
> The course of true love never did run smooth.
>
> (1.1.132–34)

Lysander interprets his own experience in the light of what he has learned from literature. He understands the particular by his knowledge of the general, and he has gained that knowledge from books, stories, and legends. Letters illuminate his love. Lysander seems to regard both his knowledge and its source as absolute or comprehensive: "For aught . . . could ever read, / Could ever hear . . . / . . . never did. . . ." The general rule admits of no exceptions. Having thus stated his immutable conclusion and its literary source, Lysander goes on to survey specific instances of true love's invariably unhappy course. His examples, like his conclusion, seem meant to be exhaustive. His list includes every instance: "But either it was . . . / Or else . . . / Or . . ." (1.1.135–41). Lysander first gives three examples, which Hermia echoes, in alternate lines, repeating both him and herself. To his examples of birth or rank ("blood" [1.1.135]), age ("years" [1.1.137]), and someone else's choice ("the choice of friends" [1.1.139]), she responds, "[T]oo high to be enthrall'd to low" (1.1.136), "too old to be engag'd to young" (1.1.138), and "to choose love by another's eyes" (1.1.140). The last, of course, includes her own situation. Lysander does not, however, say, or allow Hermia to think, that they would be happy if they were permitted to choose love with their own eyes. Proceeding to his fourth example, he declares, instead, in mock tragic style, that even if the lovers chose each other, their love was always cut short by war, death, or sickness:

> Or, if there were a sympathy in choice,
> War, death, sickness lay siege to it,
> Making it momentany as a sound,
> Swift as a shadow, short as any dream,
> Brief as the lightning in the collied night,
> That, in a spleen, unfolds both heaven and earth,
> And, ere a man hath power to say 'Behold!',
> The jaws of darkness do devour it up:
> So quick bright things come to confusion.
>
> (1.1.141–49)

Lysander describes the brevity of love as though he were a poet. Mimicking what he has read, he personifies both the lightning and the night, making the one angry and the other voracious, casts a human spectator as a witness to the act, suggests that the violent event is cosmic in scope, and employs aphorism, alliteration, wordplay, the historical present, and a series of repetitious, hyperbolic comparisons. Inspired by love, the speech, describing the weakness of the bright in the world of darkness, is, by far, Lysander's most poetic passage.

Hermia accepts Lysander's general conclusion in its absolute form: "If then true lovers have ever been cross'd, / It stands as an edict in destiny" (1.1.150–51). And, speaking much like a Stoic, she concludes that patient resignation is called for: "Then let us teach our trial patience" (1.1.152). It is "a customary cross" (1.1.153) for lovers to be "cross'd" (1.1.150), "[a]s due to love," she says, "as thoughts and dreams and sighs, / Wishes and tears, poor fancy's followers" (1.1.154–55). Being thwarted is an inevitable part of love.

Lysander's reply appears puzzling. Lysander first says that Hermia has persuaded him, that her moral lesson is a good principle to adopt ("A good persuasion" [1.1.156]). And then, as though following her thought through, he seems about to state its further consequence: "Therefore hear me, Hermia" (1.1.156). But, contrary both to her lesson and to his own previous conclusion, he proposes a plan of escape. Hermia and he can escape love's invariable rule by escaping Athens. Lysander has an aunt, he says, a dowager of great wealth, who "hath no child" (1.1.158) and who regards him "as her only son" (1.1.160). She lives seven leagues from Athens.

> There, gentle Hermia, may I marry thee,
> And to that place the sharp Athenian law
> Cannot pursue us.
>
> (1.1.161–63)

Lysander reverses Theseus's opening complaint. Where Theseus compared time's delay of his desire's satisfaction to a stepmother or a dowager consuming a young man's inheritance (1.1.4–6), Lysander says that a rich dowager will come to the aid of his desires by treating or adopting him as a son. A literal, beneficent stepmother and dowager replaces a figurative, hostile stepmother or dowager in matters concerning a young man's love. Lysander's dowager aunt is the second stepmother in the play. Because the woman's house lies beyond Athens, Lysander explains, Athens's severe patriarchal law cannot reach Hermia and him there. Lysander does not name "that place."

But its laws not only allow lovers to marry whom they wish, they also permit a childless widow to choose someone "as her . . . son" and a young man to choose someone as his mother. Choice replaces birth throughout the family. Within the family or household ("house" [1.1.159]), the love of one's own is subdued, as choice defeats both the authority of fathers and its basis, the power of natural generation.[23]

Lysander's unnamed aunt's unnamed "place" seems to be what amounts to an imaginary city—a city in thought or in speech, in which the course of true love does indeed run smooth. Not unlike a philosophical utopia, it may be a place where the only ruling compulsion is the inner compulsion of reason and love of the beautiful. Even the material conditions of a good life are fully and easily provided there. The lovers, however, never reach it. They lose their way in the woods, without explanation and without the interference of the fairies (2.2.35), soon after setting out. And, never mentioning either the city or the aunt again, they return to Athens to be married. Surpassing Athens, from which it is initially said to be a refuge, the imaginary city seems to be, literally, a utopia: a "good place" (*eu topia*) which is at the same time "no place" (*ou topia*) and is therefore unreachable.[24] It seems to be the model by which Shakespeare intends Athens to be measured or considered, though, precisely because it abstracts from natural generation, an impossible model for any real city to imitate fully.

Lysander's sudden change of mind signifies something else as well. Lysander sees love as literature. Later, he will go so far as to describe his beloved's eyes as "[l]ove's stories, written in love's richest book" (2.2.121). Lysander, characteristically, fails to distinguish between life and letters, love and art. Yet, art can imitate life only by distorting it. In poetry or drama, actions have a unity or wholeness. A play, as Aristotle says of tragedy, is "an imitation of an action that is complete and whole," and "[a] whole is what has a beginning, middle, and end" (Aristotle, *Poetics*, 1450b25–27). Unlike an action in ordinary life, a dramatic action, having an absolute beginning and end, is separated from the continuum of which it is a part. And as for its beginning and end, so too for its middle. Nothing that occurs in the drama is extraneous. Whatever happens has significance and is determined by the end or the plot. The action must end as it does, and every incident is necessary in its place. A play thus involves a double perspective—from within and from without. From the perspective of the characters, actions and choices must have the uncertainty and contingency that actions and choices in life contain. The characters must see their ends as brought about by their actions, not their actions as fated by their ends. From the perspective of the drama itself or its spectators, however, events that seem contingent to the characters must seem inevitable. The audience must see the action both from within the drama, as the characters do, and from outside or above the drama, as only the playwright and audience can. The action must seem, at once, contingent and necessary, incomplete and complete.[25] Hence, Lysander's apparent self-contradiction. Observing his life as literature, he sees it from the outside and finds his fate inevitable—"an edict in destiny," as Hermia says (1.1.151). But observing it from within as a character, he thinks that he can escape his fate and the law, and change or effect the outcome. He sees his own life with the double vision of a drama.

Lysander, echoing Egeus's accusation against him, thus tells Hermia that if she loves him she should "steal forth" (1.1.164; cf. 1.1.32, 36) her father's house tomorrow night, and he will wait for her in the woods a league outside Athens, "[w]here," he adds parenthetically, "I did meet thee once with Helena / To do observance to a morn of May" (1.1.166–67). It is not clear why the lovers wait until tomorrow night (1.1.164, 178, 209, 223, 247). Nothing in the plot requires the delay. On the other hand, it seems entirely fitting that the lovers return to where they once celebrated May Day—a day, or rather a night, associated with love and liberty, when young people go to the woods after midnight to celebrate the return of spring and often fall in love (cf. 4.1.131ff.). Xenophon mentions that the Athenians celebrated more festivals than any other Greek city (Xenophon, *Constitution of the Athenians*, 3.2). The only festival in *A Midsummer Night's Dream* is May Day.

Although Lysander does not ask for an oath, Hermia, without the slightest hesitation, swears to him that she will meet him tomorrow at the designated place. Her oath, while displaying a curious knowledge of Roman poetry,[26] playfully points to the weakness of such oaths. The oath has two major parts. In the first, Hermia swears by the powers of the divinities of love:

> [B]y Cupid's strongest bow,
> By his best arrow with the golden head,
> By the simplicity of Venus' doves,
> By that which knitteth souls and prospers loves.

(1.1.169–72)

In the second part, she swears by the betrayal of love and its tragic effect:

> And by that fire which burn'd the Carthage queen
> When the false Trojan under sail was seen;
> By all the vows that ever men have broke
> (In numbers more than ever women spoke).

(1.1.173–76)

Where in the first part she swears by what she vows, in the second she swears by what she vows against. Even the first part of her oath, however, is ambiguous. Cupid's arrow with a golden head may cause love, unlike his arrow with a leaden head, which repels it. But when shooting it, Cupid is often driven by jealousy and spite, "fierce and cruel wrath" (Ovid, *Metamorphoses*, 1.452; Golding, 1.546), as when he caused Apollo to pursue Daphane (cf. 2.1.231). War and love may not be far apart (cf. 1.1.16–17; 3.2.336–38, 401–30; 4.1.141–44). Cupid may not be as innocent or harmless as Venus's doves (cf. 2.1.155–66; 3.2.439–41). Hermia's oath is the first mention of either Cupid or Venus. And, underscoring the intimacy that she vows, it also contains the play's first rhyme, which, suitably enough, ends with "loves."

## 4. The Art of Love

Helena enters. Hermia greets her as "fair Helena" (1.1.180), a courteous form of address which Theseus has already used several times when speaking to Hermia and Hippolyta (1.1.1, 46, 67, 117), which he will use again in speaking to Hippolyta and all the four lovers (4.1.108, 176), and which Bottom will suggest that Lion use to address the women in the *Pyramus and Thisbe* audience (3.1.38). Helena, however, immediately takes the word in the strong sense and painfully rejects it as a description of herself: "Call you me fair? That fair again unsay! / Demetrius loves your fair: O happy fair!" (1.1.181–82). Helena may be, literally, fair—that is, blond with light complexion as well as tall (3.2.291–98, 343). And she may be thought throughout Athens "as fair as [Hermia]" (1.1.227). But what matters to her is only what Demetrius finds fair. Not being beautiful, but being thought beautiful by the one you love, brings happiness ("happy fair"). Helena thus goes on to describe Hermia's beauty as she imagines Demetrius sees it. She emphasizes Hermia's eyes and voice—how her eyes, like "lode-stars" (1.1.183), guide Demetrius's motion by fixing his looks, and how her voice is more melodious to him than a lark to a shepherd's ear in early spring. Helena says that she wishes that "favour" were as "catching" as "[s]ickness" (1.1.186). Soon, we will see that in an important sense it is for Demetrius. Helena says that if favor were "catching," she would "catch" "fair Hermia['s]" before she leaves (1.1.187). Her ear would "catch" Hermia's voice, her eye her eye, and her tongue would "catch" the music of her tongue (1.1.189). Helena, using the word "catch" four times in four lines with four different meanings,[27] wishes not only to acquire whatever Demetrius loves in Hermia, but to become Hermia herself: "Were the world mine, Demetrius being bated, / The rest I'd give to be to you translated" (1.1.190–91). Somehow, Helena thinks, she could become someone else and still be herself. It would be she and not Hermia whom Demetrius would love.

When Helena arrived, Hermia asked her where she was going, but Helena did not say. Instead, she railed at her use of the word "fair." Now it becomes clear that she has come to learn Hermia's "art" of love: "O, teach me how you look, and with what art / You sway the motion of Demetrius's heart" (1.1.192–93). Like Egeus (1.1.28–35), Helena believes that those who are loved are loved because they practice an art. Whether or not attractiveness ("favour") is catching, it can be taught or learned.

Hermia denies not only that she uses an art, but that she encourages Demetrius's love in any way. On the contrary, she does nothing but rebuff him. Where Helena spoke of Hermia's attractive look and voice, Hermia says that she gives Demetrius nothing but frowns, curses, and hate; yet the more she does so, the more he loves her:

> Herm.:  I frown upon him; yet he loves me still.
> Hel.:   O that your frowns would teach my smiles such skill!
> Herm.:  I give him curses; yet he gives me love.
> Hel.:   O that my prayers could such affection move!
> Herm.:  The more I hate, the more he follows me.
> Hel.:   The more I love, the more he hateth me.

> (1.1.194–99)

Shakespeare never explicitly tells why Demetrius, who wooed and won Helena's heart, has jilted her and is now pursing Hermia. We must wonder, though, whether the reason is not precisely because of, rather than despite, the opposite ways the two women are treating him, contrary to what both women, but especially Helena, seem to think. Commentators frequently say that Shakespeare hardly distinguishes the characters of Demetrius and Lysander or those of Helena and Hermia, the former differing only in name, the latter in height, hair color, and skin complexion as well as name. The lack of distinctive characterization, they say, making the lovers exchangeable, serves to heighten the puzzle (and the absurdity) of love's choices.[28] While, for reasons already mentioned, Shakespeare does not distinguish them as vividly as some characters in other plays, he nonetheless distinguishes the lovers in more than merely incidental ways. For Demetrius, who, unlike Lysander, is quick to suspect others of challenging his manhood and to accuse or deride others for their presumed lack of manhood (cf. 3.2.404–27; 5.1.232, 240–41), love proves to be more a matter of conquest than of affection. Thus, the one woman's disdain provokes his love, while the other's love provokes his disdain. It surely is no accident that Oberon will not remove the love juice from Demetrius's eyes. Without it, Demetrius can love only what he lacks or someone else has. Paradoxically, Hermia's denial inadvertently answers Helena's question. The "art" with which Hermia sways Demetrius's heart are her frowns and curses, not smiles and sweet words. This is a lesson Helena will never learn. Accordingly, concluding the stichomythia, Hermia first denies her responsibility: "His folly, Helena, is no fault of mine"; and Helena, attempting to correct her, answers as before: "None but your beauty; would that fault were mine" (1.1.200–1). Helena recognizes no cause of love other than what someone sees as beautiful.

To ease Helena's pain ("Take comfort" [1.1.202]) and perhaps her charge of guilt, Hermia discloses or promises[29] that she and Lysander will flee Athens: "[Demetrius] no more shall see my face; / Lysander and myself will fly this place" (1.1.202–3). If Hermia's beauty is her fault, removing herself from Demetrius's sight is her exoneration. But having reassured Helena, Hermia immediately disabuses her of her principal assumption—that mutual love makes for happiness:

> Before the time I did Lysander see,
> Seem'd Athens as a paradise to me.
> O then what graces in my love do dwell,
> That he hath turn'd a heaven into a hell!
>
> (1.1.204–7)

The beauty ("graces") that inspires love can also bring misery, when the law prevents the lovers from marrying. Mutual love does not guarantee happiness. On the contrary, it can turn a heaven into a hell. At the same time, Hermia implicitly adopts Helena's understanding of the fault. Hermia denied that she was responsible for Demetrius's love: "His folly . . . is no fault of mine" (1.1.200). But Helena seemed to think that fault has nothing to do with intention. Hermia's beauty is her "fault" (1.1.201), regardless of her wish or intention. Hermia, now, follows Helena's lead. "[H]e" who has turned Athens into a hell is not the jealous Demetrius or the angry Egeus, but her beloved Lysander. His graces, despite his wishes for her happiness, have caused her torture.

Lysander, taking Helena into their confidence, reveals that Hermia and he will elope tomorrow night, when Phoebe beholds her face in the sea and decks the grass with dew. That is "[a] time," he says, "that lovers' flights still conceal" (1.1.212). Phoebe (Diana)—the same goddess whom the perpetual virgin Hermia would have had to worship—will provide a dark cover for their flight. Phoebe will see her own reflection, but no one will see the fleeing lovers. Lysander, again, seems to set his own action by a universal rule which he has learned from literature: he and Hermia will flee at a time which always ("still") conceals lovers' flights. It is hard to see how he reconciles this universal rule with his earlier one.

Lysander tells when he and Hermia will flee. Hermia tells where. The place where Lysander once met Hermia and Helena to celebrate May Day, and where Hermia and Lysander will now meet, turns out also to be the place where the two women used to go to disclose their secret thoughts to each other (1.1.166–67, 214–17). The three locations are the same. Hermia also makes clear something that Lysander only implied: "And thence from Athens turn away our eyes, / To seek new friends, and stranger companies" (1.1.218–19). Running away from Athens means starting a new life—a life in the company of strangers. Perhaps not surprisingly, Hermia speaks only of friends, not of family. She speaks only of what one might choose and ignores what birth imposes. As with Lysander's description of that city, choice replaces birth. We might note here that the absence of mothers in *A Midsummer Night's Dream* does double duty. On the one hand, it emphasizes the Athenian patriarchy by simplifying the family. But, on the other, by eliminating generation it suggests the contrary principle of choice rather than birth of children. It thus points at once to Hermia's father and Lysander's aunt, and to the fundamental tension between them.

Hermia, bidding her farewell, asks Helena to "pray" for Lysander and herself, but she only wishes Helena "good luck" in winning back Demetrius (1.1.220–21). The two situations are converse: one woman keeps her friends and city, but must gain the man she loves; the other has the man she loves, but must find new friends in a new city. Hermia may think that her situation is more difficult than Helena's and needs a prayer, not just a wish for good luck. Once Hermia is gone, Demetrius's love is likely to return to Helena. But starting a new life amid strangers may require a prayer.

Hermia turns to Lysander and addresses her final words to him. Only time now keeps the lovers apart. "Keep word, Lysander; we must starve our sight / From lovers' food, till morrow deep midnight" (1.1.222–23). Hermia does not ask Lysander for an oath, but simply to keep his word. His vow needs the support only of his love. Hermia also speaks of the sight of each other as "lovers' food." Whether she means that the sight feeds the desire or the satisfaction or both, even at "deep midnight" in the woods, only three days before a new moon, the sight will feed the lovers. This is the only kind of food the lovers ever mention for themselves (2.2.137; 4.1.172–73; cf. 5.1.31).

As Hermia leaves, Lysander promises to keep his word: "I will, my Hermia" (1.1.224). As Hermia's parting words, mentioning both a vow and lovers' food, suggest, vows contain a doubleness similar to that of desire.

When a vow is made, its fulfillment is absent in reality and present only in thought or speech. As with desire, its fulfillment is not yet at hand. About to depart himself, Lysander offers Helena a wish: "As you on him, Demetrius dote on you" (1.1.225). From his effusive and indignant description earlier ("[A]nd she, sweet lady, dotes, / Devoutly dotes, dotes in idolatry" [1.1.108–9]), one might have thought that Lysander found fault with causing someone to dote. But it seems that he objects only to its one-sidedness in Helena's case, not to its excess. If the doting is reciprocal, it is to be wished for.

### 5. The Eye and the Mind
Helena, alone on stage, reflects on love. Rejecting out of hand Hermia's talk of hell, she begins by comparing Hermia's happiness to her own: "How happy some o'er other some can be!" (1.1.226). To Helena, Hermia is happy because she has Lysander's love. Mutual love assures happiness. Beauty, however, does not assure love: "Through Athens I am thought as fair as she. / But what of that? Demetrius thinks not so" (1.1.227–28). All that matters is what one's beloved thinks. Helena thus takes no comfort from the fact that Demetrius is ignorant—that he is even the only Athenian ignorant— of her beauty:

> He will not know what all but he do know;
> And as he errs, doting on Hermia's eyes,
> So I, admiring his qualities.
>
> (1.1.229–31)

Helena is concerned not with knowledge, but with love, not with truth, but with desire. Indeed, as Demetrius "errs," so does Helena herself. He errs in not loving her; she, in loving him. So little do love and knowledge go together that Helena can recognize her error in loving Demetrius and yet love him nonetheless. Even the truth about love's indifference to the truth does not diminish her love.

Helena proceeds to explain why love subverts judgment. Denying a connection between love and merit, she describes love's power to transform its object: "Things base and vile, holding no quantity, / Love can transpose to form and dignity" (1.1.232–33). Love transforms its object, creating excellent and worthy qualities even out of their extreme opposites. And it does so, precisely if perversely, because of its dependence on the mind. Love may lie in the eyes, as both Hermia and Helena have already stressed (1.1.56, 140, 183, 188, 192, 202, 204, 222–23), but it does not look with the eyes: "Love looks not with the eyes, but with the mind" (1.1.234). Normally, when we perceive something, imagination connects our sensation and thought. Through our imagination, our senses inform our intellect. Imagination presents to the mind an interpreted sensation, which allows for thought.[30] Love, however, alters the steps. Instead of our senses informing our mind through our imagination, our imagination informs our mind without the benefit of our senses. Rather than proceeding from outside in, imagination proceeds from inside out, projecting an imaginary form upon what the eyes see. It becomes projective rather than receptive. It sees what it wishes to see or imagines. Indeed, imagination is so strong for lovers and so nearly indistinguishable from thought itself that Helena can refer to it as "the mind." Under the spell of love or "fancy" (1.1.118, 155; 2.1.164; 3.2.96; 4.1.162; 5.1.25), all the mental powers collapse into "fantasy" (1.1.32; 2.1.258; 5.1.5).[31] "Love's mind" (1.1.236), Helena seems to say, is all love and imagination, and no real perception or thought.

Helena, having separated imagination and reason in a lover's mind, tacitly reunites them in an artist's mind. Describing the traditional iconography of Cupid in painting and poetry, she discusses art's apt imagery of love's unreason and folly:

> And therefore is wing'd Cupid painted blind;
> Nor hath Love's mind of any judgment taste:
> Wings, and no eyes, figure unheedy haste.
> And therefore is Love said to be a child,
> Because in choice he is so oft beguil'd.
>
> (1.1.235–39)

The artists' Cupid is an image of "Love's mind." If love transforms what the lover sees, art gives form to ("figure[s]") what the artist sees. Painted Cupid's wings and blindness fitly represent love's heedless haste, while poetry's depiction of Love as a child, likewise, represents love's easy gullibility.[32] Love and art work differently. Love takes literally what the lover imagines; art, on the other hand, presents an image, which is meant to be seen as an image. The artist's Cupid is a product of the artist's imagination imagining the lover's imagination. Unlike what it represents, the work imitates rather than creates its object. It is, as Helena emphasizes with two introductory "[a]nd therefore's" and one explicit "[b]ecause," a reasoned depiction of love's unreason.

Like Lysander and Hermia (but unlike Demetrius), Helena thinks of art and letters when she thinks of love. What she has learned from paintings and poetry explains her own situation to her. In contrast to Hermia, in particular, however, Helena places great importance on oaths of love. While Hermia mentions oaths only playfully, Helena seems no less surprised than disappointed that a lover's vow does not secure his unwavering love. Thus, having discussed what is said about love, Helena describes what Love himself says: "As waggish boys, in game, themselves forswear, / So the boy Love is perjur'd everywhere" (1.1.240–41). It is not, as before, that Love, a child, is innocently deceived, but rather that Love himself mischievously deceives. Love is no more serious about keeping his oaths than are prankish boys making oaths in jest. No vow of love is to be trusted. Helena cites Demetrius's oaths to support her conclusion:

> For, ere Demetrius look'd on Hermia's eyne,
> He hail'd down oaths that he was only mine;
> And when this hail some heat from Hermia felt,
> So he dissolv'd and show'rs of oaths did melt.

(1.1.242–45)

Helena, once again, describes Demetrius as falling in love with Hermia's eyes. Although it looks not with the eyes, love nevertheless looks at the eyes. It sees beauty in the eyes of its beloved. Helena leaves unclear what she means by saying that Demetrius "some heat from Hermia felt." Earlier, she suggested that Hermia won his heart by using some art (1.1.192–93), but nothing in the play indicates that Hermia deliberately encouraged Demetrius. It seems, rather, that Hermia and Lysander's falling in love with each other was all the encouragement Demetrius needed. The heat he felt was not Hermia's love, but his own rivalry or jealousy. Helena seems to expect—or to have expected—vows not only to be meant when made, but necessarily to remain true forever: they bind the future absolutely, not conditionally. Notwithstanding her view that love defeats reason, she seems to have expected that words govern as well as express love. It is perhaps a sign of her stress on, or trust in, words that Helena is the most loquacious of the four young lovers[33] and the one who, often using verbs of speech, most often emphasizes what has been said.[34]

Nothing better illustrates love's folly than Helena's plan of action. Helena will tell Demetrius of Hermia's flight, and then he will pursue Hermia into the woods. If Helena gains his thanks for telling him, "it is a dear expense" (1.1.249). By "dear," she seems to mean both costly to Demetrius and loved by herself. Demetrius hates her so much that he would begrudge her thanks, but she loves him so much that any thanks from him would be cherished. And even if she gets no thanks, she will be rewarded: "But herein I mean to enrich my pain, / To have his sight thither and back again" (1.1.250–51). Just the sight of Demetrius even as he chases after Hermia will be her reward. Helena is greatly hurt by Demetrius's breaking his vows, and she will later accuse Hermia of forgetting their "sisters' vows" (3.2.199). But Helena herself gives no thought at all to her betraying her friendship with Hermia for the sake of a glimpse of her beloved (cf. 3.2.307–10).

## Act One, Scene Two

The artisans have gathered to plan the casting and production of a play to celebrate Theseus's wedding. They are the only members of the Athenian common people mentioned in A Midsummer Night's Dream. Notwithstanding Athens's fame as the first democracy, the only commoners in the play seem to have nothing to do with politics. Instead, they are doubly connected to art. They are artisans who attempt to perform a drama. Shakespeare, moreover, identifies the artisans doubly by their proper crafts: "Nick Bottom, the weaver" (1.216), "Francis Flute, the bellows-mender" (1.2.38), "Tom Snout, the tinker" (1.2.57), and so on. Their names—all metonymical—derive from their crafts. "Bottom" refers to the wooden reel or spool on which a weaver's thread is wound. "Flute" refers to the church organs which a bellows-mender might repair. "Snout," meaning a nozzle or a spout, suggests the kettles that a tinker mends. "Quince" is a wooden wedge used by carpenters. "Snug" describes the close-fit a joiner tries to produce. And "Starveling" refers to the proverbial leanness of tailors ("Nine tailors make a man"[35]). Only the last is not a technical term of art.[36] Yet, although all are identified by their crafts, none of the artisans ever says a word about his trade, and all of them hope to make their fortunes by acting (4.2.17–24). The artisans may be "[h]ard-handed men that work in Athens . . . / Wh[o] never labour'd in their minds till now" (5.1.72–73), but in Theseus's Athens even the "handicraft m[e]n" think they can become "made men" (4.2.9, 18) by using their minds rather than their hands.

Quince begins the scene and, with a single exception when everyone speaks (1.2.73), delivers every other speech. He is at once producer, director, actor, and author. Bottom, however, tries to take over right away, making corrections and giving directions. When Quince initially asks whether all the company is there, Bottom, with his characteristic officiousness and aplomb, immediately corrects him: "You were best to call them generally, man by man, according to the scrip" (1.2.2–3). Bottom's confident correction contains a pair of errors. It confuses "generally" with "severally" and "scrip" with "script." The first error mistakes the collective for its individual members, the whole for the parts. The second mistakes a piece of paper for a piece of writing, the paper for what is written on it. The errors seem especially suitable for a man who will seek to play every major role in the play and who will have difficulty distinguishing between something and its theatrical imitation. The confusions between whole and part, and something real and its imitation, will characterize the artisans as a group.

Quince does as told, adding that the men to be called enjoy a distinction. They constitute all the men ("every man's name" [1.2.4]) who are "thought fit through all Athens" (1.2.5) to perform before Theseus and Hippolyta on their wedding night. The artisans are greatly given to exaggerating their reputations and abilities as dramatic performers. They will rehearse in the woods for fear that if they met in the city others would steal their material (1.2.94–97). Later, they will be certain that they would win high incomes and high praise if they performed before the Duke (4.2.17–24). And they will consider their play as chosen ("[O]ur play is preferred" [4.2.36–37]) when not only it has not yet been chosen, but Philostrate strongly urges Theseus to reject it because of its ineptness ("There is not one word apt, one player fitted. . . . It is not for you" [5.1.65, 77; also 3.1.4–5]). The artisans' self-knowledge seldom equals their self-assurance.

Bottom tries, again, to direct Quince. Quince, he says, should state what the play deals with, then read the actors' names, "and so grow to a point" (1.2.9–10). By the last, Bottom seems to mean "come to a conclusion." It is unclear, however, what conclusion or sort of conclusion he might mean. In the immediate sequel, Quince, with Bottom's coaching, will cover the first two items, but no one, including Bottom, will again suggest the last, which may in fact be little more than an inadvertent obscenity.[37]

Quince, agreeing, announces the play's title: "'The most lamentable comedy, and most cruel death of Pyramus and Thisbe'" (1.2.11–12). The artisans' play closely mirrors Hermia and Lysander's furtive flight. The one is an imitation of the other. The young lovers, Pyramus and Thisbe, prevented by their fathers from marrying, flee the city by moonlight while planning to meet in the woods. Only the outcome differs. The legendary Babylonian lovers, each mistakenly taking responsibility for the other's death, kill themselves in the woods. They die for love.[38] Their story is of course not a "comedy," as Quince says. It is neither humorous nor happy. It becomes a comedy only in the sense that it proves to be written and performed with ludicrous incompetence. Pyramus's "tragical" death "[m]ade mine eyes water; but more merry tears / The passion of loud laughter never shed" (5.1.66, 69–70). It is the actors and their script, not the plot and the characters, that are funny.

On the other hand, notwithstanding the similarity of their plots, A *Midsummer Night's Dream* is a comedy, while *Pyramus and Thisbe* is a tragedy. The one ends happily in marriage; the other, miserably in death. Lysander and Hermia avoid Pyramus and Thisbe's tragic fate thanks to Theseus's political act. Whereas the traditional tragic tale turns on the tension between the authority of parenthood and the passion of love, the love of one's own and the love of the beautiful, Theseus's deposing the ancient authority of Athenian fathers averts the same outcome. What makes Athens free also makes A *Midsummer Night's Dream* a happy comedy.

Bottom, hearing the play's title, quickly responds with the assumed authority of a learned critic: "A very good piece of work, I assure you." But then, just as quickly, Bottom displays his ignorance: "and a merry" (1.1.13–14). No one says why the play would be appropriate for the Duke's wedding celebration. Bottom, with a commanding "Now" (1.2.14), next directs Quince to call forth the actors by name and then, addressing the actors as "Masters," directs them to stand out as their names are called (1.2.14, 15). "Master" or "Masters" is Bottom's most frequent term of address. He uses it in speaking to both his fellow players and the fairies whom Titania assigns to serve him assiduously.[39] It is a term of respect or politeness, which is used here, with fitting democratic irony, by the one giving orders to those taking them.[40]

Quince begins to call the names and first calls Bottom's. Bottom, answering, again gives Quince directions: "Ready. Name what part I am for, and proceed" (1.2.17). When told that he is to play Pyramus, Bottom, despite having just passed judgment on the play, asks, "What is Pyramus? A lover, or a tyrant?" (1.2.19). Bottom is not at all surprised that he is to have a title role, but imagines that it must be the part of a lover or a tyrant. He seems to think that these are the only two leading roles.[41] And as he thinks that good drama depicts men dominated by strong passion, so great passion is Bottom's standard for excellent acting. When Quince explains that Pyramus is "[a] lover, that kills himself most gallant for love" (1.2.20), Bottom, saying that the role will require "some tears in the true performing of it" (1.2.21), proclaims that if he plays the part, he will "move [such] storms" (1.2.23) that the audience should take care lest they weep away their eyes. But as passionate as that role would be, Bottom, interrupting his next order, declares that he would prefer to play a tyrant: "—yet my chief humour is for a tyrant" (1.2.24). Bottom's example of a tyrant is Hercules. "I could play Ercles rarely, or a part to tear a cat in, to make all split" (1.2.25–26). A tyrant's part permits or demands more ranting than a lover's. To demonstrate his ability to play such a part rarely, Bottom bursts into eight lines of bombastic doggerel rhyme and blatant alliteration, describing destruction of cosmic proportions:

> The raging rocks,
> And shivering shocks,
> Shall break the locks,
> Of prison-gates;
> And Phibbus' car
> Shall shine from far
> And make and mar
> The foolish fates.

> (1.2.27–34)

Bottom, who finds either his lines or his performance, or both, "lofty" (1.2.35), explains that "[t]his is Ercles' vein, a tyrant's vein: a lover's is more condoling" (1.2.36–37). A lover's vein is sad; a tyrant's vein is thundering. A tyrant lacks limits both in style and in substance. We might note that, despite his ignorance of the Pyramus and Thisbe story, and despite the difficulty he will show in handling his part, Bottom is evidently able to draw on a dramatic passage which he has committed to memory. His reputation for know-how in acting may not be altogether unwarranted (cf. 4.2.7–10).

Quince gives Flute the part of Thisbe. Flute initially imagines that Thisbe is a wandering knight—a medieval hero—and is offended to learn that she is a woman. Flute, who has, or perhaps would like to think he has, "a beard coming" (1.2.43–44), seems to hope that his beard will disqualify him from the role. Bottom, however, is not in the least offended by the prospect of playing a woman, and he wants the part of Thisbe, too. He wants to play both lovers. And to show his qualification for playing the two parts at once, he breaks into theatrical lines again, delivering a short improvised dialogue between Pyramus and Thisbe. Soon Bottom will want the part of the lion as well. Mimicking the nature of the tyrant he wishes to play, he will want all the major parts.

After he firmly rejects Bottom's attempt and Bottom acquiesces, Quince in quick succession casts four more roles. The first three are Thisbe's mother (Starveling), Pyramus's father (Snout), and Thisbe's father (Quince himself). None of the characters appears in the play when performed. Instead, there are three others: Moonshine (Starveling), Wall (Snout), and Prologue (Quince). As already noted, even though act 5 is a wedding celebration, no parents appear in either the play within the play or its onstage audience.

The fourth assignment is the role of the lion, which is given to Snug. Snug, dumbest of the artisans, hopes that the part is already written so he will have time to learn it: "I am slow of study" (1.2.63). Quince assures him that he can play it extemporaneously, "for it is nothing but roaring" (1.1.64–65). But, in fact, Snug will have to speak eight lines of prologue as Lion (5.1.214–21), which is more than he speaks apart from the role (1.2.62–63; 4.2.15–18).[42]

Bottom wants the lion's part, too. Unlike the roles of parents, which he does not claim, that of a lion calls for a boisterous voice. Bottom wants the part because he wants to show his excellence and affect the audience:

> I will roar, that will do any man's heart good to hear me. I will
> roar, that I will make the Duke say: "Let him roar again; let him
> roar again!"
>
> (1.2.66–69)

Quince objects, however, that Bottom would act his part too well. He would roar "too terribly" —he means "too terrifyingly"—and that would "fright the Duchess and the ladies," so that they would "shriek." And that would be enough to cause all the actors to be hanged—"every mother's son," as the crew says, fearfully seconding Quince (1.2.70–73). Bottom would be so good an imitation of a lion that the women would think he was a lion. Good acting would destroy acting, by turning a resemblance into the thing which it resembles. Quince, at the same time, makes an implicit distinction between men and women. The men would not be frightened (and perhaps not deluded) by the lion, but all the women—the Amazon queen ("the Duchess") no less than "the ladies"—would. Ironically, Quince and the others express manly contempt for the women's fear just when they fear for themselves and just when they identify themselves as their mothers' offspring ("That would hang us, every mother's son" [1.2.73]). Their manliness resembles Flute's beard.

Bottom, seeing an opportunity, proposes a remedy. If earlier he boasted that he would make the audience cry so hard they might lose their eyes, now he fears that he would make the women fear so much they might lose their minds:

> I grant you, friends, if you should fright the ladies out of their wits,
> they would have no more discretion but to hang us. But I will
> aggravate my voice so, that I will roar you as gently as any sucking
> dove; I will roar you and 'twere any nightingale.
>
> (1.2.74–78)

Bottom offers to "aggravate"—he means "moderate" or "mitigate"—his voice so that his lion's roar would be as soft and meek as the sound of a gentle bird. Though the women would still be deluded into thinking that what they see and hear is real, they would not be frightened by it. It seems perfectly apt that the man who will himself become a "monster" (3.2.6; 3.1.99) sees nothing monstrous in a lion roaring like a dove.

Quince, once more, refuses, but tries to relieve Bottom's disappointment with flattery. Bottom has the looks for the leading man (cf. 4.2.11):

> You can play no part but Pyramus: for Pyramus is a sweet-faced man; a proper man as one shall see in a summer's day; a most lovely, gentleman-like man: therefore you must needs play Pyramus.
>
> (1.2.79–82)

Bottom agrees and immediately starts to think of the appearance of his face and, particularly, the color of his beard. Later, when desired as a lover, he will have whiskers (4.1.22–26). Now, as an actor playing a lover, he mulls over the proper beard for the part. Beards, a mark of manliness (1.2.43–44), seem appropriate for gallant lovers. Bottom suggests four colors for his beard. The last—"your French-crown-colour beard, your perfect yellow" (1.2.88–89)—prompts Quince, taking the name of the French gold coin or "crown" literally, to make a bawdy joke about French kings: "Some of your French crowns have no hair at all, and then you will play bare-faced" (1.2.90–91). Some French kings are bald from syphilis, and so to play with a beard like theirs—"play" meaning both "to act on the stage" and "to have sex"[43]—is to play uncovered. Confusing or conflating acting and sex, Quince jokes that the actor's private life would show through his dramatic role. Quince initially feared that the audience would take an imitation of a lion for a real lion; now he suggests that they would see only the actor and not the character. Either way, there would be no dramatic illusion. The audience would see one part but not the other of the illusion's whole.

Having cast the roles, Quince distributes the players' lines. The play, it seems, is already written. The players are to learn their parts by tomorrow night, a task whose uncertain accomplishment is underscored by Quince's triple pleading: "I am to entreat you, request you, and desire you" (1.2.92–93). Snug may not be the only one slow of study. The actors are to meet tomorrow night to rehearse "in the palace wood, a mile without the town, by moonlight" (1.2.94–95). Quince explains that they if they rehearsed in the city they would be closely followed and their plans discovered.

Quince then adds that he will draw up a list of props needed for their play. This is the first hint of the roles of Moonshine and Wall. The props—"properties" (1.2.98)—will take on a life of their own. Stage accessories will become full characters.

Bottom answers for all and vows that they will rehearse "most obscenely and courageously" (1.2.100–1). Bottom's "obscenely" may not be entirely a malapropism. If he means "seemly," it is one, though it is not easy to see why he would mean that. But Bottom may mean the word in its literal, dramaturgical sense: what is "obscene" is what happens "off stage." Whatever the case, Bottom, delivering what he seems to think will be the final word of the meeting, exhorts his fellow actors, using a theatrical term, to take pains to learn their lines perfectly, and bids them goodbye: "take pains, be perfect: adieu!" (1.2.101–2). But when Quince follows by stating more specifically where they are to meet ("At the Duke's oak we meet" [1.2.103]), Bottom, evidently intent upon having the last word, gives another order and exhortation: "Enough: hold, or cut bow-strings" (1.2.104). Bottom's final exhortation seems at once proverbial and obscure, though its sense, shrouded by its archery metaphor, appears to be "Keep your promise or suffer the consequence."[44] Forced to go beyond his initial effort at having the final word, Bottom concludes with a phrase which is, characteristically, at once confident and confused.

## Notes

1. Ernest Schanzer, "The Moon and the Fairies in A Midsummer Night's Dream," University of Toronto Quarterly, 24 (1955), 242.

2. Hans Jonas, The Phenomenon of Life (Chicago: The University of Chicago Press, 1966), 101. Note the ambiguity of Theseus's first word, "Now." Besides being emphatic, it seems to refer to both the present moment and the time directly following upon it.

3. Forty-seven times, including Starveling's role in Pyramus and Thisbe and the compounds "moonlight," "moonbeams," and "moonshine."

4. Plutarch, Theseus, 12.2–3; Apollodorus, Library; 1.9.28, Epitome, 1.5–6; Pausanius, Description of Greece, 2.3.8; Ovid, Metamorphoses, 7.404ff.

5. Lisa Hopkins, The Shakespearean Marriage (New York: St. Martin's Press, 1998), 25.

6. Chaucer, The Knight's Tale, 870; see also Boccaccio, 1.134; 2.18–24; Statius, 12.519ff. Plutarch tells of the "solemn oath" concluding the Amazon war (Plutarch, Theseus, 27.5; North's Plutarch, 8 vols. [1579; London: David Nutt, 1895], 1:58). For the "day of more solemnity" than any previous day in Athens, see Ovid, Metamorphoses, 7.425ff.; Golding, 7.447 (Ovid's Metamorphoses, The Arthur Golding Translation, ed. John Frederick Nimes [1567; London: Macmillian, 1965]); and for the fact

that the festivity was so joyous on that day that "[t]here was not to be found / In all the City any place of sadness," see Ovid, *Metamorphoses*, 7.452; Golding, 7.574–75. Throughout, I have modernized the spelling and punctuation of Golding and North.

7. In *A Midsummer Night's* Dream, "solemnity" always refers to a wedding or a wedding celebration (4.1.133, 184; 5.1.355; note also 4.1.87).

8. See Plutarch, *Theseus*, 8.2–3, 20; 26.1–2; 29.1–2; *Comparison of Theseus and Romulus*, 6.1; Ovid, *Metamorphoses*, 8.174ff.; *Heroides*, 10; Catullus, *Poems*, 64.50ff.

9. Pausanius, *Description of Greece*, 5.11.7.

10. Cf., e.g., *Coriolanus*, 2.1.176; *Julius Caesar*, 1.1.31, 51; 5.1.108, the Arden Shakespeare, ed. T. S. Dorsch, (London: Methuen, 1961); *Antony and Cleopatra*, 3.13.141; 4.12.33; 4.14.20; 5.1.66; 5.2.108, the Arden Shakespeare, ed. John Wilders, (London: Routledge, 1995).

11. Plutarch, *Theseus*, 24.2–4; 25.2; North, 1:52. See also Aristotle, *Constitution of Athens*, 41.2.

12. Boccaccio, 2.25ff.; Chaucer, *The Knight's Tale*, 893ff.; John Fletcher and William Shakespeare, *The Two Noble Kinsmen*, the Arden Edition, ed. Lois Potter (Walton-on-Thames: Thomas Nelson and Sons, 1997), 1.1.24ff. See also Aeschylus, *Seven against Thebes*; Euripides, *The Suppliant Women*; Plutarch, *Theseus*, 29.4–5; Statius, 112.464–809.

13. "[A]ll other arts . . . were discovered and even perfected well before [the art of rhetoric] was developed [in Athens]." Cicero, *Brutus*, 26; also Quintilian, *Institutio Oratoria*, 3.1.8ff.

14. Aristotle, *The Art of Rhetoric*, 3.14–19; Cicero, *De Inventione*, 1.20–109.

15. For example, 1.1.135–44; 1.2.2–65, 86–89; 2.1.34–42, 44–57, 77–114, 180–81, 249–52; 2.2.1–23, 29–30; 3.1.120–28, 157–67; 3.2.198–214; 4.1.118–25, 209–12; 5.1.9–22, 42–60, 194–97, 317–19, 357–68, 395–400.

16. Kristian Smidt, *Unconformities in Shakespeare's Early Comedies* (London: Macmillan, 1986), 212 n. 20.

17. Although he has just seven speeches, Egeus uses "my" eighteen times and "mine" another three times (1.1.23 [twice], 24, 25, 26, 27, 29, 36, 38, 42, 95, 96 [twice], 87 [twice]; 4.1.127 [twice], 136, 153, 157, 158).

18. Thucydides, 2.15–16; Plutarch, *Theseus*, 24.1.

19. Plutarch, *Theseus*, 29.1–2; North, 1:58–59.

20. See, for example, 1.1.132–49; 2.2.40–41, 46–49, 136–41; 3.2.246, 260, 264, 269–70, 279–80, 329–30.

21. See also Plutarch, *Demetrius*, 3, 5–6, 18.

22. See also Plutarch, *Lysander*, 24–26.

23. Lysander's childless aunt is the only relative of either young man and the only female relative of any of the young lovers and, in fact, of anyone we see in the play. Only the artisans refer to their own mothers, though only proverbially (1.1.73; 3.1.69), while Helena, much in the spirit of what Lysander says of his aunt, refers to close female friends as "sisters" (3.2.199). Cf. 3.2.53–55.

24. Thomas More, "Six Lines on the Island of Utopia," *Utopia*, eds. George M. Logan, et al. (1516; Cambridge: Cambridge University Press, 1995), 18–19.

25. Davis, 54–56; Jan H. Blits, *Deadly Thought: "Hamlet" and the Human Soul* (Lanham, Md.: Lexington Books, 2001), 213–14.

26. For example, Virgil, *Aeneid*, 4.591ff; Ovid, *Metamorphoses*, 1.468–72; *Heroides*, 7.181–96. Hermia might have mentioned Theseus's promises to Aegles, Ariadne, and Antiopa (2.1.79–80).

27. From contagious, to hear (and see), to make her own, and to sing a "catch" of music.

28. See Introduction, n. 36, in this volume.

29. The verbs "shall" and "will" "express a promise—*shall* in the third person, *will* in the first." ed. George Kittredge, *Sixteen Plays of Shakespeare* (Boston: Ginn & Co., 1946), 179.

30. Aristotle, *On the Soul*, 427a16ff. See, further, Eva T. H. Brann, *The World of the Imagination: Sum and Substance* (Lanham, Md.: Rowman & Littlefield, 1991), 40–44.

31. Contrary to what some contemporary scholars suppose, "fantasy" is, in general, no less serious or weighty a term than "imagination." In fact, until well after Shakespeare's day, the word "fantasy" carried greater dignity. On the reversal, see James Engell, *The Creative Imagination: Enlightenment to Romanticism* (Cambridge, Mass.: Harvard University Press, 1981), 172–83; and Brann, 18–23.

32. See, for example, Propertius, *Elegies*, 2.12; Ovid, *The Art of Love*, 2.17–20.

33. Helena has 36 speeches and 229 lines. Hermia has one-third again as many speeches (48) but only two-thirds the number of lines (165). Lysander has 50 speeches and 178 lines; Demetrius, 48 speeches and 139 lines. While Oberon has almost as many lines (224), only Theseus (240) and Bottom, including his lines as Pyramus (269), have more.

34. E.g., 1.1.181, 240–46; 2.2.88, 107, 122–23; 3.2.128–33, 135, 145–61, 168, 192–201, 216–17, 222–31, 240, 265, 286–87, 308–10. Note the first and last words of her first line ("Call . . . unsay" [1.1.181]).

35. M. P. Tilley, *A Dictionary of Proverbs in England in the Sixteenth and Seventeenth Centuries* (Ann Arbor: University of Michigan Press, 1950), T23.

36. *A Midsummer Night's Dream*, the New Cambridge Shakespeare, ed. A. T. Quiller Couch and J. Dover Wilson (Cambridge: Cambridge University Press, 1949), 102.

37. Eric Partridge, *Shakespeare's Bawdy* (New York: Dutton, 1960), s.v. Point.

38. Ovid, *Metamorphoses*, 4.55–166; Chaucer, *The Legend of Good Women*, 706–923.

39. E.g., 1.2.15; 3.1.28, 3.1.175–76, 180, 181, 184, 189; 4.2.28. See, also, 3.1.100; 4.2.15.

40. See, for example, *Coriolanus*, 1.1.61; 2.3.153; 3.1.328 (cf. 2.2.51, 77); *Julius Caesar*, 3.2.123.

41. Lowenthal, 84–85.

42. Of Snug's fifty words apart from his role as Lion, only nine are longer than four letters and only seven have two syllables. Fittingly, Snug has the shortest last name and is the only artisan without a first name.

43. Partridge, s.v. Play.

44. For a survey of interpretations and difficulties, see Brooks, 25.

# ACT TWO

~

## Act Two, Scene One

### 1. Wandering Fairies

Scene 1 is the first scene in the woods. But instead of seeing either the lovers or the artisans, we see a new group of characters—the fairies. While the lovers flee to the woods to escape Athenian law and the artisans to escape Athenian pirating, the fairies have come to celebrate the Athenian Duke and Duchess's wedding.

Puck begins by asking a nameless fairy, "How now, spirit? Whither wander you?" (2.1.1). In both a literal and a figurative sense, the fairies frequently wander and cause others to wander. It is no mere coincidence that the name Oberon, while derived (via the French Auberon) from the German Alberich or Albrich (*alb*: elf, *rich*: king), means "wander" in Latin.[1] Oberon's name, title, and activity are one and the same.

The Fairy's answer, the first of many fairy narratives,[2] forms a frontispiece of the wandering. The speech falls into two major parts. In the first (2.1.2–7), the Fairy tells where he (or perhaps she) goes; in the second (2.1.8–15), what he does. The general doubleness of the answer's two parts is repeated within each of the parts. In the first, the Fairy, speaking in a rapid rhythm which mimics the celerity he describes, replies:

> Over hill, over dale,
>   Thorough bush, thorough briar,
> Over park, over pale,

53

> Thorough flood, thorough fire,
> I do wander everywhere,
> Swifter than the moon's sphere.

> (2.1.2–7)

Nowhere else in the play is every other word in a series of lines repeated not just once but twice. And while the Fairy twice repeats every other word in his first four lines ("Over . . . , over . . . , / Thorough . . . , thorough . . . , / Over . . . , over . . . , / Thorough . . . , thorough . . ."), he alternates with these prepositions a list of nouns ("hill . . . dale, / . . . bush . . . briar, / . . . park, . . . pale, / . . . flood . . . fire"), which he then immediately generalizes in a single word ("everywhere"). The general repeats while containing the particulars. Yet, at the same time, the Fairy conflates antitheses and synonyms. The first and last pairs in his list contain antitheses ("hill . . . dale"; "flood . . . fire"), while the middle two contain synonyms ("bush . . . briar"; "park . . . pale"), but the repeated prepositions ("Over" and "Thorough") could be either antitheses or synonyms. The distinction between opposition and repetition, difference and sameness, loses force. Only the Fairy's swiftness seems to be stated singly. However, stated as a comparison ("Swifter than . . ."), it is actually a suppressed double.

In the second part, the Fairy explains that his duties are twofold: he dews the grass with the fairy queen's fairy circles, and he places dewdrops in her royal guards' ears. Both duties are concerned with ornamenting what is rooted in the ground. With both, what the Fairy ornaments contrasts with his unrestricted movement. Now, where the first part of the Fairy's answer obscured the distinction between difference and sameness, the second part obscures the difference between an imitation and its original. Continuing, the Fairy describes the queen's royal guard:

> The cowslips tall her pensioners be,
> In their gold coats spots you see,
> Those be rubies, fairy favours,
> In those freckles live their savours.

> (2.1.10–13)

According to the Fairy, the cowslips are ("be") the queen's guard; they do not merely resemble one. The description is not a personification. It is literal, not figurative. So, too, with the "rubies." The flowers' red spots are ("be") rubies; they are not imitations of rubies. Yet, even as he implicitly denies the imitative character of the rubies, the Fairy emphasizes it: "[The] spots you see, / Those be rubies." What Puck sees is one thing; what they are is something else. On the Fairy's lips, the doubleness of imitation collapses into the singleness of identity, and the singleness of identity expands into the doubleness of imitation. Neither remains what it is. The imitation and imitated, the image and the imagined, are both different and the same. This ambiguity—the ambiguity of image and reality—will characterize nearly everything concerning the fairies.

Both Puck and the Fairy have a sense of urgency. The Fairy is in a hurry to leave: "Farewell, thou lob of spirits; I'll be gone; / Our Queen and all her elves come here anon" (2.1.16–17). The Fairy seems to want to complete his tasks before Titania and her train arrive. Puck, however, has a different concern. He wants to keep Titania and Oberon apart. Telling the Fairy that "[t]he King doth keep his revels here tonight" (2.1.18), Puck urges him to take care that "the Queen come not within [the King's] sight" (2.1.19). Titania and Oberon, the only married couple until act 5, are quarreling. Puck explains that Oberon is fiercely angry "[b]ecause . . . [Titania] as her attendant hath / A lovely boy, stol'n from an Indian king" (2.1.22–23). Oberon is angry because he wants the boy for himself. His anger is really jealousy:

> She never had so sweet a changeling;
> And jealous Oberon would have the child
> Knight of his train, to trace the forests wild.
>
> (2.1.23–25)

Puck calls the boy a "changeling." A changeling normally refers to the ugly child fairies leave behind, not to the beautiful one they take. Puck inverts the word's usual sense.[3] His use of the word illustrates the word. The word "changeling" itself becomes a changeling: its ugly meaning is exchanged for a more handsome one. Puck explains that Titania "perforce withholds the loved boy, / Crowns him with flowers, and makes him all her joy" (2.1.26–27). Her reason for withholding the boy is not immediately clear. Titania will soon say that she keeps him for his mother's sake and will not give him up for all of fairyland (2.1.121–37). But, later, when finally ready to reconcile with Oberon, she will give him up without a thought for the boy or his mother (4.1.56–62). Even more surprising, after that, neither she nor Oberon will ever mention the boy again. With their reconciliation, the boy vanishes from the play—and presumably from their hearts—without the slightest trace. We must therefore wonder whether Oberon and Titania's rivalry for the boy is the consequence rather than the cause of their quarrel. Soon we will hear that Oberon is jealous of Titania's love of Theseus and Titania is jealous of his love of Phillida and Hippolyta (2.1.60–81). The boy may be a stand-in for the real object of their quarrel. Oberon may be jealous of Titania's love of Theseus, not her possession of the boy. And as he seeks the boy out of jealousy, Titania may withhold him out of spite. For the fairies, too, war may be a part of love. Puck concludes by stressing the fierceness of the royals' quarreling. The fairy king and queen now never meet, he says, "[b]ut they do square; that all their elves for fear / Creep into acorn-cups, and hide them there" (2.1.30–31). Like much else, Puck's account of the royals' quarreling will soon be countered by another.

The Fairy thinks he recognizes Puck:

> Either I mistake your shape and making quite,
> Or else you are that shrewd and knavish sprite
> Call'd Robin Goodfellow.
>
> (2.1.32–34)

Despite Puck's ability to metamorphose himself, the Fairy recognizes him by his outward appearance ("your shape and making"). Beneath Puck's transformations lies a sprite with definite looks, at least in the eyes of another fairy. And as the Fairy knows Puck's outward appearance, he also knows his inner nature or character. Puck is artful and roguish ("shrewd and knavish"), prone to playing pranks. Characterizing Puck by his pranks, the Fairy describes six of them. Puck frightens the village maidens, deprives the milk of its cream, causes the grinding of corn to fail, prevents housewives from churning butter, stops the fermentation of ale, and misleads night travelers, laughing at their harm. While all of Puck's pranks are domestic or homely, their common element is emptiness or futility: false fears, vain efforts, and misdirected travel. Puck, however, sometimes gives help. He does the work of, and brings good luck to, those who call him "Hobgoblin" and "sweet Puck" (2.1.40). At the same time that he is amused by the harm he causes (2.1.39, 42–57; 3.1.73ff.; 3.2.7–32, 110–15, 118–21, 352–53), he benefits those who conciliate him with a kind name.[4]

Puck, confirming his identity, proudly describes himself and his tricks. Corroborating that he is "that merry wanderer of the night" (2.1.43), he explains that he "jest[s] to Oberon, and make[s] him smile" at his pranks (2.1.44). Puck then describes three sorts of his tricks. All of them rest on his ability to imitate whatever shape and sound he wishes. In the first, he arouses the sexual desire of a fat, well-fed horse by neighing "in likeness" (2.1.46) of a female foal. In the second, he induces a tattling woman to spill her drink on herself by turning himself into the "very likeness" (2.1.48) of a roasted crabapple. And in the third, he causes an old lady, telling a serious tale, to fall on the floor by "mistak[ing]" (2.1.52) him for a stool. Variations on the common element in the Fairy's description, all three of Puck's pranks turn on his ability to cause a likeness to be mistaken for something real.

Oberon and Titania enter separately, evidently by chance ("Ill met by moonlight" [2.1.60]). While Puck, seeing Oberon enter with his royal train, calls for the Fairy to make room, the Fairy, seeing Titania enter at the same time, wishes that Oberon were not there: "Would that he were gone!" (2.1.59). Just as Puck's pranks produce futility and frustration, the Fairy's discussion with Puck, and about him, has thwarted his wish to leave.

## 2. Imagination

Oberon and Titania immediately berate each other, he for her pride ("proud Titania" [2.1.60]), she for his jealousy ("jealous Oberon" [2.1.61]). Titania orders the fairies in her train to leave, explaining that she has forsworn Oberon's bed and company. But Oberon, asserting his authority as her husband, orders her to stay: "Tarry, rash wanton; am not I thy lord?" (2.1.63). Titania turns Oberon's claim back against him: "Then I must be thy lady" (2.1.64). If Oberon has the right to govern his wife, Titania has the right to expect him to be faithful. Their rights are reciprocal. Titania, however, charges that Oberon has been unfaithful and makes two specific accusations. "[B]ut I know," she begins,

> When thou hast stol'n away from fairy land,
> And in the shape of Corin, sat all day
> Playing on pipes of corn, and versing love
> To amorous Phillida.
>
> (2.1.64–68)

Corin and Phillida are traditional names in pastoral poetry—Corin, for a lovesick shepherd, who attaches as much importance to his musical abilities and his love as to his flocks.[5] According to Titania, Oberon has changed into Corin's shape and spent all day playing music on corn pipes and reciting his own love poems to the loving Phillida. Love literally takes the form of literature. Not only are Phillida and Corin stock characters from poetry, but Oberon courts one by imitating the other. He imitates a poetic imitation of a lover (Corin), who is himself a poetic imitator ("Playing on pipes of corn, and versing love"),[6] in pursuit of a poetic imitation of a beloved (Phillida). Love becomes wholly translated into art.

Titania's second charge accuses Oberon of loving Hippolyta. "Why art thou here," Titania asks rhetorically,

> Come from the farthest step of India,
> But that, forsooth, the bouncing Amazon,
> Your buskin'd mistress and your warrior love,
> To Theseus must be wedded, and you come
> To give their bed joy and prosperity?
>
> (2.1.68–73)

Oberon does not deny either charge, but, instead, tries to shame Titania, accusing her, in turn, of hypocrisy. How can she, "for shame" (2.1.74), he indignantly (and rhetorically) asks, attack his good name by mentioning Hippolyta, "[k]nowing I know thy love to Theseus?" (2.1.76). Oberon then describes Titania's love for Theseus:

> Didst not thou lead him through the glimmering night
> From Perigouna, whom he ravished;
> And make him with fair Aegles break his faith,
> With Ariadne and Antiopa?
>
> (2.1.77–80)

Oberon lists four of Theseus's notorious encounters with women. All involve abduction, abandonment, and betrayal. As Oberon loves Hippolyta for her hunting and warrior qualities, so Titania is said to have led Theseus on his ravishing adventures. Although they have come to Athens to celebrate Theseus and Hippolyta's wedding and will, in fact, bless their lawful marriage bed (5.1.389ff.), Oberon and Titania, here, present each other as loving the precivilized, heroic Theseus and Hippolyta. It is not immediately clear, though, what Oberon means by saying that Titania "led" Theseus through the glimmering night. From all we can tell, Theseus knows nothing of her. Titania may love him, but Theseus never mentions any of the fairies, let alone Titania. And, far from showing any taste for, or belief in, fairies, he uses the term "fairy" disparagingly for what he considers an unreal and unbelievable story. Fairies are mere fairy tales ("fairy toys" [5.1.3]), to him.[7]

But if Titania does not exist for Theseus, she may nevertheless have led him led through the glimmering night in much the way that Puck leads, or misleads, the villagers and night-wanderers. As seems true of the fairies' powers in general, her ability to affect people may be unknown to those she affects. The power of imagination may conceal itself in the object of desire (cf., e.g., 1.1.32–35, 232–35; 2.2.103–4; 3.1.132–36; 3.2.137–44). Titania, however, rejects Oberon's accusations out of hand as "the forgeries of jealousy" (2.1.81). Like love, jealousy can counterfeit truth. The one imagines beauty; the other, fault. Rather than answer Oberon's charge, Titania describes at length the effects of his jealous quarreling. Puck said that whenever Titania and Oberon meet they quarrel so fiercely that all their elves hide in acorns from fear (2.1.28–31). Titania describes something quite different.

Never, since "the middle summer's spring" (2.1.82), she begins, do she and Oberon meet anywhere ("On hill, in dale, forest or mead," etc., [2.1.83]), "[t]o dance our ringlets to the whistling wind" (2.1.86), but Oberon disturbs their enjoyment with his quarreling.

> Therefore, the winds, piping to us in vain,
> As in revenge have suck'd up from the sea
> Contagious fogs.

> (2.1.88–90)

The winds' revenge fits Oberon's offense. The pestilent fogs, falling back to earth, have caused every paltry river to rise and overflow its banks. And, consequently, just as Oberon caused the winds to pipe "in vain," the ox, the ploughman, and the corn now all work or grow "in vain" (2.1.88, 93). What characterized Puck's pranks characterizes both Oberon's offense and the winds' revenge, though misery has replaced laughter. And now, Titania continues, the sheep-pens stand "empty" (2.1.96) in the flooded fields, and crows are "fatted with the murrion flock" (2.1.97). Only what feeds on fatally diseased carrion grows. Distinctions on the earth have also been lost. Mud has filled up the figures cut into the turf for a certain game ("The nine-men's-morris" [2.1.98]), and, owing to the lack of people to trample them down, the elaborate paths ("the quaint mazes" [2.1.99]) in the luxurious grass, laid out as another game, have become "undistinguishable" (2.1.100). As she began her description of the great flood with the destruction of the fairies' dance, Titania ends it with the destruction of human games. We might wonder whether "sport" (2.1.87) is on the same level for the fairy queen (and the winds) as pestilent fogs, floods, barrenness, disease, and death.

Oberon's disturbing the fairies' dance has also brought confusion to the seasons, Titania says. The moon, "the governess of floods," she continues,

> Pale in her anger, washes all the air,
> That rheumatic diseases do abound.
> And thorough this distemperature we see
> The seasons alter: hoary-headed frosts
> Fall in the fresh lap of the crimson rose;
> And on old Hiems' thin and icy crown,
> An odorous chaplet of sweet summer buds
> Is, as in mockery, set; the spring, the summer,
> The childing autumn, angry winter, change
> Their wonted liveries.
>
> (2.1.103–13)

And as a result of the seasons' changes, the bewildered world can no longer tell which season is which by the seasons' products: "[A]nd the mazed world, / By their increase, knows not which is which" (2.1.113–14).

Titania's narrative contains obvious discrepancies. Titania begins by recounting the peaceful and clear waterways by which Oberon and she have recently met ("By paved fountain, or rushy brook" [2.1.84]), but then describes how "every pelting river" has been "made so proud / That [all the rivers] have overborne their continents" (2.1.91–92). Similarly, she says that she and Oberon have met "on hill, in dale, forest [and] mead" (2.1.83), but then claims that the fields are "drowned" (2.1.96). Moreover, while initially saying that nothing grows, Titania subsequently says that rose buds grow but at the wrong time. Most generally and most importantly, although Oberon never questions Titania's description, nowhere else in the play is there any kind of evidence—or even hint—of such disorder. Apart from the fog that Puck produces (3.2.355–59), there are no fogs, no floods, no famine, and no signs of winter in summer. Nor does anyone seem to be at all concerned with such things, not even when deciding to go into the woods. Quite the contrary, the lovers, artisans, and fairies alike describe the woods as undisturbed. The lovers and fairies even speak of Phoebe or the fairies themselves placing dewdrops on the grass and flowers, tonight and tomorrow night (1.1.211; 2.1.14–15). Titania's narrative is at odds not only with Puck's report of the frightened elves hiding from the quarreling in acorns (2.1.30–31), but with itself and the rest of the play. Nothing else in the play allows what Titania describes. Her narrative—the longest speech in the play—seems fictitious even within the fiction of Shakespeare's play. It is an image without an original.

Like the Fairy's first speech (2.1.2–15) and so much else involving the fairies, Titania's speech, besides containing two major parts, is replete with doubles, both imperfect and perfect. While Titania describes the loss of distinctions in the natural world and consequently in men's minds (". . . and the mazed world / . . . knows not which is which"), her dual accounts of the effects of the winds' revenge and the moon's anger both stress contrasts. Where the former account emphasizes the antithesis between the empty and the full, the latter emphasizes the antithesis between the winter cheer that "[t]he human mortals want" and the "rheumatic diseases [that] do abound" (2.1.101, 105). In both, the contrast is between what is absent and what is present. On the other hand, Titania's account of the moon's anger inverts her account of the winds' revenge. Whereas the winds sucked up contagious fogs from the sea, which then fell back to earth and produced floods, the moon, by contrast, caused floods, which then produced the unhealthy air. In the one account, the pestilent fogs produce the disastrous flood; in the other, the inundating floods produce the rheumatic air. Though both are introduced by the word "[t]herefore" (2.1.88, 103; also 2.1.93), the two accounts reverse cause and effect. Further, while the causal connection between the flooding rivers and the flooded fields seems obvious, the causal connection between the rheumatic air and the seasons' changes seems to rest merely on a pun. Only the word "distemperature" links the distempered conditions of the air and the disordered temperatures of the season—and both, perhaps, initially to Oberon's bad temper. In addition, Titania echoes her own words,[8] puns on "brawls" (2.1.87; cf. 2.1.86) as well as on "distemperature," both contrasts and combines contraries,[9] characterizes Oberon's charges as "forgeries," personifies the wind, rivers, corn, moon, seasons, and (we will soon see) the evils Oberon's quarreling has produced as well as his and her own relation to them (2.1.115–17), and will conclude with the mention of their "progeny" (2.1.115) and with a pair of redundancies ("From our debate, from our dissension; / We are their parents and original" [2.1.116–17]). And while she says that all four seasons have changed their outward appearances ("liveries"), she describes one of the changes as resembling "mockery" (2.1.111). Finally, the two games that Titania names not only both involve imitation; each also contrasts with the other. "The nine-men's-morris" imitates the dancers in a "morris." Its figure consists of a square within a square, whose corners are joined by straight lines.[10] "[T]he giant mazes," on the other hand, imitate a game imitating a battle and flight (the Roman "Troy games" in honor of Anchises). Its figure is a intricate labyrinth.[11] While the former game is British, the latter is Roman.[12]

Titania, concluding her speech, claims that the natural disorder is the child of her quarrel with Oberon:

> And this same progeny of evils comes
> From our debate, from our dissension;
> We are their parents and original.

(2.1.115–17)

This is the play's only reference to Oberon and Titania's offspring. The fairy king and queen have a child only in a figurative sense. While its cause is said to be their dispute over a certain living "child" (2.1.24, 122; 4.1.58), their only "progeny" is a creature of the imagination. Titania and Oberon are the "original" of their "progeny" not only in the (redundant) sense of being its cause or "parents," but in the (nonredundant) sense of being the original in relation to its copy. Like parents, like child. While the fairy king and queen may have the power to bless the children of others (2.1.72–73; 4.1.89; 5.1.391–400), they generate directly only in the imagination and generate children only indirectly through the imagination's effect on lovers. Personifying imagination in love, they are always at least one remove from procreation.

Oberon, evidently unmoved by Titania's description of the natural upheaval, attempts to turn tables on her. Titania can amend the problem, he says. The power lies in her:

> Do you amend it then: it lies in you.
> Why should Titania cross her Oberon?
> I do but beg a little changeling boy
> To be my henchman.

(2.1.118–21)

Oberon makes light of his demand or request ("I do but beg . . .") and speaks of himself as Titania's love ("her Oberon"). While Titania's change of mind would have the effect of restoring the natural order, the action itself would be small and agreeable: Titania would do it for her love. This is not the last time that Oberon will expect the power of love to govern someone's action.

Oberon, however, is disappointed. Titania immediately refuses, in the strongest terms. She will not part with the boy for all of fairyland: "Set your heart at rest: / The fairy land buys not the child of me" (2.1.121–22). Titania explains her refusal with another lengthy narrative. The child's mother, she says, was "a votress of my order" (2.1.123). A votress of Diana wears the habit of a nun, lives in isolation, remains a virgin, and chants passionless hymns to the passionless moon (1.1.70–73). A votress of Titania does nothing of the kind. While the woman's vows (if any) are obscure, Titania's votress was a "mother" (2.1.123), who lived "in the spiced Indian air" (2.1.124), "gossip'd by [Titania's] side" at night (2.1.125), sat with her on the shore, and, watching trading ships at sea, laughed with Titania "to see the sails conceive / And grow big-bellied with the wanton wind" (2.1.128–29). Intimacy, laughter, and sensuality mark her worship (cf. 3.2.7). At the same time, mimicry marks the woman herself. Just as Titania and she would laugh at her pregnant belly as a metaphor for the ships' sails, so the votress, copying ("[f]ollowing" [2.1.131]) the ships, would "imitate" (2.1.132) their movement at sea with her pretty "swimming gait" on land:

> [S]he, with pretty and with swimming gait
> Following (her womb then rich with my young squire),
> Would imitate, and sail upon the land
> To fetch me trifles, and return again
> As from a voyage rich in merchandise.
>
> (2.1.130–34)

The woman would mimic what mimicked her. Similar in certain respects but quite different in others, she and the ships were reciprocal metaphors. Each was a figure for the other, she for the fullness of the ships' sails, the ships for the smoothness of her motion. Moreover, as the word "metaphor"—itself a metaphor—means, literally, a "carrying over" or a "transferring," the woman herself was not only carried over or exchanged for the ships, and the ships for her, but both she and the ships were engaged in traffic or "trade" (2.1.127). While metaphors for each other, they enacted the nature of a metaphor. Doubling back upon themselves, they enacted what they figured.[13] It seems no wonder that the woman, the personification of a metaphor, was Titania's votress, or that her son is a "changeling" (2.1.23, 120; 4.1.58).[14]

"But," Titania concludes, suddenly shifting to monosyllabic words,

> she, being mortal, of that boy did die;
> And for her sake do I rear up her boy;
> And for her sake I will not part with him.
>
> (2.1.135–37)

Death replaces generation. The boy's birth is, in fact, the mother's death. The two acts are one and the same. To be human means to be mortal ("[t]he hu-

man mortals" [2.1.101]). Titania, the third stepmother in the play, has taken
the mother's place and raised the boy "for her sake" and will not part with him
"for her sake," as she declares in parallel, closing lines. Although Puck said
that the boy had been stolen from an Indian king (2.1.22), Titania seems to
suggest that she adopted the boy at his mother's death. From all that Shakespeare tells us, it is impossible to determine whether the twin accounts are
complementary parts of a single story or rival versions of events. On the other
hand, Titania's account seems not to be repetitious in one respect in which we
might expect it to be. Oberon has evidently never heard the story before.

Already planning his plot, Oberon asks Titania how long she intends to
stay in the woods. Titania, unsuspecting, tells him that she may be there until after Theseus's wedding day. She speaks with a note of uncertainty ("Perchance" [2.1.139]). It seems that she would rather leave before Theseus's
wedding than endure Oberon's continued quarreling. Titania thus sets strict
conditions on Oberon's behavior. If he will calmly dance in the fairies' round
and attend their moonlight revels, he may go with them. If not, he should
avoid Titania, and she will keep away from him. Titania seems to want either
the concord of dancing or the silence of distance. Oberon, however, replies
with a condition of his own. He will go with her if she gives him the boy. Titania can enjoy dancing with him again only at the cost of surrendering the
child. Titania immediately and emphatically refuses. "Not for thy fairy king-
dom," she answers, repeating her former refusal (2.1.144; cf. 2.1.122) and
again commanding her fairies to leave, this time to avoid a larger quarrel:
"Fairies away! / We shall chide downright if longer I stay" (2.1.144–45; cf.
2.1.61). Notwithstanding the apparent finality of her closing couplet, she
will, of course, relent.

## 3. Love Juice
Oberon, speaking to himself, vows to torment Titania: "Well, go thy way;
thou shalt not from this grove / Till I torment thee for this injury"
(2.1.146–47). It is not immediately evident whether Oberon intends simply
to punish Titania for her refusal or to force her to give up the boy. His language suggests revenge, but soon he will say that he intends to extort her
concession (2.1.185). The love juice, or the strange torment it causes, he
seems to think, may accomplish both at once.

Addressing Puck for the first time, Oberon narrates the history and the
power of the love juice. Beginning by emphasizing Puck's remembrance of an
episode long ago ("Thou rememb'rest / Since . . . ?" [2.1.148–49]), he describes how he

once . . . sat upon a promontory,
And heard a mermaid on a dolphin's back
Uttering such dulcet and harmonious breath
That the rude sea grew civil at her song
And certain stars shot madly from their spheres
To hear the sea-maid's music.

(2.1.149–54)

The mermaid's voice was so sweet and harmonious that it was able to affect both the sea and the stars. Its effects on each, however, were opposite. While the rough sea, hearing the sound, was calmed, the ordered stars, desiring to hear, became disordered. The violent, made satisfied, grew civil; the ordered, made desirous, become mad. Oberon emphasizes that he, too, heard the mermaid's song. But although he describes—and even personifies—its effects on the sea and the stars, he says nothing about its having any effect on him. He speaks as though he had been an impassive spectator, simply observing the extraordinary scene. Some commentators suggest that Oberon's story echoes the legend of the singer-poet Arion.[15] But where Arion leaped into the sea in order to escape from murderous sailors (and was saved by a dolphin),[16] Oberon is silent about the mermaid's circumstances and intention. We have no idea why she was singing her song.

When Puck confirms that he remembers, Oberon goes on to tell him of another event. The relation between the two events is left dark. Apart from their closeness in time, we know nothing of the connection between the mermaid's song and Cupid's taking aim at the vestal virgin. We do not know whether the mermaid's song caused or in any way influenced Cupid's action. In fact, even their temporal relation, though close, is uncertain. "That very time I saw" (2.1.155) could mean either that the two events were simultaneous or that one followed upon the other. As with the twin accounts of the Indian boy, it is not clear how the two parts of Oberon's narrative fit together. They are parts which may or may not form a whole. Nor is it clear whether Puck remembers what he saw or what he only heard about. While we know that he was unable to see Cupid's action ("That very time I saw [but thou couldst not]" [2.1.155]), we can only guess whether he saw the mermaid herself or heard about her secondhand. The distinction between witnessing something extraordinary and hearing it recounted is blurred.

Oberon's account of Cupid's action contains the play's most extensive description of a god's action. It is no surprise that the god is Cupid, but it is curious that Oberon describes Cupid's failure, not his success. Despite being "all arm'd" (2.1.157), taking sure ("certain" [2.1.157]) aim, and shooting his golden arrow ("love-shaft" [2.1.159]) so strongly ("smartly" [2.2.159]) that it could "pierce a hundred thousand hearts" (2.1.160), Cupid missed his target. His target was a "vestal" "votress" (2.1.158, 163)—a virgin under a vow of chastity, for whom love would have been a curse, not a gift.

> But . . . young Cupid's fiery shaft [was]
> Quench'd in the chaste beams of the watery moon;
> And the imperial votress passed on,
> In maiden meditation, fancy free.
>
> (2.1.161–64)

If Cupid's golden arrow could overcome the virgin's vow, the moon's chaste beams were able to extinguish the god's fiery shaft. The virgin, who remained wholly unchanged, was able to proceed, free from the power of love. Piety and virginity are not always helpless against Cupid, though they appear to need superterrestrial aid (cf. 4.1.72–73). Oberon continues by describing the effect of the errant arrow:

> Yet mark'd I where the bolt of Cupid fell:
> It fell upon a little western flower,
> Before milk-white, now purple with love's wound:
> And maidens call it "love-in-idleness."
>
> (2.1.165–68)

Cupid's loss was Oberon's gain. The wandering arrow passed its power on to the wounded flower and gave Oberon Cupid's power:

> Fetch me that flower; the herb I show'd thee once.
> The juice of it, on sleeping eyelids laid,
> Will make or man or woman madly dote
> Upon the next live creature that it sees.
>
> (2.1.169–72)

By protecting the pious maiden, the moon's chaste beams, paradoxically, permitted Oberon to acquire the magical art of love—the power to cause anyone to fall madly in love at first sight with any living creature. The chaste moon's victory over Cupid is also its loss.

Oberon, again, orders Puck to "[f]etch [him] this herb" (2.1.173). It seems that he has held the drug in readiness for a long time, waiting for the right moment. Oberon then orders Puck to return "[e]re the leviathan can swim a league" (2.1.174). Puck, emphasizing his obedience and perhaps guessing Oberon's purpose, vows even greater speed: "I'll put a girdle round the earth / In forty minutes" (2.1.175–76). The Fairy at the beginning of the scene boasted of his ability to circle the earth in a day (2.1.7). Puck will do it in forty minutes.

Oberon's account of the love juice recalls much of Titania's account of the Indian boy and mother, to which it responds. Both Titania and Oberon sat on the edge of the land, looking out on the sea (2.1.126–27, 149–54). The one tells of a mother who was her "votress" (2.1.123); the other, of a virgin who was Diana's "votress" (2.1.163). Both speak of motion on the sea (2.1.127, 130–34, 150, 174) and of the sea itself (2.1.127, 152). Both mention "swim[ming]," Titania using the word metaphorically (2.1.130), Oberon implying as well as explicitly mentioning the literal activity (2.1.150, 174), and both speak of someone returning (2.1.133, 173–74). Both also emphasize antitheses, stressing sitting and moving, seeing and hearing. But where Titania tells of birth and death, Oberon tells of love and virginity. Both, however, sharply distinguish between the past and now ("But she, being mortal, of that boy did die; / And for her sake I do rear up her boy" [2.1.135–36]; "Before milk-white; now purple . . ." [2.1.167]). Titania's tale ends with a woman's death and Titania's acquiring her child. Oberon's ends with a god's failure and Oberon's acquiring his power. While Titania describes the woman and the ships imitating each other, Oberon describes a flower duplicating the power of Cupid's arrow. And, further, while the woman and the ships, doubling back upon themselves, enact the nature of a metaphor, the arrow and the flower, doubling back upon themselves, enact the nature of imagination in love. The flower, itself struck by a straying arrow, arouses love which is blind to person or merit. Accordingly, just as Helena said that love looks not with the eyes but with the mind (1.1.234), maidens call the flower "love-in-idleness"—which is to say, "pansy" or "thought."[17] Its juice, made powerful by Cupid's aberrant arrow, is the reification of desire aroused entirely by the imagination.[18]

After Puck leaves to fetch the love juice, Oberon explains what he intends to do. He will watch Titania when she is asleep and drop "the liquor" of the "juice," as he says redundantly, "in her eyes" (2.1.178, 176). Then, the next thing that she "waking looks upon" (2.1.179), she will "pursue . . . with the soul of love" (2.1.182). Oberon describes the juice's effect as "the soul of love." He identifies the quintessence of love with the power of love. Love, he seems to mean, is naturally unrestrained in its measure even when it is indiscriminate in its object. Its madness is not merely metaphorical. Oberon mentions six kinds of beasts that Titania might fall in love with. The first four—"lion, bear, or wolf, or bull" (2.1.180)—are all dangerous, while the last two are characterized as more mischievous than deadly ("meddling monkey, or . . . busy ape" [2.1.181]). Oberon says nothing about an ass, which is neither dangerous nor mischievous. Nor does he say anything about a human. Oberon's plan is to extort the Indian boy from Titania:

> And ere I take this charm from off her sight
> (As I can take it with another herb)
> I'll make her render up her page to me.
>
> (2.1.183–85)

We must wonder why Oberon's plan would work. Its prospects appear puzzling. Why would Titania give up something she wants (the boy) in order to rid herself of something she madly desires (her love)? If Oberon expects Titania to be so shamed by her mad passion that she would want to give it up, its very madness would seem to work against her feeling such shame. In fact, she will not feel any shame until after Oberon removes his charm (4.1.78). On the other hand, Oberon may expect that Titania's love will not be returned and that she will relinquish the boy in order to free herself from her fruitless desire. Oberon will, in fact, soon suggest that Titania will "[l]ove and languish" for her love's sake (2.2.28), though, again, the very power of her passion would seem to work against her wishing to be rid of it, despite her pain, as the lovelorn young lovers will soon show. Whatever the case, Oberon's plan will, of course, work, but only for a completely unexpected and accidental reason.

Oberon no sooner states his plan than Demetrius and Helena enter. By pure chance, the two plots—that of the royal fairies and that of the young Athenian lovers—converge. Without knowing who has come, and without explaining why he might be interested, Oberon chooses to make himself "invisible" (2.1.186) so he can overhear them. As he could see what is invisible (2.1.155ff.), he can make himself invisible. Without the former he would not possess the love juice; without the latter he would not affect the lovers.

### 4. Love's Chase

This is the first time we have seen Demetrius and Helena together. Just as he is chasing Hermia, Helena is chasing him. The pursuer is being pursued. Pursuit and reversal are the themes of the young Athenians' exchange.

Demetrius contradicts himself right away. He tells Helena not to pursue him because he does not love her: "I love thee not, therefore pursue me not" (2.1.188). But he pursues Hermia even though she does not love him:

"Where is Lysander and fair Hermia?" (2.1.189). Demetrius's locution of reasoning, with which he begins and ends the speech, only underscores his self-contradiction: "I love thee not, therefore pursue me not"; "Hence, get thee gone, and follow me no more" (2.1.188, 194). Reason, he seems to say, should perfectly govern desire. Yet, Demetrius himself declares how his love for Hermia has driven him mad: "And here am I, and wood within this wood / Because I cannot meet my Hermia" (2.1.192–93). Demetrius goes so far as to call Hermia "my Hermia." His love for her, not hers for him, makes her his. Even as his desire bemoans not having what it seeks, it speaks as though it already possessed its object. At least in speech, love, it seems, tends to confuse longing and fulfillment.[19]

Demetrius's self-contradictory speech, while confusing desire and its object, juxtaposes pairs or opposites at least once in each of its five sentences. Its central sentence, in particular, organized around a strong central caesura, balances "the one" and "the other," while the rest of the sentence forms a chiasmus, "I'll slay . . . slayeth me," varying the same word and reversing subject and object (2.1.190). The juxtaposition of pairs and opposites generally characterizes Demetrius's manner of speaking throughout the play. In addition, here, to other balanced breaks (2.1.188, 190, 192, 194) and a pair of epiphora (2.1.188, 191–92), Demetrius plays on a double, a triple, and, finally, a quadruple meaning: First: "The one I'll slay, the other slayeth me" (2.1.190). As Demetrius would kill for love, so he is killed by love.[20] The former is literally true; the latter, figuratively true. Then: "And here am I, and wood within this wood" (2.1.192). Demetrius is at once wooed ("wood") by Helena and madly frantic ("wood") because he cannot find Hermia in this forest ("wood"). As with his play on "slay," Demetrius's play on "wood" is partly literally and partly figuratively true. Finally: "Hence, get thee gone, and follow me no more" (2.1.194). "Hence," here, has a fourfold meaning. It is a synonym for "therefore" and a command to leave, and it means "from now on" and "away from here." It is, at once, both temporal and spatial, and both a conclusion and a consequent command.

Helena rejects Demetrius's command and blames him for her pursuit. "You draw me, you hard-hearted adamant—" (2.1.195). Helena, too, plays on words. "Adamant" means both a magnet and the hardest metal. Demetrius, Helena suggests, both draws and resists her. Then, correcting half of her metaphor, while implicitly contrasting their hearts, Helena assures Demetrius that her own heart is not hard, like iron, but true as steel: "But yet you draw not iron, for my heart / Is true as steel" (2.1.196–97). But notwithstanding her true heart, Helena is unable to obey Demetrius's command: "Leave you your power to draw, / And I shall have no power to follow you"

(2.1.197–98). Helena is entirely blameless because she is entirely helpless. She cannot help doing what she is doing, for while Demetrius has the "power to draw," she has only the "power to follow." Her passivity compels her pursuit.

Sounding much like Hermia earlier (1.1.194–201), Demetrius denies his responsibility and claims that he does nothing to attract Helena:

> Do I entice you? Do I speak you fair?
> Or rather do I not in plainest truth,
> Tell you I do not, nor I cannot love you?
>
> (2.1.199–201)

Demetrius seems to think that only words of love can attract ("entice") and plain words of rejection must repel. Love cannot be aroused unless it is returned. Demetrius appears to have forgotten Hermia's treatment of him.

Echoing Hermia, but to the opposite effect, Helena confesses that the more Demetrius rebuffs her, the more she loves him: "And even for that do I love you the more" (2.1.202; cf. 1.1.194–99). Demetrius's rejection only increases her love. It seems that words of scorn can arouse the love they rebuff, while words of love can repel the love they seek. As in her discussion with Hermia, Helena, however, fails to recognize her own point. Instead of considering why Demetrius is not pursuing the woman who has declared her love for him, but rather the woman who has spurned him, she begs for the chance to follow him and supplicate him like his spaniel. Earlier, she was going to tell Demetrius of Hermia's plan just so she could see him even chasing after Hermia (1.1.246–51). Now, having accomplished that, she is reduced to begging him for permission to beg him like his dog:

> I am your spaniel; and, Demetrius,
> The more you beat me, I will fawn on you.
> Use me but as your spaniel, spurn me, strike me,
> Neglect me, lose me; only give me leave,
> Unworthy as I am, to follow you.
> What worser place can I beg in your love—
> And yet a place of high respect with me—
> Than to be used as you use your dog?
>
> (2.1.204–10)

The worst place in Demetrius's love would be a place highly regarded by Helena. If Oberon would debase Titania by making her fall in love with a beast, Helena would debase herself by turning herself into her love's fawning dog.

Demetrius cautions her not to tempt his hatred too much, "[f]or I am sick when I do look on thee" (2.1.212). Helena, turning his words back upon him, repeats them with a contrary meaning: "And I am sick when I look not on you" (2.1.213). Where Demetrius meant that he is nauseated when he sees her, Helena means that she is lovesick when she does not see him. The closeness of their words marks the distance between them.[21]

Demetrius now warns. Soon he will threaten to do Helena "mischief in the wood" (2.1.237). Now, however, he warns not that he might do her violence if she stays, but that she calls her "modesty" (2.1.214) into question by putting herself in the hands of someone who does not love her,

> . . . trust[ing] the opportunity of night
> And the ill counsel of a desert place
> With the rich worth of your virginity.

> (2.1.217–19)

The danger is not rape, but reputation. For Helena to stay with Demetrius alone, at night, in the woods "impeach[es]" her "modesty too much" (2.1.214) by making her appear to think that her virginity is worth little.

Helena defends herself and her modesty by praising Demetrius's qualities. His "virtue" is her immunity or "privilege" (2.1.220). Answering each of his reproaches, Helena insists that Demetrius's qualities render her safe. For her seeing his face turns night into day, and her being with him is, to her mind, being with the whole world. So, because Demetrius lights the night and is all the world, she is not alone with him at night in the woods: "[A]ll the world is here to look on me" (2.1.226). While we might wonder how literally Helena means her metaphorical answer, we should note that she qualifies what she says: "I think I am not in the night" (2.1.222); "For you, in my respect, are all the world" (2.1.224). Helena seems to distinguish what is from what she thinks is. Yet, the distinction does not seem to matter. If anything, it seems only to strengthen her conviction (cf. 1.1.230–31).

Having failed to arouse Helena's concern for her modesty, Demetrius tries to make her fear for her life. He says that he will run away, hide in the thickets, and leave her to the mercy of wild beasts. Helena, again turning his words around, accuses Demetrius of having a heart less merciful than a wild beast's: "The wildest hath not such a heart as you" (2.1.229). But then, going further, she inverts his warning and challenges him to run away, making explicit the reversal implicit in her pursuing him:

> Run when you will; the story shall be chang'd:
> Apollo flies, and Daphane holds the chase;
> The dove pursues the griffin, the mild hind
> Makes speed to catch the tiger—bootless speed,
> When cowardice pursues and valour flies!
>
> (2.1.230–34)

Helena, as before, sees her own situation in light of a "story" (cf. 1.1.235–41)—as the myth of Apollo and Daphane, in reverse. While exchanging the roles of Apollo and Daphane (and hence of Cupid's two arrows),[22] she also reverses the natural effects of courage and speed. Love, she suggests, has the power to render speed useless and to make cowardice strong. It does the one by doing the other: love makes the slow swift by making the cowardly brave. It seems ironically fitting, however, that Helena refers to the story of Apollo and Daphane, for Apollo failed to win Daphane's love, even though he was swifter and nearly overtook her. Helena has already caught up to her love once and did not win his heart. What she lacks is not speed.[23] Apart from love's endless hope, it is hard to see why she should expect Demetrius to be different next time.

Demetrius, refusing to continue to talk, threatens violence. Unless she lets him go, Helena should expect him to do her "mischief in the wood" (2.1.237). Helena, still once more turning Demetrius's words back on him while shifting their sense, dismisses his threat by claiming that he already does her mischief: "Ay, in the temple, in the town, the field, / You do me mischief" (2.1.238–39). Demetrius does her mischief everywhere. The mischief is not just making her fall in love with him, but compelling her to act in a scandalous way—in a way that has humiliated not only her but women, in general:

> Fie, Demetrius!
> Your wrongs do set a scandal on my sex.
> We cannot fight for love, as men may do;
> We should be woo'd, and were not made to woo.
>
> (2.1.239–42)

Demetrius forces Helena to act in a way that is scandalous for a woman, by forcing her to act like a man. While generalizing both the cause and its effect, Helena speaks as though nature agrees perfectly with convention. What men may do or should do, they can do; what women may not or should not do, they were not made to do. Helena goes further, however. She suggests that a woman can do nothing proper to win a man. Not able or allowed to fight or to woo, women must be entirely passive or else become unnatural mimics of men. There is nothing respectable or natural that a woman can do to attract or win a man. Helena's helplessness is every woman's fate.

When Demetrius leaves, Helena, addressing him as "thee" for the first time, vows to follow: "I'll follow thee, and make a heaven of hell, / To die upon the hand I love so well" (2.1.243–44). Helena appears to take Demetrius's warning of violence at face value. She speaks of following Demetrius and dying by his hand. Both she and Hermia complain of being in hell. Helena, however, inverts what Hermia said. Hermia spoke of turning "a heaven into a hell" (1.1.207); Helena speaks of making "a heaven of hell." For Hermia, being unable to marry the man she loves has transformed Athens from a heaven into a hell. But, for Helena, being killed by the man she loves would transform her hell into a heaven. Death, it would seem, is her only hope, though it is by no means evident that Helena seriously means it.

## 5. Flower Power

The invisible Oberon, who has overheard the exchange, takes sympathy on Helena and promises to reverse the chase before Demetrius goes far: "Fare thee well, nymph; ere he do leave this grove / Thou shalt fly him, and he shall seek thy love" (2.1.245–46). It is not yet certain whether Oberon seeks to reunite the former lovers or, instead, to punish Demetrius by turning tables on him. From what he says here, we know only that Demetrius will pursue Helena and she will flee him.

Puck, greeted by Oberon as "wanderer" (2.1.247), enters with the magical flower, brought from the far ends of the earth. The love juice will now do double service. That it will be used in connection with the young lovers is altogether a consequence of chance, depending on the convergence of the two quarreling couples in the woods and Oberon's plot against Titania.

Oberon describes a fragrant, flowery bank in the forest where Titania sometimes sleeps at night. His lyrical description of her canopy and couch tends to mingle what it describes, much like the plants and scents themselves. Oberon uses a singular verb with a plural subject, while, in addition, stating one of the two subjects in the plural and the other in the generic singular: "Where oxslips and the nodding violet grows" (2.1.250). Moreover, one of the flowers ("oxslips") is itself a hybrid. Oberon also names three flowers which form Titania's canopy. The three are easily confused: "Quite over-canopied with luscious woodbine, / With sweet musk-roses, and with eglantine" (2.1.251–52). While eglantine is, like a musk-rose, a rose, owing to its sweet fragrance it is also often associated with woodbine (honey-suckle), with which it is rhymed here.[24] Oberon explains that he will streak Titania's eyes with the juice of his magical "flower" (2.1.247), while she is "[l]ull'd in these flowers with dances and delight" (2.1.254). Amid the bank's flowers, he will use his flower to make her love what she should hate ("And make her full of hateful fantasies" [2.1.258]).

It now becomes clearer that Oberon intends to reunite Helena and Demetrius. Describing them as "[a] sweet Athenian lady . . . in love / With a disdainful youth" (2.1.260–61), he says that while Puck should do the same to Demetrius's eyes, he should "[e]ffect it with some care, [so] that [Demetrius] may prove / More fond on [Helena] than she upon her love" (2.1.265–66). Demetrius and Helena will love each other, but their loves will be unequal. As we shall see in a moment, Oberon knows very little about Demetrius, but he understands the connection between his lovelessness and his disdain. Un-like Helena, he recognizes that Demetrius needs to be loved less in order to love at all. Demetrius can love only what he lacks and can only disdain what he has. Strictly speaking, reciprocal love is impossible for him.

Although stressing that Puck should apply the love juice "with some care," Oberon himself takes little care in giving his instructions. Unlike with Titania, he does not know where to find Demetrius, so Puck must "seek [him] through this grove" (2.1.259). But Oberon's description of Demetrius is no help: "Thou shalt know the man / By the Athenian garments he hath on" (2.1.263–64). Oberon's description says either too much or too little—too much if Demetrius is the only Athenian young man in the woods, for then Puck would not need to recognize him by his clothing; too little if he is not, for then his Athenian garments would not adequately distinguish him. As it happens, Oberon should know that his description is insufficient, for Demetrius's first words to Helena spoke of Lysander's being in "this wood" (2.1.189–93). Much of what happens to the young lovers will result from Oberon's careless error.

## Act Two, Scene Two

### 1. Harm and Charm

Oberon just said that he would apply the love juice to Titania's eyes when she was "[l]ull'd . . . with dances and delight" (2.1.254). Titania, entering with her royal train, calls for a dance and fairy song. The dance, a "roundel" (2.2.1), is a circular dance, like other fairy dances (e.g., 2.1.86, 140). Titania's attendants apparently join hands and dance around her, while singing a song. The song is also called a "roundel" ("roundelay")—a type of song which has a refrain recurring frequently or at fixed intervals. In this instance, the song is a lullaby, consisting of two quatrains, each followed by a six-line refrain. It is meant to lull Titania to sleep.

The fairies are to dance and sing, and then, within "the third part of a minute" (2.2.2), leave to perform various tasks. The brevity of time seems to suit their diminutive world.[25] The fairy world is at once speeded up and (mostly) pared down.[26] The two seem to go together. Titania assigns the fairies three tasks:

> Some to kill cankers in the musk-rose buds;
> Some war with reremice for their leathern wings,
> To make my small elves coats; and some to keep back
> The clamorous owl, that nightly hoots and wonders
> At our quaint spirits.

> (2.2.3–7)

The fairies are not without their natural enemies. They must "kill" canker worms to protect the roses they love and make "war" on bats to provide the coats the elves need. Both their loves and their needs require them to kill. Nor are the fairies free from frightening dangers. Their dainty ("quaint") spirits attract the hooting and wonder of dangerous owls. What sets the fairy world apart from the natural world adds to the fairies' dangers.

Accordingly, the fairies' song, which is meant to sing Titania to sleep, is also meant to protect her while sleeping. It is a charm to ward off evils as well as a lullaby. The two quatrains, which are couched entirely in the negative, are to keep certain creatures away:

> You spotted snakes with double tongue,
> Thorny hedgehogs, be not seen;
> Newts and blind-worms, do no wrong,
> Come not near our fairy queen.

> (2.2.9–12)

> Weaving spiders, come not here;
> Hence, you long-legg'd spinners, hence!
> Beetles black, approach not near;
> Worm nor snail, do no offence.

> (2.2.19–22)

And while the quatrains are intended to fend off harmful or repulsive creatures of the woods, the refrain bids Philomel to join the fairies in singing their lullaby:

> Philomel, with melody,
> Sing in our sweet lullaby.
> Lulla, lulla, lullaby; lulla, lulla, lullaby.
> Never harm, nor spell, nor charm,
> Come our lovely lady nigh;
> So goodnight, with lullaby.
>
> (2.2.13–18)

Philomel—whose name in Greek means "love of lyric song"—was transformed into a nightingale to escape her sister's murderous husband, who had torn out her tongue after raping her to keep her from revealing his crime (Ovid, *Metamorphoses*, 6.424–614). Later, in Athens, Titania will emphasize the words rather than the melody of a song in offering a blessing (5.1.383–86). Here in the woods, her fairies emphasize the sweet, speechless sound of a melody in singing a charm to protect her.

When Titania falls asleep, a fairy, dismissing the singers, declares, in a tone of certainty and assurance, "Hence, away! Now all is well; / One aloof stand sentinel" (2.2.24–25). Yet, although Titania will avoid physical harm, neither the song nor the sentinel will be proof against the spell of the fairy king's stronger charm.

Oberon, applying the love juice, chants what is to happen when Titania awakes:

> What thou seest when thou dost wake,
> Do it for thy true love take;
> Love and languish for his sake.
>
> (2.2.26–28)

Oberon distinguishes between love-juice love and true love. Titania, he says, will "take"—that is, mistake—what she sees for her "true love." At the same time, Oberon seems to presume that Titania's passion will not be returned ("[l]ove and languish"). Beasts by nature desire only members of their own kind. Titania will pine away with love. Oberon then names five possible objects of her love, all known for ferocity (cf. 2.1.179–81):

Be it ounce, or cat, or bear,
Pard, or boar with bristled hair,
In thy eye that shall appear
When thou wak'st, it is thy dear.
Wake when some vile thing is near.

(2.2.29–33)

Titania will make two mistakes, which are really the same. As she will mistake her true love, she will also mistake its beauty. Though vile in itself, what she sees will appear most beautiful in her eyes ("it is thy dear"). Neither her love nor her beloved's beauty will be as it appears.

## 2. Together and Apart

Lysander, concerned that Hermia has grown faint from their "wand'ring in the wood" (2.2.34), confesses that, "to speak troth" (2.2.35), he has lost their way. Their journey to his aunt's house has proved to resemble a maze. Lysander suggests that they rest and wait for day, "if [Hermia] think[s] it good" (2.2.36). He does not command, but seeks her consent. Neither of them ever mentions their original destination again.

Hermia agrees to wait the night, but asks Lysander to find his own bed and sleep apart from her. Lysander objects: "One turf shall serve as pillow for us both; / One heart, one bed, two bosoms, and one troth" (2.2.40–41). While two in body ("two bosoms"), they are one in mutual love ("[o]ne heart") and one in faithful vows ("one troth"), and so they should share one bed. Hermia, however, insists: "Nay, good Lysander; for my sake, my dear, / Lie further off yet; do not lie so near" (2.2.42–43). Lysander, at least claiming to have been misunderstood, declares his innocence: "O take the sense, sweet, of my innocence! / Love takes the meaning in love's conference" (2.2.44–45). Although words can have more than one sense or meaning, in lovers' conversation love lets the lovers understand each other. Love listens as well as speaks. Yet, notwithstanding that love understands a lover's words, Lysander finds it necessary to explain what he means:

I mean that my heart unto yours is knit,
So that but one heart we can make of it:
Two bosoms interchained with an oath,
So then, two bosoms and a single troth.
Then by your side no bed-room me deny;
For lying so, Hermia, I do not lie.

(2.2.46–51)

Lysander repeats, only more strongly, what Hermia did not want him to say: as they are one in heart, one in troth, but two in body, their bed should overcome their bodies' separateness. Lysander's closing play on the two senses of "lie" attempts to turn the question entirely to that of his truthfulness: since he does not lie, they should lie together. Lysander mentions the word "troth" thrice in the exchange (2.2.35, 41, 49). No one speaks of troth or truth nearly so often as he.[27]

Hermia compliments Lysander on his clever wordplay: "Lysander riddles very prettily" (2.2.52). Her compliment, ironically, tops him. It turns Lysander's play on the twin meanings of "lie" into puns on his name. Hermia then, more seriously, explains her objection by implicitly distinguishing between conventional propriety ("manners" [2.2.53]) and "human modesty." While she mildly curses the former (and her pride) if she meant to say that Lysander lied, she appeals to the latter to explain her meaning:

> [F]or love and courtesy,
> Lie further off, in human modesty;
> Such separation as may well be said
> Becomes a virtuous bachelor and a maid,
> So far be distant.
>
> (2.2.55–59)

Hermia governs herself in the name of "love and courtesy," "human modesty," and what "[b]ecomes a virtuous bachelor and a maid." In act 1, scene 1, she meant, by her "modesty" (1.1.60), a lack of presumption or impudence. Here, she means a sense of self-restraint springing from an appreciation of what is seemly. As it stands in contrast to mere "manners," so it also stands in contrast to mere reputation, which Demetrius meant by the word when he warned Helena that she "impeach[es] her modesty too much" by trusting her virginity to him at night in the woods (2.1.214). Here, on Hermia's lips, "modesty" combines the morality of a fixed principle and the sweetness of love. It unities reason and passion. It is also not limited to women. "[H]uman modesty" applies to "a virtuous bachelor" as well as to "a maid."

Throughout the play, but particularly here, Hermia seems to live up to her name. Hermes, after whom she is named, is the god both of boundaries and of the transgression of boundaries. He both respects and crosses them. Whereas Dionysus, his rival, blurs and dissolves limits, Hermes maintains hierarchies and distinctions, even as he traverses them.[28] Just as Hermes crosses boundaries and yet preserves them, Hermia defies her father's authority and yet preserves her own modesty. Though she contravenes boundaries, she keeps her restraint intact.

At once together and apart, Hermia and Lysander get ready to sleep. Hermia offers a brief prayer for Lysander's unchanged love until his death: "[G]ood night, sweet friend: / Thy love ne'er alter till thy sweet life end!" (2.2.59–60). And Lysander seconds her prayer and offers a vow: "Amen, amen, to that fair prayer say I; / And then end life when I end loyalty!" (2.2.61–62). Neither lover thinks that Hermia's love needs a prayer or a vow. Except for Titania (at least when under the influence of the love juice), it is men, not women, whose loves are inconstant in the play. Hence, in the corresponding passage when she and Lysander planned to flee Athens in the opening scene, Hermia could playfully swear, "By all the vows that ever men have broke / (In numbers more than ever women spoke)" (1.1.175–76). The lovers, in their final words before falling asleep, emphasize their closeness in their separation by sharing a wish:

> Lys.:  Here is my bed; sleep give thee all his rest.
> Herm.: With half that wish the wisher's eyes be press'd.
>
> (2.2.63–64)

The wisher's eyes will indeed be pressed, but with Oberon's love juice as well as with sleep. The next time Lysander speaks, just thirty lines from now, he will instantly break his vow.

## 3. Eros and Error

Puck enters, complaining that he has gone through the forest, but has found no Athenian. Suddenly, however, he sees Lysander and Hermia. "Night and silence—Who is here?" (2.2.69), he asks, juxtaposing the absence of light and sound in his fruitless search with the abrupt, apparent presence of what he has been seeking. Seeing Lysander wearing Athenian clothes ("Weeds of Athens he doth wear" [2.2.70]) and Hermia lying on "the dank and dirty ground" (2.2.74), Puck takes his cue from Oberon ("This is he my master said . . . / And here the maiden . . ." [2.2.71–73]) and immediately jumps to the wrong conclusion. To Puck, the distance between the sleepers is a sign that the man disdains the woman and she dares not lie near him: "Pretty soul, she durst not lie / Near this lack-love, this kill-courtesy" (2.2.75–76). What was done from "love and courtesy," Puck sees as having been caused by "this lack-love, this kill-courtesy." Modesty means nothing to him. Puck quickly becomes angry at the man:

> Churl, upon thy eyes I throw
> All the power this charm doth owe:
> When thou wak'st, let love forbid
> Sleep his seat on thy eyelid.
>
> (2.2.77–80)

Oberon told Puck to make the man fonder of the woman than she is of him. Puck seems to exceed his instructions. Using all the power that the charm possesses, he will punish the "lack-love," in the name of love, with sleepless love. Puck's anger may seem surprising. Unlike Oberon, Puck has shown no interest in setting love right. Later, that will change, though not before he fully enjoys watching the lovers' foolish wrangling. Puck's anger is aroused here, however, not by his concern for any lover, but by the sight of someone he takes to be a loveless impediment to love and hence to his most enjoyable sport ("[T]his their jangling I esteem a sport" [3.2.353; also 3.2.118–21]). He is thinking of his own amusement, not of the lovers' happiness.

## 4. Appearance and Reality

Just as Helena and Demetrius crossed Oberon's path (2.1.188ff.) and Puck crossed Hermia and Lysander's (2.2.65ff.), Helena and Demetrius now cross Hermia and Lysander's path. Their brief exchange consists, again, in reversals (cf. 2.1.188–244). Although Demetrius orders Helena to leave ("I charge thee, hence" [2.2.84]), he is the one who goes ("I alone will go" [2.2.86]). And Helena's urging him to "[s]tay, though thou kill me," (2.2.83) becomes his commanding her to "[s]tay, on thy peril" (2.2.86). We might note that, despite everything, to Helena, Demetrius is still "sweet Demetrius" (2.2.83). And, unlike earlier, she now uses familiar pronouns in addressing him to his face.

It is not immediately clear whether Helena stays after Demetrius leaves because she is "out of breath" or because she has given up her "fond chase" (2.2.87). She seems at first to recognize that the more she pursues Demetrius, the less he wants her: "The more my prayer, the lesser is my grace" (2.2.88). But Helena no sooner says this than, as when she first appeared (1.1.180–251), she compares herself unfavorably to Hermia and attributes her own unhappiness not to her actions but to her looks. Hermia is happy, she says, because she has "blessed and attractive eyes" (2.2.90). No longer distinguishing between the ways Demetrius and the rest of Athens see her (cf. 1.1.227–29), Helena now seems to think that he is right. He sees her as she is. Thus, Helena plaintively asks, "How came [Hermia's] eyes so bright?" (2.2.91). And with more than a touch of self-pity, she concludes that it was not because of Hermia's tears, for if it were, Helena's own eyes would be as bright. "No, no; I am as ugly as a bear" (2.2.93). Demetrius, she says, does only what beasts do. Since they run away from her for fear of her ugliness, it is "[t]herefore no marvel" that Demetrius flees "[her] presence thus," as if she were "a monster" (2.2.95, 96). Her ugliness excuses Demetrius's action as well as her own. As he cannot help fleeing her, she can do nothing to prevent it. All she can do is cry.

Further shifting responsibility, Helena blames her mirror for her vying with Hermia: "What wicked and dissembling glass of mine / Made me compare with Hermia's sphery eyne?" (2.2.97–98). Blaming her mirror for deceiving her, Helena tells of seeing a false reflection of her own eyes and claims that that reflection made her a rival of Hermia, a rivalry which she now apparently quits. In doing so, Helena draws a double comparison. She compares her own eyes to Hermia's and Hermia's to the heavenly spheres ("Hermia's sphery eyne"). The former is a comparison of difference; the latter, a metaphor, of likeness. Helena is unlike Hermia, while Hermia resembles the heavens. It seems telling that although Helena blames her mirror for deceiving her about her relative beauty, she seems to take for granted that she can know herself only by comparing herself to another. Beauty, for her, is always a matter of comparison (cf. 1.1.181–201, 226–29; 3.2.232). In this important respect, she and Demetrius form a pair. For her, beauty, for him, love, are essentially rooted in rivalry. Comparisons are everything.

Helena discovers Lysander on the ground. In *Pyramus and Thisbe*, Thisbe finds Pyramus on the ground and, initially thinking him asleep, discovers that he is dead (5.1.311–12). Here, the story is reversed. Helena initially thinks that Lysander is dead, but, seeing "no blood, no wound" (2.2.100), proceeds to wake him up.

Lysander wakes, and immediately and madly falls in love with Helena. This is the play's first example of love at first sight:

> *Hel.*: Lysander, if you live, good sir, awake!
> *Lys.*: And run through fire I will for thy sweet sake!
>
> (2.2.101–2)

Love speaks in perpetual hyperbole. Where Helena just accounted herself ugly, Lysander sees in her nothing but perfect beauty: "Transparent Helena! Nature shows art, / That through thy bosom makes me see thy heart" (2.2.103–4). Lysander uses "transparent" in twin senses. He means both brilliant and diaphanous. The blonde, sweet Helena is gloriously radiant and entirely ingenuous. While her outward looks radiate beauty, her inward goodness is wholly visible to Lysander's eyes. Lysander, while supposing art to be superior to nature, at once states and cancels their usual antithesis. Bodies, by nature, are opaque. They are impenetrable to sight. Art, however, reveals the inside by means of the outside, the soul by means of the body. It exhibits the natures of its characters by imitating or representing their actions and words.[29] In Helena's case, however, nature shows directly what art shows indirectly. Nature imitates art imitating nature. It allows at least the loving Lysander to see Helena's heart right though her body ("bosom") as clearly as her outward looks. Her body in no way obscures what she truly is. Her appearance and true nature are the same.

Lysander, in his next breath, speaks of killing: "Where is Demetrius? O how fit a word / Is that vile name to perish on my sword" (2.2.105–6). Just as art is his standard for nature, Lysander confuses the man and his name. He speaks as though what stands for the man is the man, and to kill the "word" or the "name" is to kill the man himself. Lysander, accordingly, calls Demetrius's name vile. Plutarch explains that he wrote the life of Demetrius because proper moral education requires young men to see what is base as well as what is noble. Medicine deals with diseases and music with discord in order to remove them and produce their opposites. Similarly, the "arts [of] temperance, justice, and wisdom do not only consider honesty, uprightness, and profit, but examine withal the nature and effects of lewdness, corruption, and damage" (Plutarch, Demetrius, 1.2; North, 5:372). Lysander seems to have studied Plutarch's cautionary tale all too well. Once again seeing letters as life, he confuses Plutarch's character and Helena's scornful beloved. And taking the namesake for the original, he not only finds the name itself vile but, thinking the name equivalent to what it names, wants to strike it rather than the man himself.

Helena, for good reason, misunderstands. She thinks that Lysander curses Demetrius because both of them love Hermia: "What though he love your Hermia? Lord, what though? / Yet Hermia still loves you; then be content" (2.2.108–9). It should not matter to Lysander that Demetrius is his rival in love, so long as Hermia continues to love him. In fact, however, Lysander threatens Demetrius, not for loving Hermia, but for hurting Helena—for scorning her love. He is indignant not that Demetrius is (or was) his rival for Hermia, but, paradoxically, that he is not his rival for Helena. Killing Demetrius (or his name) would be his act of love for Helena.

Lysander thus immediately forswears his love for Hermia and harshly disparages her. Where Helena urged him to be "content," that is, calm, Lysander shifts the sense of her word and, repeating and twice rhyming it, vehemently denies that he ever was satisfied with Hermia: "Content with Hermia? No, I do repent / The tedious minutes I with her have spent" (2.2.110–11). In a moment, Lysander will try to explain his change of heart as a matter of his having matured. Here, however, with egregious revisionism, he claims that he never enjoyed Hermia's company—that he always found her wearisome and boring. If love distorts what it sees in the present, it no less distorts what it remembers of the past.

In his first words to Helena upon awakening, Lysander spoke of the correspondence between her outward beauty and her inward goodness. Now, he does something similar as he contrasts Hermia and Helena with a pair of metaphors: "Not Hermia, but Helena I love: / Who would not change a raven for a dove?" (2.2.112–13). Dark-haired and of dark complexion (3.2.257, 263), Hermia is a raven, a bird proverbial for both blackness and noisy, aggressive omnivorousness. And, blond and of fair complexion (1.1.182), Helena is a dove, a bird proverbial for both whiteness and harmless innocence. Having fallen in (and out of) love for no reason other than the love juice, the love-smitten Lysander believes that the outside—indeed, the most superficial aspect of the outside—reflects and reveals the deepest moral inside. The identification of outward appearances and inner qualities is complete for Hermia as well as for Helena.

Lysander proceeds to claim to be acting in accordance with reason. He not only contends that reason has guided his change of affections, however. As though to corroborate his claim, he tries to set forth his explanation in a fully rational or logical manner. Lysander first states a general principle and then its particular instance (cf. 1.1.132–49): "The will of man is by his reason sway'd, / And reason says you are the worthier maid" (2.2.114–15). One might ask, though, why reason did not tell him this earlier. If a man's desire is swayed by his reason, did reason tell Lysander to love Hermia? Lysander answers the question by maintaining that he was previously not mature enough to be capable of reason. Again, he states a general principle and the particular instance: "Things growing are not ripe until their season: / So I, being young, till now ripe not to reason" (2.2.116–17). Then, continuing his formal argument, he offers the obverse of his particular instance, with a positive predicate: "And, touching now the point of human skill, / Reason becomes the marshal to my will" (2.2.118–19). Lysander having reached the peak of human judgment, reason now guides his will. Entirely mature, he is entirely rational, and reason now fully governs his desire. Love, it would seem, is only sometimes like a child (cf. 1.1.238–39). Lysander, who mentions reason four times in this speech (2.2.114, 115, 117, 119) and nowhere else, is never less rational than when claiming to be nothing but rational. His claim to reason amounts to love's mockery of reason.

True to form, Lysander concludes his "reasoned" account by telling Helena that "[r]eason" ". . . leads me to your eyes, where I o'erlook / Love's stories, written in love's richest book" (2.2.119–21). Lysander, still again confounding love and letters, says not only that Helena illustrates "[l]ove's stories, written in love's richest book," but that she is the book itself. For Lysander, looking at his love's eyes is tantamount to reading the richest book of love. Love turns his beloved into art's presentation of love. Love becomes, literally, a love story.

Helena takes Lysander's words as mockery—as a derisive imitation of love—and angrily denies that she deserves such treatment: "Wherefore was I to this keen mockery born? / When at your hands did I deserve this scorn?" (2.2.122–23). Helena never did anything to Lysander to deserve his scorn. She does think, however, that she deserves Demetrius's scorn:

> Is't not enough, is't not enough, young man,
> That I did never, no, nor never can
> Deserve a sweet look from Demetrius' eye,
> But you must flout my insufficiency?
>
> (2.2.124–27)

Helena does not deserve to be mocked by Lysander for not deserving to be loved by Demetrius. Owing to her unattractiveness ("insufficiency"), she does not deserve to be loved by Demetrius. But good character or good taste should prevent Lysander from mocking her deficiencies. Lysander, however, insults her, she says, by the way he woos her, because he does not really mean his professions of love and praise: "Good troth, you do me wrong, good sooth, you do, / In such disdainful manner me to woo" (2.2.128–29). Love's hyperbolic speech may be (unintentionally) comic when meant, but it is insulting when not meant. The praise becomes mockery, ridiculing as absent the very qualities it pretends to praise as present. Helena thus accuses Lysander of not being the gentleman she had thought he was: "But fare you well; perforce I must confess / I thought you lord of more true gentleness" (2.2.130–31). Lysander is not truly a gentleman, because he merely pretends to love her. And so, departing, Helena voices her distress: "O that a lady, of one man refus'd, / Should of another therefore be abus'd!" (2.2.132–33). Oberon, intending to end Demetrius's disdainful treatment of Helena, has only compounded it, in her eyes, with Lysander's abuse.

When Helena leaves, Lysander explains to himself that she mistook his love because she failed to see Hermia asleep on the ground: "She sees not Hermia" (2.2.134). Had she seen her, Lysander seems to think, Helena would have realized that he no longer loves Hermia. Lysander appears to imagine that Helena—or anyone else—would view Hermia as he now does and would therefore recognize that he does not love her anymore. Accordingly, Lysander, wanting Hermia never to come near him again, explains his revulsion, which he wishes to be shared by "all":

> For, as a surfeit of the sweetest things,
> The deepest loathing to the stomach brings;
> Or as the heresies that men do leave
> Are hated most of those they did deceive;
> So, thou, my surfeit and my heresy,
> Of all be hated, but the most of me!

> (2.2.136–41)

Lysander presents two analogies—of surfeit and of conversion. The first concerns appetite and pleasure; the second, belief and truth. Despite the obvious tension between them, Lysander seems to consider the analogies alike. Appetite and belief, pleasure and truth, go together. Moreover, what Lysander loathes and hates, everyone should loath and hate, he says, though he most of all. Love, it seems, does not simply fade or disappear, but rather changes into its equally strong opposite. And while a lover does not want everyone to love what he loves, a former lover seems to want everyone to hate what he hates. Love is exclusive; hatred and loathing are not.

Lysander concludes by apostrophizing "all [his] powers" and exhorting them to apply all "your love and might / To honour Helena, and to be her knight!" (2.2.142–43). Addressing his powers in the second person, he enacts his reason directing his will (cf. 2.2.114–15). He impersonates his own soul. Lysander then exits, presumably to pursue Helena.

At the sound of Lysander's self-exhortation, Hermia, starting out of her dream, cries to Lysander for help. Hermia's dream is the only real dream in A Midsummer Night's Dream, and it is a lover's nightmare: "Help me, Lysander, help me! Do thy best / To pluck this crawling serpent from my breast!" (2.2.144–45). The deception of a dream lies in the dreamer's mistaking a resemblance for what it resembles, an appearance for a reality. When we dream, we believe that we see what we only dream of. We become literal-minded and take a likeness for the thing itself. It is only after waking that we recognize the dream as a dream. We see it with a double vision. Thus, now awake, realizing that she had dreamt, and stressing how strongly she believed what she dreamt, Hermia describes both her dream and her fear to (the absent) Lysander:

> Ay me, for pity! What a dream was here!
> Lysander, look how I do quake with fear.
> Methought a serpent ate my heart away,
> And you sat smiling at his cruel prey.

> (2.2.146–49)

Hermia's dream was a likeness in two respects. Like any dream, it was only an image, not the thing itself. And it was only figuratively true. Hermia did not dream that Lysander renounced his love for her and declared his love for someone else. She dreamt that a serpent ate her heart and Lysander did nothing but sit and smile at the snake's preying upon her. In a double sense, her dream was not what it was and was what it was not: it was only an appearance, which was only metaphorically true. Notwithstanding its frightening vividness, the dream involved a double absence.

Hermia's fear is quickly replaced by an even stronger fear, however, as she discovers that Lysander is gone:

> Lysander! What, remov'd? Lysander! lord!
> What, out of hearing? Gone? No sound, no word?
> Alack, where are you? Speak, and if you hear;
> Speak, of all loves! I swoon almost with fear.

> (2.2.150–53)

Lysander's absence is marked by his silence—the absence of the man, by the absence of his sound. His double absence replaces the double absence of Hermia's dream, though, in contrast to her understanding of the dream, Hermia still believes that Lysander loves her. Then, interpreting the silence with a negative question which serves as a confirming answer, Hermia concludes the worst: "No? Then I well perceive you are not nigh. / Either death or you I'll find immediately" (2.2.154–55). Hermia's desperate thought is uncertain. She may mean death by her own hand or death by her loss and pain. Her death could be by choice or by compulsion. Whatever the case, unlike Helena, who also talked of death (2.1.244), Hermia seems to mean what she says.

# Notes

1. See Frank Sidgwick, *The Sources and Analogues of "A Midsummer-Night's Dream"* (New York: Duffield, 1908), 35–36. The name Oberon appears first in English literature as the name of the fairy king in Lord Berners' translation of *Huon of Bordeaux* (1534; London: The Early English Text Society, Trübner, 1882), 21.12ff., and later in Edmund Spenser's *The Fairie Queen*, 2.1.6.9; 2.10.75.8.

2. The fairies speak in virtually continuous narratives throughout the scene: 1) a nameless Fairy, of himself and of Titania's royal guard (2.1.2–13); 2) Puck, of Oberon's wrath, and its cause (2.1.18–31); 3) the Fairy, of Puck's pranks (2.1.34–42); 4) Puck, of his own pranks (2.1.44–57); 5) Titania, of Oberon's philandering and his coming from India (2.1.64–73); 6) Oberon, of Titania's leading Theseus through the glimmering night (2.1.77–80); 7) Titania, of her quarrel with Oberon and its effects (2.1.82–117); 8) Titania, of the Indian boy and his mother (2.1.123–37); 9) Oberon, of the history and power of the love juice (2.1.148–72); 10) Oberon, of the love juice and Titania (2.1.176–85); and 11) Oberon, of the bank where Titania sleeps (2.1.249–58).

3. Puck's use of the word is the only such instance in the *Oxford English Dictionary*: s.v. Changeling, 3.

4. "The term Goodfellow was not a family name nor a proper name, but a propitiatory term bestowed upon him, in accordance with the universal belief that such complimentary appellations, as good fellow and good neighbor, would propitiate any anger and render the spirit addressed both agreeable and kind." Minor White Latham, *The Elizabethan Fairies*, Columbia University Studies in English and Comparative Literature (New York: Columbia University Press, 1930), 223. Accordingly, "Puck" (or "pouke") is an old word for fiend or devil; see, e.g., Reginald Scot, *The Discoverie of Witchcraft* (1584), 7.2. Hence, the epithet "sweet puck" is "by no means superfluous." Furness, 54. Cf. 3.2.398.

5. The names come from Virgil, *Eclogues*, 2, 7, and, before that, from the first pastoral poet, Theocritus, *Idylls*, 4, 5.6.

6. Note the pun on and parallel placement of Corin's identity and musical instrument: "shape of Corin" / "pipes of corn" (2.1.66, 67).

7. Hippolyta never says the word "fairy" or anything like it.

8. "[I]n vain" / "in vain" (2.1.88, 93); "wanton" / "want" (2.1.99, 101); "mazes" / "mazed" (2.1.99, 113); "anger" / "angry" (2.1.104, 112); "which is which" (2.1.114). The first use of "maze" is a metonymy, where the effect ("mazed") gives its name to the cause, the state of mind to the labyrinth. For a similar use of "wood," cf. 2.1.192; 3.1.143–44; 4.1.139.

9. "On hill, in dale, forest or mead" (2.1.83); "paved fountain, or . . . rushy brook" (2.1.84); "sea . . . land" (2.1.89–90), "pelting . . . proud" (2.1.91); "hoary-headed frosts / Fall in the fresh lap of the crimson rose" (2.1.108–9).

10. Cecil J. Sharp and Herbert C. Macilwaine, *The Morris Book* (London: Novello and Co., 1907).

11. Virgil, *Aeneid*, 5.714ff.

12. An ancestral observance, the Troy games were part of Julius Caesar's triumph (Suetonius, *Julius Caesar*, 39.2), favored by Augustus (Suetonius, *Augustus*, 43.2), and performed or offered by the next four emperors (Suetonius, *Tiberius*, 6.4; *Caligula*, 18.3; *Claudius*, 21.3; *Nero*, 7.1).

13. David Marshall, "Exchanging Visions: Reading A *Midsummer Night's Dream*," *ELH*, 49 (1982), 569.

14. Titania's description of the woman is, once again, suffused with a variety of doubles. Titania speaks of a "child" and his "mother" (2.1.122, 123, 135, 136), of the ships' "sails" on the water and the woman's "sail[ing]" upon the land (2.1.128, 132), of Titania's not trading the child ("buys not" [2.1.122]) and of "traders" embarked on the sea (2.1.127), of the votress both "[f]ollowing" and "imitat[ing]" the ships (2.1.131, 132), of the woman's womb "rich with [Titania's] young squire" and of the ships "rich with merchandise" (2.1.131, 134), and of the woman's "fetch[ing] . . . and return[ing] again" (2.1.133). In addition to repeating, or half repeating, words and phrases, Titania uses a hendiadys ("with pretty and with swimming gait" [2.1.130]), anaphora (2.1.136–37) and alliteration (2.1.128–32) as well as metaphors and explicit comparisons. She also stresses the antitheses of land and sea (2.1.126–34), sitting and moving (2.1.126, 130–34), seeing and hearing (2.1.125ff.), and conception and death (2.1.128–31, 135).

15. See, e.g., R. A. Foakes, A *Midsummer Night's Dream*, the New Cambridge Shakespeare (Cambridge: Cambridge University Press, 1984), 67.

16. Herodotus, 1.24.

17. Esther Singleton, *The Shakespeare Garden* (New York: William Farquhar Payson, 1931), 200.

18. Like Titania's account, Oberon's is full of doubles, both exact and inexact. Oberon twice mentions "fell" (2.1.165, 166), "west[ern]" (2.1.158, 166), "[f]etch me" (2.1.169, 173), "moon" (2.1.156, 162), "sea" (2.1.152, 154), "shaft" (2.1.159, 161), "madly" (2.1.153, 171), "maiden[s]" (2.1.164, 168), "flower" (2.1.166, 169), "once" (2.1.149, 169), "love" (2.1.167, 168), and "certain" (2.1.153, 157). Of these, "maiden[s]," "sea," and "west[ern]" are each once an adjective and once a noun; and "certain" means "some" one time and "unerring" another. Oberon also uses the homonym "sea" / "see" (2.1.152, 161) and numerous synonyms, including "breath" and "song" (2.1.151, 152), "mermaid" and "sea-maid" (2.1.150, 154), "love-shaft," "fiery shaft" and "bolt" (2.1.159, 161, 165), "maiden meditation" and "fancy free" (2.1.164), "flower" and "herb" (2.1.166, 169). He also frames his tale by beginning with a mermaid on a dolphin's back and concluding with a leviathan swimming a league. Besides prompting Puck's memory (2.1.148, 154) and telling him partly what he already knows and partly what he has not heard before, Oberon speaks of error, intended and unintended results, the combination of a mermaid and a dolphin, the contrasting changes in the sea and stars, what he but not Puck could see, both Cupid and his arrow flying between the moon and the earth, a fiery shaft quenched by

the watery moon, the change in the flower, the contrast between the changed flower and the unchanged virgin, and his love juice duplicating Cupid's arrow.

19. Cf., e.g., 1.1.122, 217, 224; 4.1.74, 75; 5.1.1, 187 with 1.2.221; 2.1.119; 3.2.62.

20. The point would hold, as well, if one retains the Folio and Quartos' "stay . . . stayeth." For the reading, see Furness, 93.

21. As these parallel lines point up, throughout the exchange Helena uses the respectful personal pronoun "you," but Demetrius alternates from speech to speech between "you" and the scornful "thee." Only his last speech (2.1.235–37) breaks the pattern.

22. Ovid, *Metamorphoses*, 1.452–567.

23. For Helena's speed, see 3.2.343; for her cowardice, 3.2.299, 305, 342.

24. Frances S. Osgood, *The Poetry of Flowers and the Flowers of Poetry* (New York: J. C. Riker, 1848), 178–79. Milton goes so far as to identify eglantine as honeysuckle (woodbine), see Milton, *L'Allegro*, 48.

25. Furness, 101.

26. E.g., 2.1.7–15, 30–31, 173–76, 256; 2.2.4–5; 3.1.183–89; 3.2.94, 100–1; 4.1.96–97; 5.1.369–72.

27. Ten times: 1.1.134; 2.2.35, 41, 49; 3.2.125, 127, 286; 4.1.148, 149; 5.1.121.

28. *The Homeric Hymn to Hermes*; see, further, Jenny Strauss Clay, *The Politics of Olympus: Form and Meaning in the Major Homeric Hymns* (Princeton, N.J.: Princeton University Press, 1989), 95–151.

29. Aristotle, *Poetics*, 1449b37–50a7.

# ACT THREE

~

## Act Three, Scene One

### 1. Literalism

Quince, who initially suggested that the artisans meet in the woods to rehearse (1.2.94–99), is delighted with the players' punctuality ("Pat, pat"
[3.1.2]) and with the convenience of their location. A green plot can be
their stage, he says, and a hawthorn-break their dressing room. What resembles a theater can be a theater. Quince told the players to meet "a mile
without the town" "[a]t the Duke's oak" (1.2.94–95, 103). We soon learn
that that turns out to be close to the bank where Titania is sleeping. Once
again, paths in the woods fortuitously cross. Quince, confident that their
play will be chosen, says that the rehearsal will be a complete performance
of what the artisans will put on before the Duke: "[W]e will do it in action, as we will do it before the Duke" (3.1.4–5). But nothing that they
practice here is performed there. Their "rehearsal" (3.1.3) does not rehearse the play.

Nor do the artisans begin right away. Before they start, Bottom raises a concern about "things in this comedy of Pyramus and Thisbe that will never
please" (3.1.8–9). Before act 5, the players always refer to the play as a comedy
(1.2.11; 3.1.8; 4.2.42). In act 5, they always call it a tragedy (5.1.57, 45–47).
The difference between comedy and tragedy may be lost on them. What matters more, it seems, is what pleases the audience, and that could be tears as well
as laughter (1.2.21ff.)—but not fear, at least not among the ladies.

Thus Bottom, whose roaring as a lion Quince had warned would frighten the ladies and get all the players hanged (1.2.70–78), now warns Quince that Bottom's own part as Pyramus will frighten them: "First, Pyramus must draw a sword to kill himself; which the ladies cannot abide" (3.1.9–11). When Snout seconds Bottom's concern ("Byrlakin, a parlous fear" [3.1.12]), Starveling, proposing a change that would destroy the plot and rob the play of meaning, declares that they "must leave the killing out, when all is done" (3.1.13–14). To Starveling, it seems, a play is not a whole with a beginning, middle, and end, but merely a collection of episodes or parts, any of which can be dropped for any reason. Bottom, trying, as always, to be resourceful, says he has a device to remedy the problem. Quince should add a prologue saying that the players do no harm with their swords and that Pyramus is not killed "indeed" (3.1.18). Even better ("for the more better assurance"), the prologue should "tell them that I, Pyramus, am not Pyramus, but Bottom the weaver. This will put them out of fear" (3.1.18–21). Bottom garbles his assurance. He means to distinguish the actor from his character and to say that he, Bottom, is not really Pyramus, but is merely playing the part of Pyramus. Instead, he says both that he is and is not Pyramus, first identifying himself with his part ("I, Pyramus,") and then distinguishing himself from the part ("am not Pyramus"). Afraid that the women will mistake his impersonation for what he impersonates, he repeats the very confusion he attempts to remove.

Quince agrees to add such a prologue. But when he states that it shall be written in the common meter for ballads, namely, alternating lines of "eight and six" syllables, Bottom contradicts him: "No, make it two more; let it be written in eight and eight" (3.1.22–25). Bottom, as usual, wants more. "More" is, in fact, nearly his most frequent word.[1]

Snout then repeats the concern that Quince originally raised in the casting scene: "Will not the ladies be afeard of the lion" (3.1.26; cf. 1.2.70–78). And after Starveling, expressing his fear of the ladies' fear, supports Snout's concern, Bottom, speaking of an imaginary griffin ("wild-fowl") as a "lion living," and again confusing what he wants to distinguish, warns with alarm that bringing in a lion is so horrible that the very thought of it needs God's protection:

> [T]o bring in (God shield us!) a lion among ladies is a most dreadful thing; for there is not a more fearful wild-fowl than your lion living; and we ought to look to't.
>
> (3.1.28–32)

Snout, who often echoes what others have said, concludes that they must add another prologue "to tell he is not a lion" (3.1.33–34). But Bottom goes further. It is not enough to say that the figure on the stage is not a lion. The prologue must tell the actor's name, half the actor's face must show through his costume, and the actor himself must address the women directly and explain—in words to this "defect," as Bottom puts it (3.1.38)—that they should not fear and that he fears for his life that they might fear for theirs: "'[M]y life for yours! If you think I come hither as a lion, it were pity of my life'" (3.1.40–41). If Starveling would break up wholeness of a dramatic plot into a collection of parts, Bottom would break up the wholeness of dramatic illusion into two separate parts—the actor and his character, the real and the unreal. But that is not all. Bottom says that the actor must also explain that he is a human and tell his name:

> "No, I am no such thing; I am a man, as other men are": and there, indeed, let him name his name, and tell them plainly he is Snug the joiner.
>
> (3.1.42–44)

The ladies might not only confuse an actor playing a lion with a real lion, they might also not realize that the actor speaking to them is human.

Snug took the part of Lion because, "slow of study," he could do it "extempore" since it was "nothing but roaring" (1.2.63–65). Now he is to have an elaborate prologue. Fittingly, the slow and silent Snug says not a word when the others decide that he must deliver a prologue. He remains completely silent throughout the scene.

Quince agrees to write such a prologue, but brings up two difficulties of a different sort. The first is the need for moonlight on stage, "for you know, Pyramus and Thisbe meet by moonlight" (3.1.46–47). Bottom, taking a hint from Snout, makes the first of two suggestions for dealing with the problem. Snout asks whether the moon shines the night of the play. No one thinks of looking up at the moon above them. Instead, Bottom, with great excitement, calls for a calendar: "A calendar, a calendar! Look in the almanac; find out moonshine, find out moonshine!" (3.1.49–50). And Quince, who happens to have an almanac with him, consults its calendar and reports that the moon will shine that night. "Yes, it doth shine that night" (3.1.51). The young lovers are not the only bookish Athenians. Quince's report is of course puzzling. The moon will shine, even though it will be a new moon (1.1.1–4). Hearing the report, Bottom offers his solution. The players, he says, should leave open the casement of a window in the room where they play, and the moon can shine in. No one explains why anything is needed for the moon-light. But while Bottom proposes using the moonlight itself, Quince, al-though approving Bottom's proposal, suggests something else:

> Ay; or else one must come in with a bush of thorns and a lantern, and
> say he comes to disfigure or to present the person of Moonshine.
>
> (3.1.55–57)

An actor should not only appear with the traditional trappings of a personi-fied moon—the man-in-the-moon. He should also explain his dramatic function. The only two possibilities, the players seem to think, are either the moon itself or an actor explicitly impersonating a personified symbol of the moon. Both possibilities would destroy dramatic illusion, though in opposite ways: the one by presenting the real thing, the other by expressly announc-ing the imitation as an imitation.

Quince's second difficulty concerns the wall: "[W]e must have a wall in the great chamber; for Pyramus and Thisbe, says the story, did talk through the chink of a wall" (3.1.58–60). This time, Snout rules out bringing in the real thing: "You can never bring in a wall. What say you, Bottom?" (3.1.61–62). And Bottom, following Quince's lead on the moonshine (and ignoring his own), suggests a solution:

> Some man or other must present Wall; and let him have some plaster, or
> some loam, or some rough-cast about him, to signify wall; and let him hold
> his fingers thus, and through that cranny shall Pyramus and Thisbe whisper.
>
> (3.1.63–67)

As with the moonshine, a player should represent the wall, though the ma-terials of an actual wall replace those of a symbol of the moon. The players will impersonate the play's props or scenery as well as its characters.

Satisfied, Quince orders the rehearsal to start. All the players, he says, are to speak their speeches and then enter into the break, according to each one's cue. Quince, curiously, proceeds as though there were not to be any changes in the script. Yet, three new characters—Prologue, Moonshine, and Wall—have been added, and the part of a fourth—Lion—has been greatly expanded. The players seem oblivious to their own changes.

## 2. Imagination

Puck enters, just as the rehearsal begins. Although himself a country lout among spirits (2.1.16), Puck has nothing but contempt for rustics dressed in homespun cloth, "swaggering" (3.1.73) so near where the fairy queen sleeps. Even before he knows of their theatrical pretensions, he finds the artisans full of boastful bluster. Then, as soon as he discovers that they are preparing for a play, Puck decides not simply to observe, but to be perhaps both an audience and an actor: "I'll be an auditor; / An actor too perhaps, if I see cause" (3.1.75–76). Dramatic illusion depends on a clear separation of the stage and the audience. As we have seen, the audience must see the play's action from within the drama, as the characters do, but also from outside or above the drama, as only the audience can. The doubleness of the imitation—at once real and unreal—must be matched by the doubleness of the audience's perspective. Puck, however, who characteristically makes no distinction between theater and life, is ready to ignore the distinction between a play and its audience. Soon he will go further and turn stage acting into real action.

Pyramus (Bottom) and Thisbe (Flute) take the stage. Pyramus, speaking first, declares his love for Thisbe in the first two lines and explains his sudden and unexpected momentary departure from her in the next two lines. Although the second and fourth lines of Pyramus's quatrain rhyme ("dear" / "appear"), the first and third do not ("sweet" / "awhile"). The faulty rhyme pattern is evidently unique in a Shakespearian dialogue.[2] As Quince the poet gets off to a clumsy start, so does Bottom the actor. Bottom, intending to affirm Pyramus's love, begins with a malapropism: "Thisbe, the flowers of odious savours sweet; / So hath thy breath, my dearest Thisbe dear" (3.1.78–80). Malapropisms, to which the artisans are prone, go together with their literalism. Both the one, a blunder of speech, and the other, a blunder of thought, mistake similarity for sameness. They combine what should be distinguished. While literalism takes an image for that of which it is an image, a malapropism replaces one word by another which is similar in sound but inappropriate in meaning. Here, Bottom replaces "odorous" or perhaps "odours"[3] with "odious" (3.1.79). A lover's sweet breath becomes a hateful scent. It seems no accident that not only do the artisans model their dramatic art on their productive arts, which make or repair real things rather than imitations of things. But all of their productive arts join things together: two construct, two mend, one weaves, and one sews.[4] The artisans do inappropriately with words in drama and speech what is appropriate to do with their hands in their trades.

For reasons best known to Quince himself, his plot requires that Pyramus suddenly leave and promise Thisbe that he will return right away. Pyramus's departure and promised return alter the traditional Pyramus and Thisbe story, in which the lovers leave each other only to meet in the woods near Ninus's tomb (Ovid, Metamorphoses, 4.83ff.). To permit the unexpected departure,

Quince relies on the lame theatrical expedient of having the character hear an unexpected voice near-by[5]: "But hark, a voice! Stay thou but here awhile, / And by and by I will to thee appear" (3.1.81–82). When Flute, unsure of his cue, asks whether Thisbe must now speak, Quince, confusing the senses, explains that she must: "for you must understand [Pyramus] goes but to see a noise that he heard, and is to come again" (3.1.85–87). Quince's needless change in the story's traditional plot has a crucial effect on Shakespeare's plot. Pyramus's exit provides the quick-thinking Puck, who finds Bottom "[a] stranger Pyramus than e'er played here" (3.1.83), the opportunity for mischief.

Before we see Puck's prank, Thisbe replies:

> Most radiant Pyramus, most lily-white of hue,
> Of colour like the red rose on triumphant briar,
> Most brisky juvenal, and eke most lovely Jew,
> As true as truest horse that yet would never tire;
> I'll meet thee, Pyramus, at Ninny's tomb.

> (3.1.88–92)

The paucity of Quince's poetry is evident, again. Thisbe's first four lines, which apostrophize and describe her love, contain seriatim superlatives and hyperbole ("Most radiant," "most lily-white," "Most brisky," "most lovely," "truest"), unsuited modifiers and comparisons (a "triumphant" wild rose; a love as "true" as an unwearied horse), and affected poetic diction ("brisky," "juvenal"). The verses are also stretched with idle fillers (the needless "eke," "brisky" for "brisk," "juvenal" for "youth") and seem hopeless attempts to rhyme ("Jew" with "hue," "tire" with "briar").[6] Most of all, although Pyramus just told Thisbe to "[s]tay thou but here awhile, / And by and by I will to thee appear," Thisbe announces, in a spirit of complete faithfulness, that she will leave and "meet thee, Pyramus, at Ninny's tomb"—an unexplained inconsistency which returns Quince's play to the traditional story.

Quince corrects Flute's last line for both his malapropos misnomer ("'Ninus' tomb', man!" [3.1.93]) and his poor stage-timing: "Why, you must not speak that yet; that you answer to Pyramus. You speak all your parts at once, cues and all" (3.1.93–95). Quince's second correction is incorrect. Flute does not speak "cues and all."[7] Rather, Bottom has missed his cue, and Flute reads two of Thisbe's speeches as though they were one.[8]

Directed by Quince to enter, Bottom reenters with the head of an ass, reciting what appears to be his missed line: "If I were fair, Thisbe, I were only thine" (3.1.98). The humor of Bottom's words is not limited to the irony of a man with the head of an ass speaking to his love, if only wishfully, of his handsome looks. The humor also includes Bottom's speaking the line without understanding its sense.[9] A reply to Thisbe's repeated "As true as truest horse that yet would never tire" (3.1.91, 97), the line probably should read, "If I were, fair Thisbe, I were only thine," that is, "If I were even so supremely true as that, fair Thisbe, I and all my truth would be only yours."[10] But Bottom, apparently misplacing the comma, turns his profession of true love into an ironically true comment on his monstrous looks. Instead of promising to be "[a]s true as truest horse," he shows himself to be half-assed.

Quince leads the panic: "O monstrous! O strange! We are haunted! Pray, masters! Fly, masters! Help!" (3.1.99–100). And all the other players except Bottom follow as he flees. Puck, however, is not content with the tumult he has just caused. Having turned the play into a panic, play acting into action, he now calls for more:

> I'll follow you; I'll lead you about a round!
> Through bog, through bush, through brake, through briar;
> Sometimes a horse I'll be. Sometimes a hound,
> A hog, a headless bear, sometimes a fire;
> And neigh, and bark, and grunt, and roar, and burn,
> Like horse, hound, hog, bear, fire, at every turn.
>
> (3.1.101–6)

A "round," here, is the frightened, unavailing flight of men being chased in a circle by a headless bear and other terrifying sights. Not surprisingly, Puck confuses what he will "be" and what he will be "[l]ike." And while he treats the two as the same, his stanza conspicuously echoes what the fairies have said of their own activities. Besides directly repeating the Fairy's "through bush, . . . through briar" and the general tone of the Fairy's description of what he does (2.1.2–6), the stanza echoes Puck's own description of his mischievous ability to adopt the shape and sound of anything (2.1.44–57) and Titania's mention of the delicate fairy dance of which she is so fond (2.1.140; also 2.2.1). Even more strongly, the stanza echoes itself, with its combination of repeated alliteration and frequent reiteration of words, its anaphora and contrasting combination of polysyndeton and asyndeton, and (covering more than half its lines) its series of five nouns, followed by a series of the five corresponding verbs, followed by the original series of five nouns. Its imitative diction mimics Puck's imitative action.

Bottom, unaware, thinks the others are trying to frighten him. He does not realize that he is frightening them. "Why do they run away? This is a knavery of them to make me afeard" (3.1.107–8). When Snout, returning, exclaims, "O Bottom, thou art changed! What do I see on thee?" (3.1.109–10), Bottom describes himself without knowing what has happened to him: "What do you see? You see an ass-head of your own, do you?" (3.1.111). Bottom, thinking that they are only pretending to see him changed, means that they see only what their asinine heads have made up or imagined to scare him. His figurative insult of them is both literally and figuratively true of himself. Having, literally, the head of an ass, he is all the more an ass for not knowing it.

Quince, like Snout, running at once away from and toward Bottom, enters and, seeing him, cries out, "Bless thee, Bottom, bless thee! Thou art translated" (3.1.113–14). It is hard to know whether Quince is wishing to protect Bottom from some supernatural evil or, on the contrary, pronouncing him as being supremely happy, or both. The uncertainty of his thought matches the confusion of his motion.

Bottom, only confirmed in his suspicion, claims to understand ("see" [3.1.115]) what his skulking colleagues are doing. "See" is a key word in the exchange. Snout first uses it to mean what he perceives ("What do I see on thee?" [3.1.109–10]). Bottom, repeating his words but shifting the sense, uses the word to mean both what Snout perceives and what he invents or imagines: "What do you see? You see an ass-head of your own, do you?" (3.1.111–12). Finally, Bottom uses it to mean what he understands or thinks he knows of the others' intention: "I see their knavery: this is to make an ass of me, to fright me, if they could" (3.1.115–16). The word, here, combines, in order, the triple levels of perception, imagination, and understanding. Yet, Bottom is of course wrong. Mistakenly certain of their intention, he believes that the others want to do to him, figuratively, what, unbeknownst to him, is now true of him literally and what has always been true of him figuratively. Figuratively an ass, he has become literally an ass. He has become what he has always resembled. His new body, while also a pun on his name, reveals rather than transforms his true form (cf. Ovid, *Metamorphoses*, 1.1–2).

Bottom sees being falsely frightened as being made an ass. Defending his manhood from his colleagues' imagined attack, he says that he will defy them and stand his ground, no matter what they do: "But I will not stir from this place, do what they can" (3.1.116–17). But staying in place is not enough. Bottom thinks he must actively show his lack of fear, so he decides to "walk up and down here, and . . . [to] sing, that they shall hear I am not afraid" (3.1.117–19). His singing will demonstrate his courage.

Bottom's song—a crude catalogue of singing birds—begins much like Thisbe's reply to Pyramus, only with the colors reversed (". . . most lily-white of hue" [3.1.88]; ". . . so black of hue" [3.1.120]). And, remarking on the birds' colors and calls, Bottom concludes with the cuckoo:

> The plain-song cuckoo gray,
> Whose note full many a man doth mark,
> And dares not answer nay—
>
> (3.1.126–28)

Both the cuckoo's name and call sound like "cuckold." Many a man, Bottom sings, hopes the bird's mocking cry that his wife is unfaithful does not apply to him, but none is sure that it does not. "[F]or indeed," Bottom explains, with all the wisdom he can summon (and suddenly settling the husband's doubts), "who would set his wit to so foolish a bird? Who would give a bird the lie, though he cry 'cuckoo' never so?" (3.1.129–30). Who would be so foolish as to use his intelligence to confute a foolish mocking beast? Bottom, however, seems to be committing just such folly, using his wit to answer what he thinks is the foolish mocking of his "ass-head" (3.1.111) colleagues.

The episode of Puck and the players is the central section of the central scene of A Midsummer Night's Dream. It pits a fairy whose nature consists in imagination and whose activities involve imitation against a crew of artisan-actors who are entirely literal-minded. Each is the opposite of the other. While Puck causes people to believe the reality of the images that he produces, the artisans ordinarily see the world that way. They see things as his mischief would have them. Excessive literalism and excessive imagination appear as one. The episode is central to the play in another way as well. Without Bottom's transformation, Titania would not fall in love with him, she and Oberon would not become reconciled, and the fairies would not bless the newly married couples. All that concerns the fairy king and queen depends upon Puck's action. Yet, despite what we have just seen and will soon see with our own eyes, Shakespeare will force us to wonder whether the episodes between Puck and the players, and hence between Bottom and Titania, at least on some level or in some way, ever really occurred.

## 3. Love at First Sight

Bottom's singing wakes Titania, who falls madly in love with him at first sight. "What angel wakes me from my flowery bed?" (3.1.124). Having been lulled to sleep by her fairies' singing of the nightingale, Philomel (2.2.1–23), Titania is roused by the boisterous Bottom's raucous song of homeier birds.[11] The low enthralls the high; to the fairy queen, an "ass-head" appears as an "angel." Titania, awakening to Bottom's verse about men with unfaithful wives, wants to hear more of his fine music and to see more of his handsome shape:

> I pray thee, gentle mortal, sing again:
> Mine ear is much enamour'd of thy note;
> So is mine eye enthralled to thy shape;
> And thy fair virtue's force perforce doth move me
> On the first view to say, to swear, I love thee.
>
> (3.1.132–36)

Titania is forced by the force of Bottom's excellence ("virtue's force perforce") to love him at first sight, and not only to say but to swear her love. She is helplessly overpowered by love.

Bottom makes a surprisingly sensible reply: "Methinks, mistress, you should have little reason for that" (3.1.137–38). Then, partly shifting the meaning of "reason" from "cause" to "good sense," and generalizing, he separates reason and love: "And yet, to say the truth, reason and love keep little company together nowadays" (3.1.138–39). Bottom, appearing sententious, and implicitly contradicting Lysander's claim that reason guides his love for Helena (2.2.114ff.), denies that anyone brings reason and love together nowadays: "The more the pity that some honest neighbors will not make them friends" (3.1.139–41). And having discussed and defended reason with an air of gravity and worldly wisdom, Bottom, boasting of his versatility,[12] announces that he can also make witty jests when occasion calls: "Nay, I can gleek upon occasion" (3.1.141). Bottom can be both wise and witty, serious and playful, weighty and comic. He has the soul, he seems to say, of a philosophical, comic poet. Titania, for her part, finds him "as wise as [he is] beautiful" (3.1.142). Having fallen in love with Bottom for the sound of his voice and shape of his looks, Titania comes to love him no less for his wisdom as soon as she hears his first thought.

Despite the fairy queen's passionate and growing love for him, Bottom wants to escape. With an uncharacteristic mien of modest self-depreciation, he denies his wisdom and says he wants to get out of this wood: "Not so neither; but if I had wit enough to get out of this wood, I have enough to serve mine own turn" (3.1.143–44). "[T]his wood" is ambiguous. As Demetrius indicated (2.1.192), it could mean "forest," "madness," or "wooed." Here, Bottom seems to mean "madness": if he had enough intelligence to get out of his present mad confusion, he could take care of himself. Titania, however, understands him to mean "forest" and perhaps "wooed." Admonishing Bottom imperiously not to "desire" to leave this wood, she tells him, "Thou shalt remain here, whether thou wilt or not" (3.1.145, 146). Her power does not depend upon love. Bottom must stay, whether he wants to or not. Titania, however, tries to persuade him to desire to do what she says he has no power or freedom not to do. Without disclosing her precise identity, she describes her rank and royal presence:

> I am a spirit of no common rate;
> The summer still doth tend upon my state;
> And I do love thee: therefore go with me.
>
> (3.1.147–49)

Titania tries with her words to make herself more attractive to Bottom. But Bottom seems immune to her beauty and charm and even to her royal presence. Titania therefore offers to give him fairies who will attend him.

> And they shall fetch thee jewels from the deep,
> And sing, while thou on pressed flowers dost sleep:
> And I will purge thy mortal grossness so,
> That thou shalt like an airy spirit go.
>
> (3.1.151–54)

Like Puck, Titania will transform Bottom. While the fairies will fetch him jewels and sing while he sleeps, she will purge his "mortal grossness" so that he will move "like an airy spirit." No one mentions mortality as much as Titania does. It is nearly her first word to Bottom ("gentle mortal" [3.1.132]); it is at the heart of her descriptions of her Indian votress ("But she, being mortal, of that boy did die" [2.1.135]) and of the effects of her quarreling with Oberon ("The human mortals want their winter cheer" [2.1.101]); and it will be her only word to describe the young lovers ("these mortals" [4.1.101]).[13] Titania does not seem to mean that she will purge Bottom of his mortality, but rather that she will purge him of his living body's grossness. As with the Indian woman, so, too, it seems, with Bottom. The fairy queen—even the daughter of Titans—may love human beings, but she cannot take away their mortality. Titania thus promises only that Bottom will move "like an airy spirit," not that he will become one. He would resemble, not be, an airy spirit. Just as Bottom now combines the human and the ass, so he would combine the human and the fairy. Notwithstanding Puck's transformation of Bottom, the fairies' power over the corporeal world is limited. Confined to the imagination, it is always at least one remove from the bodily.

Titania summons four fairies, who promptly respond. All have British names, like Robin Goodfellow and the artisans. Those in the play who serve have British names; those who rule or belong to the noble class have classical names. The fairies' names are all common nouns. All but one (Peaseblossom) are the names of things that are insubstantial, tiny, or tenuous. One of the names, however, is ambiguous. "Moth" is a common Elizabethan spelling of "mote."[14] The two words were also pronounced alike.[15] If Shakespeare intends "mote," then two of the fairies are paired by their tiny size: a speck of dust and a mustardseed, "the least of all seeds" (Matthew, 13.32; Mark, 4.31 [Bishops' Bible; 1568]); and two are paired by their insubstantiality: a speck and a cobweb.[16] Moth says nearly nothing on his own—two speeches, three words—and, unlike the other three, is never described or discussed in the dialogue. He seems characterized by his virtual absence.

The four fairies briskly announce that they are ready and ask, in unison, "Where shall we go?" (3.1.156). They expect to be ordered to go somewhere for Titania.[17] Titania, however, gives them different orders. Her orders begin by telling the fairies to be kind and courteous to "this gentleman" (3.1.157)—something that evidently needs to be said and cannot be taken for granted. Titania says that they should "[h]op in his walks, and gambol in his eyes" (3.1.158). If moving is a distinctive fairy activity, it is, more particularly, a stylized form of movement. The fairies "skip" (2.1.61), "gambol" (3.1.158), "hop" (3.1.158; 5.1.380), "trip" (4.1.95), "trip away" (5.1.407), and of course dance (2.1.86, 140; 2.2.1, 254; 4.1.88; 5.1.382), just as they typically speak with lyrical diction and in narrative form. Mere walking and running are mostly left to humans.[18] As poetry differs from ordinary speech, the fairies' movement differs from humans'. Titania directs the fairies to feed Bottom with sweet, rare fruits. And they are to hunt and steal from living creatures (cf. 2.2.3–5), so that they can attend to him when he goes to bed, when he is asleep, and when he arises:

> The honey-bags steal from the humble-bees,
> And for night-tapers crop their waxen thighs,
> And light them at the fiery glow-worms' eyes,
> To have my love to bed, and to arise;
> And pluck the wings from painted butterflies
> To fan the moonbeams from his sleeping eyes.
>
> (3.1.161–66)

Finally, concluding as she began, Titania reminds the fairies to treat Bottom with respect: "Nod to him, elves, and do him courtesies" (3.1.167). Despite his appearing so handsome and so wise to her, Titania seems to recognize that, to her fairies, Bottom may not appear to deserve such treatment.

Hailed by the fairies as "mortal!" (3.1.168), Bottom, begging their pardon for taking the liberty to inquire and addressing them twice with a term of respect ("your worships" [3.1.172–73]), asks Cobweb, Peaseblossom, and Mustardseed their names. None of the fairies, including Titania, ever asks his. Bottom tries to be genteel and witty. Hearing the name Cobweb, he replies: "I shall desire you of more acquaintance, good Master Cobweb: if I cut my finger, I shall make bold with you" (3.1.175–77). Bottom's reply, in fact, shows nothing so much as his homespun prosaicness: cobwebs were used to stop bleeding. Bottom tries again with Peaseblossom. Here, his attempt at urbane wit turns bawdy: "I pray you, commend me to Mistress Squash, your mother, and to Master Peascod, your father" (3.1.179–80). While "squash," as a verb, means to press or to crush, "peascod" is a quibble on "codpiece," its syllables reversed.[19] After complimenting Cobweb on his utility and Peaseblossom on his parentage, Bottom praises Mustardseed for his patience, which stands in direct contrast to his size:

> Good Master Mustardseed, I know your patience well. The same cowardly giant-like ox-beef hath devoured many a gentleman of your house: I promise you, your kindred hath made my eyes water ere now.
>
> (3.1.184–88)

Bottom muddles his praise. It becomes a confession. On the one hand, Mustardseed has shown his patience in enduring the loss of kinsmen, who have been cowardly devoured as mustard. But, on the other, Bottom himself has devoured the beef which cowardly devoured his kinsmen. Thus, Mustardseed's kin have made Bottom's "eyes water." His eyes have teared in sympathy, even as they smarted from the pungency of the mustard which he ate.

After telling the fairies to wait upon Bottom and lead him to her bower, Titania talks of the moon's looking with a watery eye. Like Hippolyta and Lysander (1.1.9–11, 209–11), she speaks of the moon seeing rather than being seen:

> The moon, methinks, looks with a watery eye,
> And when she weeps, weeps every little flower,
> Lamenting some enforced chastity.
>
> (3.1.191–93)

These are Titania's first words since awaking which are not explicitly spoken to or in regard to Bottom. They are the only ones of the sort she will utter until Oberon removes the effect of the love juice (4.1.75ff.). Yet, the difference may be largely apparent. Love compels Titania to sound like her love as well as to celebrate love. Thus she repeats (and elevates) Bottom's mention of his watering eyes and at the same time sympathizes with those forced ("enforced") to avoid love. Love compels what she says and how she says it. Nevertheless, concluding the scene, Titania wants to silence Bottom: "Tie up my love's tongue, bring him silently" (3.1.194). She may no longer be so sure that he is so wise. Titania will praise Bottom's amiable cheeks, smooth head, and large ears (4.1.1–4), but she will never again praise his wisdom.

## Act Three, Scene Two

### 1. Mimic, Madness, and Monster

Oberon, alone on stage, wonders what has happened to Titania, and Puck immediately enters, as though on cue, to report the news. Oberon seems to expect Puck, his "messenger" (3.2.4), to know about all nocturnal events ("What night-rule . . . ?" [3.2.5]) in the grove. Puck, in fact, knows (or thinks he knows) not only about the two Athenians, but about Titania as well. Puck had a hand in what he reports. His actions, however, had nothing directly to do with Titania. After applying the love juice to the young Athenian, Puck, by chance, came upon the players and, for no reason having anything to do with Titania or with love, transformed Bottom's head and frightened both the other players and Bottom; then Bottom, trying to parry what he incorrectly imagined to be the other players' ploy, sang and awoke Titania, who instantly fell in love with him. Just like his misapplying the love juice to Lysander's eyes, Puck's role in Titania's falling in love with Bottom is the result of pure accident or chance.

Puck's report is another of the fairies' many narratives. It differs from the others, however, in narrating actions which we have seen for ourselves, yet, actions which may never have happened. It may narrate wholly imaginary events. That seems true also in a more limited sense. The speech, twice-over, describes performed drama. While implicitly describing a play in which Puck was both "auditor" and "actor" (3.1.75, 76), it explicitly describes the artisans' rehearsal of "a play" (3.2.11). The artisans' rehearsal becomes a play within Puck's play. Accordingly, the narrative's principal themes are imitation and imagination.

The speech, though delivered by a "mad spirit" (3.2.4), has a clear, symmetrical structure. The first (3.2.6) and last (3.2.31–34) parts report Titania's falling in love with a monster. The second (3.2.7–12) and fifth (3.2.27–30) describe the artisans' dramatic rehearsal and their fearful imaginations, respectively. And the third (3.2.13–17) and fourth (3.2.18–26) tell, in particular, what Puck did to Bottom and what the other players did when they saw him.

Puck begins by summarizing the very pleasing outcome: "My mistress with a monster is in love" (3.2.6). Then, setting the scene, he describes the artisans' rehearsal near Titania's bower. As he depicts them, the men are doubly related to art. The only characters in the play who work in order to eat, they are men of various trades, who make their living by their arts: "A crew of patches, rude mechanicals, / That work for bread upon Athenian stalls" (3.2.9–10). But, now having left their manual arts to take up the art of acting, they "[w]ere met together to rehearse a play" (3.2.11). Characterizing Bottom as "[t]he shallowest thick-skin of that barren sort" (3.2.13), Puck recounts the particular circumstances of his transforming his head. As we have seen, the pointless departure in Quince's script from the traditional Pyramus and Thisbe story gave Puck his chance:

> . . . Pyramus . . .
> Forsook his scene, and enter'd in a brake,
> When I did him at this advantage take:
> An ass's nole I fixed on his head.
>
> (3.2.14–17)

Puck, shifting to the historic or dramatic present tense, describes the actors' consequent madness as though it were still before his eyes: "Anon, his Thisbe must be answered, / And forth my mimic comes" (3.2.18–19). Puck calls Bottom a "mimic." Bottom is actually a triple "mimic." He is a ludicrous imitation of an actor, of Pyramus, and of an ass. While all that happened to Bottom seems vividly present, everything concerning him is absent: he is not really an actor, or Pyramus, or an ass, but, rather, a likeness of an ass, simulating an actor, impersonating a lover. Just as Puck typically ignores the distinction between an image and a reality (and, here, ignores the difference between Pyramus the character and Bottom the actor), Bottom, "[his] mimic," combining transformation, emulation, and imitation, is nothing but mimicry.

In the spirit of mock-heroic narrative, Puck continues with an elaborate, double simile—his only simile until nearly the close of the play (5.1.372):

> When they him spy—
> As wild geese that the creeping fowler eye,
> Or russet-pated choughs, many in sort,
> Rising and cawing at the gun's report,
> Sever themselves, and madly sweep the sky,
> So, at his sight, away his fellows fly;
> And at our stamp, here o'er and o'er one falls;
> He murder cries, and help from Athens calls.

(3.2.19–26)

Puck's simile mingles seeing and hearing—what one bird saw and what the other bird heard. The simile's mingling matches the players' confusion. The terrified players, however, not only tripped and fell. They also believed that the various hindrances were deliberate wrongs:

> Their sense thus weak, lost with their fears thus strong,
> Made senseless things begin to do them wrong:
> For briars and thorns at their apparel snatch;
> Some sleeves, some hats, from yielders all things catch.

(3.2.27–30)

Fear needs a particular object and will therefore imagine one if its object is unknown. Fear also tends to personify its imagined object, accusing it of deliberate harm. Fear of the unknown thus ultimately transforms even "senseless things"—briars and thorns—into moral beings capable of intending the fear and harm they cause or seem to threaten, and hence of committing injustice or "wrong." Significantly, the two topics of Puck's report—the artisans' madness and Titania's falling in love with a monster—concern fear of the unknown and love. Fear and love may be contraries, fear leading one to flee and love leading one to pursue its object. But both fear of the unknown and love depend crucially on imagination for their objects and for the shaping of their objects (cf. 5.1.4–22). Fear of the unknown and the love juice are mirror images of each other. Accordingly, Puck, returning to the past tense, concludes by summing up the twin events:

> I led them on in this distracted fear,
> And left sweet Pyramus translated there;
> When in that moment, so it came to pass,
> Titania wak'd, and straightway lov'd an ass.

(3.2.31–34)

Oberon is delighted: "This falls out better than I could devise" (3.2.35). Chance may surpass planning. The contrary, however, may also be true. Oberon asks whether Puck has "latch'd the Athenian's eyes" (3.2.36) with the love juice. And Puck, confident of his success, proudly announces that he has:

> I took him sleeping—that is finish'd too—
> And the Athenian woman by his side,
> That when he wak'd, of force she must be ey'd.
>
> (3.2.38–40)

But error nullifies necessity. Demetrius and Hermia enter, and Puck discovers his mistake:

> Ob.:  Stand close: this is the same Athenian.
> Puck: This is the woman, but not this the man.
>
> (3.2.41–42)

This is, and is not, the man.

## 2. Love Turned

The last time we saw Demetrius, he was spurning his lover, who was chasing him (2.2.83–86). This time, he is chasing his beloved, who is spurning him. The irony of the reversal seems entirely lost on him. Helena thought that she could win Demetrius's love by declaring her love for him (2.1.202ff.). Demetrius, despite having rejected Helena's love ("I love thee not, therefore pursue me not" [2.1.188]), seems to think that he can win Hermia's love by offering her his own: "O why rebuke you him that loves you so? / Lay breath so bitter on your bitter foe" (3.2.43–44). Contrary to what he told Helena, only bitter enmity, not unwanted love, he now seems to think, deserves bitter words.

Hermia threatens to do worse: "Now I but chide, but I should use thee worse, / For thou, I fear, hast given me cause to curse" (3.2.45–46). At the end of act 2, Hermia vowed to find either Lysander or death (2.2.155). Now, unable to find Lysander, she fears that Demetrius has killed him and bids him to plunge deeper into blood and kill her as well:

> If thou hast slain Lysander in his sleep,
> Being o'er shoes in blood, plunge in the deep,
> And kill me too.
>
> (3.2.47–49)

Lysander must be dead because nothing else would explain his absence. "The sun was not so true to the day / As he to me," Hermia says, underlining her belief that he is dead by speaking in the past tense. "Would he have stol'n away / From sleeping Hermia?" she asks rhetorically.

> I'll believe as soon
> This whole earth may be bor'd, and that the moon
> May through the centre creep, and so displease
> Her brother's noon-tide with th'Antipodes.
>
> (3.2.50–55)

Hermia will not believe that Lysander has left her until a hole is bored through the center of the earth and the moon tumbles through it, bringing night to the opposite side of the world at noon. Hermia intends her analogy to state impossible conditions for her believing that Lysander has been untrue: the moon would have to pass through the solid earth, and the moon would have to bring night. Hermia could no sooner believe that Lysander's love was not whole or that his absence was caused by his own motion than she could believe that the earth could become empty through its center and that the moon's motion rather than the sun's could cause night. Thus she concludes, with an intensifying double negative, "It cannot be but thou hast murder'd him" (3.2.56), adding that Demetrius shows the face of a murderer: "So should a murderer look, so dead, so grim" (3.2.57). A killer's looks should mirror his victim's.

Demetrius, seizing upon Hermia's comparison, turns her words around, while making them a metaphor: "So should the murder'd look, and so should I, / Pierc'd through the heart with your stern cruelty" (3.2.58–59). Hermia is the killer; Demetrius, her victim. Although "heart" is mentioned often in *A Midsummer Night's Dream* (some twenty-seven times), apart from Pyramus's dying words (5.1.288) this is the only time it refers to the source of life, though it does so only figuratively. By denying Demetrius her love, Hermia takes his life with her cruelty. "[F]air Hermia / . . . slayeth me" (2.1.190). To Demetrius, however, Hermia does not resemble her own description of a killer: "Yet you, the murderer, look as bright, as clear, / As yonder Venus in her glimmering sphere" (3.2.60–61). Hermia is not pale, but bright, not grim, but cheerful. Hermia may be distraught with the thought of Lysander's murder, but to Demetrius's loving eyes she is as beautiful and sparkling as the evening star.

Hermia dismisses Demetrius's words of love because they have nothing to do with Lysander's absence: "What's this to my Lysander? Where is he?"

(3.2.62). Despite her talk about his having been murdered, Hermia now appears to think that Lysander is alive. Thus wheedling rather than rebuking him, she now asks "good Demetrius"—something she calls him no where else—to "give him [to] me" (3.2.63). She evidently means "alive." Demetrius, however, answers as though he might have killed Lysander: "I had rather give his carcase to my hounds" (3.2.64). Like Creon, Demetrius would treat his enemy's corpse with contempt. Hermia, no longer cajoling, turns tables on Demetrius, calling him a dog ("Out, dog! out, cur!" [3.2.65]) and, rhyming his "hounds" with her "bounds," declares that she is out of "maiden's patience" (3.2.65–66). Demetrius's contemptuous answer has evidently made her more ready to believe that he has murdered Lysander: "Hast thou slain him then?" (3.2.66). And, in effect, answering her own question, Hermia carries out her threat to curse Demetrius: "Henceforth be never number'd among men!" (3.2.67). But Hermia is still unsure. She no sooner curses Demetrius than she reverses herself again and asks him to tell her the truth, once and for all, for love ("even for my sake" [3.2.68]). Just as quickly, however, she reverts to accusations, this time forcefully adding the charge of cowardice to that of murder (cf. 3.2.47). Demetrius must have killed Lysander cowardly in his sleep:

> Durst thou have look'd upon him, being awake,
> And hast thou kill'd him sleeping? O brave touch!
> Could not a worm, an adder, do so much?

> (3.2.69–71)

And having lowered Demetrius to the level of a spineless snake, Hermia concludes that a snake did, and did not, kill Lysander: "An adder did it; for with doubler tongue / Than thine, thou serpent, never an adder stung!" (3.2.72–73). A metaphorical snake—namely, Demetrius—did it, for no literal snake, even with a forked or duplicitous tongue, would ever do it. Demetrius is more murderous than a treacherous snake.

Demetrius finally denies killing Lysander. Telling Hermia that she wastes her anger on a misunderstanding, he declares, "I am not guilty of Lysander's blood; / Nor is he dead, for aught that I can tell" (3.2.75–76). Hermia, however, wants to hear more. She wants to hear that Lysander is well. Earlier, she was certain that he would never have left her while she was sleeping. Now, she evidently thinks that he might have. Demetrius asks what Hermia would give him if he could tell her that Lysander is well. It is hard to know what he might expect. Ironically, Demetrius seems to be in much the same situation as Helena when, against her own interests, she told him of Hermia's plan to elope (1.1.246–51). Demetrius, in any event, gets the only reward that he might:

> A privilege, never to see me more.
> And from thy hated presence part I so:
> See me no more, whether he be dead or no.

(3.2.79–81)

If Helena hoped just to catch a glimpse of Demetrius chasing after Hermia, Demetrius will get even less, as Hermia, exiting, emphasizes with her repeated "no."

Much like Helena, who stopped pursuing Demetrius partly because she recognized the foolishness of her chase and partly because she was out of breath (2.2.87ff.), Demetrius pauses in pursuing Hermia because, he says, there is no talking to her in her angry mood and he is tired and sleepy from sorrow. Had Helena continued her chase, she would not have discovered Lysander sleeping on the ground, and he would not have fallen in love with her. Now, Demetrius's delay will allow Oberon to cancel or correct the unintended, unwanted outcome of Helena's halt. Demetrius, however, puts a limit on his sorrow:

> So sorrow's heaviness doth heavier grow
> For debt that bankrupt sleep doth sorrow owe;
> Which now in some slight measure it will pay,
> If for his tender here I make some stay.

(3.2.84–87)

Demetrius's sorrow is not as bad as it feels. Because of his sorrow, Demetrius has been unable to sleep. And because he has been unable to sleep, his sorrow feels worse. While his sadness makes him tired, his tiredness makes him feel sadder, as he underscores by playing on the two meanings of "heavy." Demetrius at the same time uses the mercenary and legalistic metaphor of bankruptcy and legal repayment for his sorrow and his sleeplessness. His most elaborate metaphor apart from when he wakes up influenced by the love juice (3.2.137–44), the trope transforms the language of love into the language of borrowed money.

When Demetrius lies down to sleep, Oberon reproaches Puck for his mistake. Puck, he says, applied the love juice to a true lover ("some true love's sight" [3.2.89]), and because of his mistake, "[s]ome true love turn'd, and not a false turn'd true" (3.2.91). Earlier, when imagining Titania falling in love with a vile beast, Oberon distinguished between true love and love caused by the love juice (2.2.27). Now, he corrects or refines the distinction. If Lysander's love of Hermia was "true," while his love of Helena is "false," Demetrius's love of Hermia is "false," while his love of Helena would be "true." True love as well as false love may be caused by love juice. For Oberon, it seems, true love is not so much love that is constant or love that is returned as love of the proper object. It is true in its suitability at least as much as in its constancy, reciprocity, or source.

Puck, who cares nothing about true love in any sense, makes light of his error. If some true love turned false, "[t]hen fate o'r-rules" (3.2.92). By "fate," Puck means "what usually occurs": "[T]hat, one man holding troth, / A million fail, confounding oath with oath" (3.2.92–93). Faithless love is the virtually invariable rule; faithful love, the rare exception. Puck may have erred, but his mistake, he says, fully agrees with human nature.

Oberon orders Puck to go very swiftly ("swifter than the wind" [3.2.94]) and find "Helena of Athens" (3.2.95). Oberon somehow knows Helena's name, even though no one has mentioned it within his hearing. The name "Helena of Athens" suggests Helen of Troy. Yet, Oberon's description of Helena hardly fits her namesake: "All fancy-sick she is, and pale of cheer / With sighs of love, that costs the fresh blood dear" (3.2.96–97). To be lovesick is to become physically sick (cf. 2.1.213). A broken heart loses life-blood.[20] Oberon will change this, however, by turning Helena of Athens, in effect, into Helen of Troy.[21] He will make her, in Demetrius's eyes, the most beautiful woman of Greece (cf. 4.1.169–70; 5.1.11). Oberon thus orders Puck to bring Helena by his usual power ("[b]y some illusion" [3.2.98]), and Oberon will charm Demetrius's eyes with love juice. Puck gladly obeys: "I go, I go, look how I go! / Swifter than arrow from the Tartar's bow" (3.2.100–1). Once more, Puck will go even more swiftly than Oberon orders (cf. 2.1.175–76).

Oberon, applying the love juice, delivers another incantation. The incantation, referring at once to the pupil of Demetrius's eye and to what he most cherishes, calls for the juice to "[s]ink in apple of his eye" (3.2.104). His eye and its loved object are to be one and the same. Yet, despite this identity, Oberon borrows Demetrius's words of love for Hermia. As Hermia appeared to Demetrius "as bright, as clear / As yonder Venus in her glimmering sphere" (3.2.60–61), so Helena will "shine as gloriously / As the Venus of the sky" (3.2.106–7). In Demetrius's eyes, his new love may merely fill the place of his old love, as, indeed, happened once before, in reverse (cf. 1.1.106–10, 242–45). Helena may become Hermia "translated" (1.1.191).

Puck, as promised, returns promptly, with Helena behind him, pursued by Lysander. Far from showing any concern for the lovers, Puck's speed seems to reflect the fact that he can fulfill his desire and duty at a single stroke. While satisfying Oberon and correcting his mistake, he can produce more mischief and observe more folly:

> Shall we their fond pageant see?
> Lord, what fools these mortals be!

> (3.2.114–15)

Just as he was both "an auditor" and "[a]n actor too" in the artisans' rehearsal (3.1.75–76), Puck views the lovers' turmoil as a comic play ("fond pageant"), in which he is both spectator and stage manager. Once again, the distinctions between the play and the audience, on the one hand, and the play and life, on the other, vanish. Life becomes theater imitating life. It is not hard to see why Puck identifies love and folly. But it is less obvious why he appears to limit the foolishness to mortals. He seems to have forgotten Titania's mad love for Bottom, which he has just recounted.

Oberon tells Puck to stand aside; the noise that Lysander and Helena make—their quarrel—will awaken Demetrius. Earlier, Puck described what he does (2.1.43–57). Now, he describes what he most enjoys. The four lines are Puck's most explicit remarks about his pleasure:

> Then will two at once woo one.
> That must needs be sport alone;
> And those things do best please me
> That befall prepost'rously.

> (3.2.118–21)

What most pleases Puck are things that happen "prepost'rously"—literally, when front and rear are reversed. Contrary to Oberon's concern for the young lovers, Puck is most pleased by things that happen counter to proper order. And what, in particular, pleases him most is when "two at once woo one," especially, it seems, when the wooing involves a sudden, inexplicable reversal. Two at once wooing one, he says, is "sport alone," by which he means not only enjoyable in itself ("alone"), but enjoyable above all else ("alone").[22] Nothing is as comic as passionate rivalry in love.

### 3. Two at Once Woo One

Helena still thinks Lysander woos her in scorn. She thinks his vows are meant to humiliate her by leading her to believe them. Lysander, at a loss to show what is inside himself, protests that his visible tears prove his love:

Scorn and derision never come in tears.
Look, when I vow, I weep; and vows so born,
In their nativity all truth appears.

(3.2.123–25)

When Helena first suspected Lysander of mocking her, she plaintively asked, "Wherefore was I to this keen mockery born?" (2.2.122). Lysander, now answering her, borrows her metaphor. As his vows are born in tears, their truthfulness can be seen in their nativity. In Theseus's Athens, love leads to the birth of speech or vows. Lysander, hoping to show what is internal by what is external (cf. 2.2.103–4), implicitly denies the possibility of play-acting, at least in connection with love. While he may be correct in saying that scorn and derision never come in tears, he overlooks the possibility that scorn and derision might prompt feigned tears. He speaks as though tears are always true—as though tearfulness is always truthfulness in love. Helena, perhaps partly fearing that Lysander's tears are meant to mock hers (cf. 2.2.91–92), dismisses his protest as just another clever ploy. But then, shifting from his assumed mockery to his assumed untruthfulness, she returns to her original indictment of Love's oaths (cf. 1.1.240–45) and directly disputes Lysander's vows: "When truth kills truth, O devilish-holy fray!" (3.2.129). If true, Lysander's vows to Helena destroy the truth of his vows to Hermia. The truth of his present vows kills the truth of his former vows, and vice versa. One truth destroys the other, in a conflict ("fray") that is "holy" because it involves truths, but "devilish" because it destroys both truths. Accordingly, Helena continues:

Weigh oath with oath, and you will nothing weigh:
Your vows to her and me, put in two scales,
Will even weigh; and both as light as tales.

(3.2.131–33)

Two vows amount to no vows. A second vow denies both itself and the first, turning both into mere "tales"—into stories that cannot be trusted.

Lysander unwittingly made Helena's point, even as he first declared his love. When he awoke and fell in love with Helena, he said that reason guided his love (". . . reason says you are the worthier maid" [2.2.115]). He was silent about his previous vow to Hermia, which, like any vow, promised to bind the future to the present ("And then end life when I end loyalty!" [2.2.62]). By appealing to reason, Lysander implicitly canceled not only his vow to Hermia, but vows as such. "[T]hen end life" became "unless reason says that I made a mistake." As Helena recognizes, vows on Lysander's lips are indeed no vows at all. They may be canceled by reason. Fully in character for both, what Lysander considers the elevation of love to "reason," Helena regards as the reduction of vows to mere "tales."

Lysander again explains, "I had no judgement when to [Hermia] I swore" (3.2.134). Then, reasoning with Helena, he tries to persuade her to love him rather than Demetrius: "Demetrius loves [Hermia], and he loves not you" (3.2.136). Ironically, on his own principle, Lysander should love Hermia and not Helena, for the one but not the other loves him. No less ironically, Demetrius wakes at the mention of his name and instantly falls madly in love with Helena: "O Helen, goddess, nymph, perfect, divine!" (3.2.137). Love's idealization becomes deification. And declaring Helena perfect, Demetrius explicitly seeks for something to which he can compare her eyes—the same eyes that she thought so dull in comparison with Hermia's (1.1.183, 188, 230; 2.2.89–98)—and sees them as exceeding even his extravagant standard: "To what, my love, shall I compare thine eyne? / Crystal is muddy" (3.2.138–39). Demetrius compares Helena's eyes, lips, and hand to metaphors for their beauty and finds them to equal or surpass the metaphors taken literally. Helena's hand not only makes high Taurus's "pure congealed white . . . snow" look black ("turns to a crow"); it is the quintessence ("[the] princess") of pure white (3.2.141, 142, 144). It is purer than the purest snow. Helena's hand is something else, as well. Demetrius, asking to kiss her hand, describes it as "this seal of bliss" (3.2.144). Under the influence of the love juice, this "spotted and inconstant man" (1.1.110) no sooner falls in love with Helena than his hopes turn to marriage, which he thinks of as bliss.

Helena, who has no way of knowing what is going on, sees the men's vows and praise as their conspiracy to make fun of her for their amusement. Where Bottom thought his friends were conspiring to demean him by frightening him (3.1.107ff.), Helena thinks her friends are conspiring to demean her by mocking her. Indignantly, she accuses the men of being uncivil and unmanly. If they were civil or courteous, she says, they would not heartily unite ("join in souls" [3.2.150]) to mock her. And if they "were men, as men [they] are in show" (3.2.151), they would not "vow, and swear, and superpraise [her] parts" (3.2.153), when in fact they hate her. If a woman may not pursue a man without setting a scandal on her sex (2.1.240–42), a man may not mock a woman without giving up his claim to being a man. "You both are rivals, and love Hermia; / And now both rivals to mock Helena" (3.2.155–56). Lysander and Demetrius are still rivals, only now their rivalry has a new purpose and a new object. Helena's sole means of self-defense is to attempt to shame the men, with a combination of sarcasm and blame:

A trim exploit, a manly enterprise,
To conjure tears up in a poor maid's eyes
With your derision! None of noble sort
Would so offend a virgin, and extort
A poor soul's patience, all to make you sport.

(3.2.157–61)

It is of course the shameless Puck, not Lysander and Demetrius, who is guilty of Helena's charge.

Instead of answering Helena, Lysander, taking her side, immediately accuses Demetrius of being "unkind" to her (3.2.162). While not saying whether he thinks Demetrius is merely mocking her, he proposes an exchange: "In Hermia's love I yield you up my part; / And yours of Helena to me bequeath" (3.2.165–66). Lysander said something like this once before. In his first words in the play, on the premise that one should marry someone who loves one, he scornfully proposed that he should marry Hermia and Demetrius should marry Egeus (1.1.93–94). Now, in a different spirit, he proposes the converse: a man should pursue only the woman he loves. "For you love Hermia; this you know I know" (3.2.161), and "I do love [Helena], and will do till my death" (3.2.167). Lysander's previous words were the first time he spoke to Demetrius. These are only the second.

While Helena considers Lysander's attempt at gallantry and dissuasion more mockery, Demetrius corrects his main premise, telling him that he does indeed love Helena, not Hermia:

Lysander, keep thy Hermia; I will none.
If ere I lov'd her, all that love is gone.
My heart to her but as guest-wise sojourn'd,
And now to Helen is it home return'd,
There to remain.

(3.2.169–73)

Despite having single-mindedly pursued Hermia, Demetrius now seems unsure whether he ever loved her, though he is certain that if he did, all that love is now gone. As we saw with Lysander (2.2.110–11), love seems to recognize fully only the love that is present, which eclipses from memory a love that is past. On the other hand, love seems as sure of the future as of the present. While his heart, Demetrius says, only visited Hermia as a guest, it now returns home to Helena, there to remain. What has not yet happened seems more certain, to Demetrius, than what already has.

Lysander, again addressing Helena, accuses Demetrius of lying: "Helen, it is not so" (3.2.173). Lysander does not explain why Demetrius's profession of love cannot be true. His own reversal would seem to work against his unsupported contention. Demetrius, evidently catching sight of Hermia approaching, thinks he sees a chance to force Lysander to drop his pursuit of Helena. "Disparage not the faith thou dost not know," he darkly warns; "Lest to thy peril thou abide it dear. / Look where thy love comes; yonder is thy dear" (3.2.174–76). Lysander must now give up his pursuit of Helena or else lose Hermia. Lest he pay dear by losing his dear, he can pursue only one.

## 4.  Union in Partition

Hermia enters. Never before have all four young Athenians been together, awake. But none of them understands what is happening. Puck told of his great pleasure in watching two at once woo one. Now that the four are together, the imbroglio becomes only more entangled. Originally, the two wooing one were Lysander and Demetrius, wooing Hermia. And the last time Hermia saw any of the other three—fewer than a hundred lines ago (3.2.81)—Helena loved Demetrius, who loved Hermia, who loved Lysander, who (so she thought) loved her. Now, Hermia and Helena have changed places, though no one realizes that. The two wooing one are Lysander and Demetrius, wooing Helena. Neither man believes that the other loves Helena, and both women believe that both men love Hermia.

Quince confused hearing and seeing, as Bottom and Pyramus will do (3.1.85–87; 4.1.209–12; 5.1.190–91, 338–40). Hermia, despite the urgency of her asking Lysander why he left her, prefaces her one-line question with six lines describing how the senses naturally compensate for one another—four lines on the general tendency of one sense to make up for another, impaired sense, and two lines on the application of that principle to her finding Lysander in the dark night. Quince had confounded the objects of seeing and hearing ("he goes . . . to see a noise that he heard" [3.1.86]). Hermia, mentioning in alternate lines "the eye" and "[t]he ear," "the seeing sense" and "the hearing," and "mine eye" and "[m]ine ear," carefully distinguishes the two senses according to their perceptual organs and proper activities. For Hermia, unlike Quince (and Bottom), the unity of the senses does not destroy their plurality. Hermia's first four lines—her theoretical lines—discuss the effect of the absence of light on the senses:

> Dark night, that from the eye his function takes,
> The ear more quick of apprehension makes;
> Wherein it doth impair the seeing sense,
> It pays the hearing double recompense.

(3.2.177–80)

Dark night impairs the one sense but strengthens the other. It nullifies the one but doubles the other. The external world thus helps order our senses. Not only is man related to the external world by his senses, the external world supports the requirements of his sensing. Even darkness—the absence of what externally allows us to see—compensates for what it denies us. Turning to her own situation, Hermia tells Lysander that she found him not by her eye but by her ear: "Thou art not by mine eye, Lysander, found; / Mine ear, I thank it, brought me to thy sound" (3.2.182–83). The paths of the characters have crossed in the woods numerous times. This is the first time a crossing has been explained. Hermia says that darkness "pays the hearing double recompense." Yet, despite having sharpened her hearing, the darkness does not seem to have allowed her to hear what Lysander said. Hermia heard his voice or "sound," but not his words: "But why unkindly didst thou leave me so?" (3.2.183). She does not have a clue.

Lysander, referring to himself in the third person, replies with a rhetorical question: "Why should he stay whom love doth press to go?" (3.2.184). The last word Hermia had previously said to him, following his vow to "end life when I end loyalty" (2.2.62), was "press'd": "With half that wish the wisher's eyes be press'd" (2.2.64). Lysander's eyes, however, were soon pressed with the love juice, and love now presses him to break his vow and leave. Hermia, utterly unable to understand, asks, using his word, while also referring to him in the third person, "What love could press Lysander from my side?" (3.2.185). Love should press him to stay, not to leave. Lysander answers by naming Helena:

> Lysander's love, that would not let him bide—
> Fair Helena, who more engilds the night
> Than all yon fiery oes and eyes of light.

(3.2.186–88)

Just as Demetrius compared Hermia to bright Venus in her glimmering sphere (3.2.61), and Oberon spoke of Helena shinning as gloriously in

Demetrius's eye as Venus in the sky (3.2.106–7), Lysander compares Helena to the glittering stars. Contrary to what Hermia just said, some things
are more easily seen at night: the night's darkness adds to their brightness.
Lysander, however, seems to confuse seeing and its object. The two become one. Besides being puns on the plurals of the vowels *i* and *o*, "eyes"
are organs of sight, while "oes" are ornamental spangles. The stars, while
brightening the night with golden light, both see and are seen (cf.
1.1.9–11, 209–10). Dropping the third person, Lysander continues by asking, apparently in genuine wonder, "Why seek'st thou me? Could not this
make thee know / The hate I bear thee made me leave thee so?"
(3.2.189–90). We might expect Lysander to say that he left Hermia because he loves Helena. That is not what he says. He says he left Hermia
because he hates her. As we have already seen, to Lysander, a past love is
indistinguishable from a present hate (cf. 2.2.135–41). Moreover, as we
have also already seen, Lysander seems to think that his new passion
speaks for itself, that Hermia should somehow know it without his having
to say so much as a word (cf. 2.2.134).

When Hermia, incredulous and pained, exclaims that Lysander cannot be
speaking as he thinks, Helena, mistaking the sign of her innocence as evidence of her guilt, angrily concludes from Hermia's hurt words that she is part
of the plot to deride her:

> Lo, she is one of this confederacy!
> Now I perceive they have conjoin'd all three
> To fashion this false sport in spite of me.
>
> (3.2.192–94)

Helena's speech—the rest of which is directed entirely to Hermia—is the
loquacious Helena's longest. Its subject is friendship. While Helena prefaces
it with the accusation that her friends have joined in a conspiracy against
her, the speech is the play's fullest discussion of the union or oneness of
friends. Its main body falls into three sections. The first (3.2.195–97) and
last (3.2.215–19) deal with the present and contain Helena's charge that
Hermia has joined with men in tormenting her. The second deals with the
past and recounts what Helena and Hermia shared as one (3.2.198–202),
what they did together as one (3.2.203–8), and how they consequently grew
together as one (3.2.208–14). While the opening and closing sections emphasize the opposition of "you" and "me" (3.2.196, 197, 215, 216, 218
[twice], 219), the central section, claiming that the women were once one
despite being or seeming to be two, uses no singular pronoun, but repeatedly

speaks, instead, of "we," including "we two" (3.2.198, 199, 200, 203, 208), "us" (3.2.201), "our" (3.2.204, 207 [twice]), and "both" (3.2.204, 205, 206 [twice]). Thematically, the crux of the speech lies in the natural ambiguity of the pronoun "we."

After prefacing her speech by blaming all three, Helena turns to Hermia and accuses her of having joined "with these" (3.2.196) to bait her with foul derision. Helena never mentions either Demetrius or Lysander by name anywhere in the speech. In the preface, she spoke only of "they . . . all three," and, here, she refers to the men only by the demonstrative pronoun "these." Later, she will be even less specific. Only the two women matter.

Helena begins recounting what she and Hermia once shared by stressing not only the time they spent together but also their conversation. As she emphasized "all" when describing the three conspirators, she thrice stresses "all" in describing what the women shared. And as she emphasized words beginning with the connective prefix "con" ("confederacy," "conjoin'd," "conspir'd," and "contriv'd" [3.2.192, 193, 196]) when describing the three, she stresses the word "counsel" in describing what the women shared (cf. 1.1.214–16; 3.2.308):

> Is all the counsel that we two have shar'd,
> The sisters' vows, the hours that we have spent
> When we chid the hasty-footed time
> For parting us—O, is all forgot?
> All school-days' friendship, childhood innocence?
>
> (3.2.198–202)

Like lovers, young girls ("sisters") can make and break "vows." Friendship as well as love can be forgotten.

Sharing secret thoughts, making sisters' vows, and chiding the quick-paced time for parting them were not Helena and Hermia's only activities. Besides speaking, they shared sewing, sitting, and singing:

> We, Hermia, like two artificial gods,
> Have with our needles created both one flower,
> Both on one sampler, sitting on one cushion,
> Both warbling of one song, both in one key,
> As if our hands, our sides, voices and minds,
> Had been incorporate.
>
> (3.2.203–7)

Helena says that, as they were one in activity, so it was as if they were one in mind and body. Like "two artificial gods," they "both" created "one" flower, "[b]oth" on "one" sampler, while sitting on "one" cushion, "[b]oth" singing "one" song, "both" in "one" key. Just as an "artificial god" is at once a god making art and a god made by art,[23] the girls, at once active and passive, grew to resemble what they did:

> So we grew together,
> Like to a double cherry, seeming parted,
> But yet an union in partition,
> Two lovely berries moulded on one stem;
> So, with two seeming bodies, but one heart;
> Two of the first, life coats in heraldry,
> Due but to one, and crowned with one crest.
>
> (3.2.208–14)

Helena clearly wants to emphasize their union, their oneness. Where originally she said that Hermia and she had chided the time "[f]or parting us," now she says they were only "seeming parted." And where she first said that it was "[a]s if" they had been incorporate, now she says that they were only seemingly separate bodies ("two seeming bodies"). Yet, she cannot emphasize their union without at the same time acknowledging their separateness, their twoness. She does, and does not, distinguish between two and one. Nor can she. "We" implies both "union" and "partition"—both "one" and "two" (or "many").[24] The union is a union of parts, which must remain parts in order to be part of the union. The parts' pairing implies or presupposes their apartness. Indeed, were the parts to lose their separateness, "we" would become "I." Despite the inseparability that Helena tries to stress, "we"—"we two"—always means "you and I." The pronoun is plural.

Helena concludes by returning to her accusation and to the singular "you" and "I." If love and friendship conceal separateness, anger brings it to the fore. Helena, however, continues to group Hermia and herself, though differently now:

> And will you rent our ancient love asunder
> To join with men in scorning your poor friend?
> It is not friendly; 'tis not maidenly;
> Our sex, as well as I, may chide you for it,
> Though I alone do feel the injury.
>
> (3.2.215–19)

Helena uses "our," here, to opposite effects. "Our sex," which she allies with "I" in opposition to "you," may chide Hermia for tearing "our ancient love" asunder. "Our" both unites and sets the women at odds. Hermia is both inside and outside the circle of "our." And just as Helena complained that Demetrius forced her to bring a scandal on "my sex" (2.1.240), she now not only speaks of "our sex" chiding Hermia, but says they will do it for her joining "with men" in scorning a female friend. Characteristically stressing the unity or sharing of women, Helena by the same token reduces Demetrius and Lysander to generic "men."

## 5. Mockery and Scorn

Each of the women thinks the other is scorning her. Hermia thinks so, because she knows she is not part of any plot to humiliate Helena by having the men feign their love: "I am amazed at your passionate words: / I scorn you not; it seems that you scorn me" (3.2.220–21). And Helena thinks so, owing to the sudden and otherwise inexplicable reversal of the two men, both of whom have expressed their love for Hermia, and one of whom "even but now did spurn [Helena] with his foot" (3.2.225). Fickle though love may be, the only thing that could do what the love juice has done would indeed be a plot hatched by Hermia: "[B]y your setting on, by your consent" (3.2.231). Helena, however, quickly resorts to another self-pitying comparison of herself and Hermia:

> What though I be not so in grace as you,
> So hung upon with love, so fortunate,
> But miserable most, to love unlov'd?
> This you should pity rather than despise.
>
> (3.2.232–35)

If to love unloved makes one most miserable, it is in fact Hermia who now deserves that unhappy distinction.

When Hermia denies that she understands Helena's meaning, Helena, mistaking the others' deep division for their collusion, imagines that they are play-acting. They are feigning sad looks to her face, and making faces at her and winking at one another behind her back. An imitation of unloved love ("counterfeit sad looks" [3.2.237]), their theatrical performance ("this sport" [3.2.240]), she says, will be written up in history ("be chronicled" [3.2.240]), if they can keep it up. Where Puck sees the young lovers's entanglements as an unwitting stage play, Helena sees them as a deliberate performance. Accusing the others, again, of lacking "pity, grace, [and] manners" (3.2.241), Helena, abruptly stopping herself and bidding farewell, admits her partial blame for the mockery and makes what seems intended as an ominous threat or prediction: "But fare ye well; 'tis partly my own fault, / Which death, or absence, soon shall remedy" (3.2.243–44). Helena does not specify her fault. Nor does she leave. On the contrary, she stays for another hundred lines (cf. 3.2.343), making one wonder whether her foreboding words are not themselves merely histrionic. A person who constantly cares about appearances, Helena is not above putting one on. This, at any rate, is not the first time that she has spoken of dying for love (cf. 2.1.244).

Helena's words have an immediate effect. Lysander begs Helena to stay and to hear his defense, calling her "[m]y love, my life, my soul, fair Helena" (3.2.246)—terms of love stronger than he ever used for Hermia (cf. 1.1.128, 179; 2.2.34). But the stronger the terms, the stronger Helena's skepticism. "O excellent!" she exclaims (3.2.247), sarcastically praising Lysander for his acting performance. Hermia, too, thinks that Lysander is scorning Helena and asks him to relent. Demetrius, as usual the last to speak, threatens to use force to stop Lysander if Hermia fails with words: "If she cannot entreat, I can compel" (3.2.248). Lysander, however, dismisses Demetrius's threat: "Thou canst compel no more than she entreat; / Thy threats have no more strength than her weak prayers" (3.2.249–50). Then, to show why threats cannot compel him, Lysander vows to give his life to prove his love:

> Helen, I love thee, by my life I do;
> I swear by that which I will lose for thee
> To prove him false that says I love thee not.

> (3.2.251–53)

Lysander's vow amount to a triple negative. Swearing as strongly as he can imagine, Lysander swears by that which he will lose for Helena that he will lose it to prove him wrong who says he does not love her. His love is measured by his willing loss. Demetrius, aroused by Lysander's spirited vow, declares that he loves Helena more than Lysander can. And Lysander, daring him to make good his word, challenges him to a duel to prove what he says. Demetrius quickly takes the challenge and wants to duel right away. Men can "fight for love" (2.1.241). If compulsion is stronger than prayers, duels may nevertheless confirm speech. The physical force that can overpower speech may also ratify speech.

When Hermia, worried, asks him where all of this is leading, Lysander contemptuously dismisses her, insulting her and her looks: "Away, you

Ethiope!" (3.2.257). As when he first fell in love with Helena, Lysander not only prefers the blonde to the brunette, but identifies the brunette with her looks and exaggerates them in the most extreme way (cf. 2.2.113). The brunette Athenian becomes a black African. Lysander's judgments, like his passions, seem to admit of no moderation. Demetrius, however, taunting his willingness to fight, describes Lysander as merely pretending to want to free himself from Hermia, who is holding him to keep him from fighting (cf. 3.2.335).[25] While Helena thinks the men are feigning love, Demetrius thinks Lysander is feigning courage. Demetrius thus mockingly advises Lysander to rant as though he really wanted to follow him but, once free, not to show up for the fight. "You are a tame man, go!" (3.2.259). Taunted by Demetrius for pretended bravery, Lysander, continuing to vilify Hermia, tries to free himself from her so he can prove his courage: "Hang off, thou cat, thou burr! Vile thing, let loose / Or I will shake thee from me like a serpent" (3.2.260–61). Hermia, still managing to call him "[s]weet love" (3.2.263; also 3.2.247, 272), cannot understand why Lysander has "change[d]" and grown so "rude" (3.2.262). Lysander is never more abusive, however, than in reply: "Thy love? Out, tawny Tartar, out! / Out, loathed medicine! O hated potion, hence!" (3.2.263–64). Hermia, still perplexed, still thinks that Lysander is jesting ("Do you not jest?" [3.2.264]). Helena, still thinking she understands, answers not only for Lysander, but also for Hermia herself: "Yes sooth, and so do you." (3.2.265). While the men, affected by the love juice, find nothing strange in their new situation, the women, who attempt to understand it, can understand the strange changes only as a cruel hoax.

Lysander, replying to Demetrius's insult that he is faking his willingness to fight, declares that he will "keep my word with thee" (3.2.266)—an assertion that only provokes Demetrius's further insult. Quibbling on "bond" to refer both to a binding agreement and to a restraint (being held in Hermia's clutches), Demetrius denies that Lysander's bond is as good as his word: "I would I had your bond, for I perceive / A weak bond holds you; I'll not trust you" (3.2.267–68). Lysander is at once a coward and a liar. His word is weak, for the restraint that he says binds him is not strong but weak. The weakness of Hermia's restraint implies the weakness of Lysander's courage and word.

Lysander pleads his inability to break free without harming Hermia, which he refuses to do, despite hating her: "What, should I hurt her, strike her, kill her dead? / Although I hate her, I'll not harm her so" (3.2.269–70). Hermia, echoing Lysander's question, asks bewilderedly, "What, can you do me greater harm than hate?" (3.2.271). Harm to the soul far outweighs harm to the body. Unable even to begin to understand, Hermia asks why Lysander says he hates her and what could possibly have caused his change:

> Hate me? Wherefor? O me! what news, my love?
> Am not I Hermia? Are not you Lysander?
> I am as fair now as I was erewhile.
> Since night you lov'd me; yet since night you left me.
>
> (3.2.272–75)

Something must have changed to cause Lysander's change, but nothing has. Hermia, nevertheless, finally allows herself to ask whether Lysander is serious: "Why, then you left me—O the gods forbid!— / In earnest, shall I say?" (3.2.276–77). And Lysander replies unequivocally and brutally. Swearing by his life again—the thing he most often swears by (cf. 3.2.246, 251)—and emphasizing both the negative and the finality of what he swears, he answers:

> Ay, by my life!
> And never did desire to see thee more.
> Therefore, be out of hope, of question, of doubt;
> Be certain, nothing truer; 'tis no jest
> That I do hate thee, and love Helena.
>
> (3.2.277–81)

Hermia, finally certain of Lysander's change of heart, turns to Helena and blames her for the change. Change must have a cause, and the cause of Lysander's change must be Helena, who has stolen his heart:

> You juggler! You canker-blossom!
> You thief of love! What, have you come by night
> And stol'n my love's heart from him?
>
> (3.2.283–84)

Hermia's accusation against Helena, ironically, recalls Egeus's accusation against Lysander: she is a trickster who stole a heart by night (cf. 1.1.26ff.). Helena's seduction, not Lysander's inconstancy, is to blame.

Helena continues to assume that Hermia is conspiring with the others to mock her. Now, however, she seems to think that the plot has reached a new phase, with Hermia pretending to believe that Lysander loves Helena and that Helena has stolen his love away from Hermia. With mock praise for her acting performance, she, once again, accuses Hermia of lacking maidenly modesty in joining with men to scorn a friend (cf. 3.2.217–18):

> Fine, i'faith!
> Have you no modesty, no maiden shame,
> No touch of bashfulness?
>
> (3.2.284–86)

Only the likeness of a friend, Hermia is only the likeness of a modest maiden. "Fie, fie, you counterfeit! You puppet you!" (3.2.288). Just as the men are men only in show (3.2.151), Hermia is only the imitation of a woman. This is Helena's first direct insult of her.

Hermia misunderstands the insult and, taking "puppet" literally to mean a small figure or small person,[26] makes the further mistake of concluding that Helena won Lysander's heart by comparing their heights. To Hermia's mind, Helena's insult suddenly makes everything clear: "'Puppet'! Why so? Ay, that way goes the game! / Now I perceive . . ." (3.2.289–90). Hermia then compounds her error by taking her own literal understanding figuratively. If being a puppet means being short, being tall means being held in high esteem: "And are you grown so high in his esteem / Because I am so dwarfish and so low?" (3.2.294–95). According to Hermia's hermeneutics, littleness is tantamount to lowliness. Helena has often compared herself to Hermia (cf., e.g., 1.1.181–201, 226–29; 2.2.89–98; 3.2.232–34). This is the first time Hermia has compared herself to Helena. Hermia, demanding that Helena tell her how low she is, threatens her—"thou painted maypole" (3.2.296)—with scratching out her eyes: "I am not yet so low / But that my nails can reach unto thine eyes" (3.2.297–98). Being tall not only fails to guarantee safety. It might also be something to disparage. A maypole is skinny as well as overtall, and being painted may mean being phony.

Helena, responding to Hermia's threat rather than to her insult, appeals to the two men to protect her. Denying that she was ever a shrew but acknowledging that she is a coward (cf. 2.1.232–34), she first asks them not to let Hermia strike her. But then she, once again, rubs Hermia where she is touchiest:

> You perhaps may think,
> Because she is something lower than myself,
> That I can match her.
>
> (3.2.303–5)

Hermia's response is predictable: "'Lower'? Hark, again!" (3.2.305).

Helena admits to one misdeed. Asking "[g]ood Hermia" (3.2.306) not to be so bitter with her, she explains that she at all times loved her, always kept her counsels and never wronged her, "[s]ave that, in love unto Demetrius, / I told him of your stealth unto this wood" (3.2.309–10). Without that single breach of confidence, of course, none of the lovers' embroilments in the woods would have occurred. Helena, in effect, justifies her lapse as an act of love which painfully failed. Her justification is twofold: she did it for love ("in love unto Demetrius" [3.2.309]), and she gained nothing from it except pain ("But he hath chid me hence, and threaten'd me / To strike me, spurn me, nay to kill me too" [3.2.312–13]). Both love and painful failure tend to excuse, Helena suggests. Owing to the one, she could not help doing what she did. And owing to the other, she has nothing but regret. Accordingly, Helena ends hers speech by repenting her coming to the woods and asking to be allowed to return to Athens:

> And now, so you will let me quiet go,
> To Athens will I bear my folly back,
> And follow you no further. Let me go:
> You see how simple and how fond I am.
>
> (3.2.314–17)

Earlier, Helena announced her departure, while admitting some partial (and unspecified) fault (3.2.243–44), but made no effort to leave. Now, she specifies her fault and asks for permission to leave. Again, however, she remains.

Hermia, reasonably enough, thinks that Helena is speaking merely for effect, that her repentance is nothing but theatrics. "Why, get you gone! Who is't that hinders you?" (3.2.318). But Helena replies, "A foolish heart that I leave here behind" (3.2.319). Helena has not changed. What caused her to go into the woods, now keeps her from leaving the woods. She still loves Demetrius and still thinks he hates her. The two men, however, respond as if Hermia were indeed threatening to harm Helena, though they do so differently. Lysander tells Helena not to fear; Hermia will not harm her. Demetrius, in effect challenging Lysander, says that Hermia will not harm her even if Lysander takes Helena's part: Demetrius is the only protector Helena needs.[27] Helena, evidently encouraged by the men's chivalrousness and Hermia's resentment at being called little, increases her warning about Hermia while repeating her description of her height:

O, when she is angry, she is keen and shrewd;
She was a vixen when she went to school,
And though she be but little, she is fierce.

(3.2.323–25)

In her initial complaint, Helena emphasized the two women's former likeness and closeness. But once Lysander says that he is not jesting and Hermia consequently blames Helena for stealing his heart (3.2.277–84), the two women stress only their differences in character or temper as well as in height. According to Helena, Hermia is impatient, immodest, and shameless, while, according to Hermia, Helena is a thieving trickster, and, according to Helena herself, she, unlike Hermia, is defenseless and cowardly. And now, according to Helena, even as schoolgirls the two were like night and day. One was tall but cowardly, the other little but fierce. Nothing remains of the "union in partition." In friendship, the women see only their sameness; in anger, only their differences. And they exaggerate both.

Taking the bait, Hermia becomes furious, not at being called a vixen, but at being called little: "'Little' again? Nothing but 'low' and 'little'?" (3.2.326). And as if to corroborate the charge of fierceness, she wants to go after Helena for calling her little and blames the men for protecting her: "Why will you suffer her to flout me thus? / Let me come to her!" (3.2.327–28). Lysander quickly joins the chorus of growing belittlement. "Get you gone, you dwarf," he dismisses Hermia; "You minimus, of hindering knot-grass made; / You bead, you acorn" (3.2.328–30). Shrinking as he speaks, Hermia's stature dwindles until she is barely visible underfoot—hardly bigger than the frightened, fleeing elves, whose smallness in size reflects their slightness in being (2.1.30–31). Demetrius, rather than speaking to Hermia or echoing Helena, addresses Lysander and, picking up where he left off (cf. 3.2.322), objects to Lysander's "officious" (3.2.330) service in her behalf, threatening once again to make him pay ("aby") for his actions (cf. 3.2.175, 426; also 3.2.84–87):

Let her alone; speak not of Helena;
Take not her part; for if thou dost intend
Never so little show of love to her,
Thou shalt aby it.

(3.2.332–35)

Helena talked of men fighting for love (2.2.241). Two men, both of whom she thinks hate her, now go to fight for her love. Lysander, no longer held back by Hermia (3.2.335), challenges Demetrius to a trial by combat: "Now follow, if thou dar'st, to try whose right, / Of thine or mine, is most in Helena" (3.2.336–37). In his opening words, Demetrius claimed his "right" to Hermia, based on the ancestral Athenian law (1.1.91–92). Now, Lysander speaks of their trying their right to Helena, based on their own manly courage. Not to be outdone, Demetrius fully accepts the challenge: "Follow? Nay, I'll go with thee, cheek by jowl" (3.2.338). The two schoolgirls' sitting side by side has been replaced by the two suitors' fighting side by side. War is indeed part of love.

With the men running off to duel, Hermia blames Helena for the turmoil. It is all because of her ("all this coil is long of you" [3.2.339]), she says, by which she seems to refer to the original cause of the chase though the woods as well as to the object of the present fight. Hermia knows nothing, of course, of Puck's and Oberon's roles. Nor does she seem to notice that her accusation suggests the sneer that she hates and has threatened to punish. "Long" in the sense of "owing to" promptly becomes "long" in the sense of "tall." Helena, afraid of Hermia's hands, flees, flinging her favorite slight: "Your hands than mine are quicker for a fray: / My legs are longer though, to run away" (3.2.342–43). Hermia, never before or again at a loss for words, is "amaz'd, and know[s] not what to say" (3.2.344). Mocking her (presumed) mocker seems to be Helena's revenge.

## 6. Doting's Antidote

Oberon blames the fracas squarely on Puck: "This is thy negligence" (3.2.345). Puck, he says, always makes mistakes or else wilfully commits his mischievous pranks. He is never reliable or trustworthy. Puck agrees that he made an error, but pleads his innocence. He did exactly what Oberon told him to do. Oberon told him that he would recognize the man by his Athenian clothing, and Puck is blameless insofar as he anointed an Athenian's eyes. Puck's innocence lies in his doing what Oberon said rather than what he meant. Just as Oberon identified the man entirely by generalities and externals ("Thou shalt know the man / By the Athenian garments he hath on" [2.1.263–64]), Puck acted entirely by generalities and externals. He followed the spirit as well as the letter—if not the intent—of Oberon's order. Helena pled her innocence by citing her painful regret (3.2.312–13), but Puck, notwithstanding his claim to innocence ("so far blameless" [3.2.350]), declares that he is delighted with his error. He is glad that things came out this way, for he considers the lovers' wrangling "a sport" (3.2.353). The last time we saw him, Puck said that, for him, two at once wooing one was the most enjoyable "sport" (3.2.119). Now, he brings out an important implication of that remark and of his actions, so far, in general. The outcome of the duel between the two Athenian men is altogether unknown to him. It could end well or badly, for any or all concerned. But Puck does not care. That lovers' quarrels are amusing in no way depends, for him, on their having a happy outcome. Folly suffices. If the difference between tragedy and comedy, tears and laughter, is lost on the artisans, the difference between human happiness and human misery counts for nothing with Puck.

Oberon, on the other hand, wants to avoid a real fight between Lysander and Demetrius. Unlike Puck, he cares about people and the effects of his actions. Oberon therefore comes up with a new plan. Puck is to overcast the night with "drooping fog, as black as Acheron" (3.2.357), and lead the rivals astray, so that neither man harms the other. In the utter darkness, Puck will impersonate each lover's voice in order to stir up the other and lead them in different directions until they give up their pursuit of each other, overcome with sleep. As Puck mistook one of the Athenians for the other, the two Athenians will mistake him for each other. Where he was misled by their clothing, they will be misled by his impersonation, ventriloquism, and the darkness. Contrary to what Hermia suggested (3.2.177–80), the night's utter absence of light will not heighten their hearing. Puck is then to apply a new drug to Lysander's eye, "[t]o take from thence all error with his might / And make his eyeballs roll with wonted sight" (3.2.368–69). Literally an antidote, the drug will end Lysander's doting over Helena. It will return him to his accustomed sight.

Still, none of the lovers will be free from error: "When they next wake, all this derision / Shall seem a dream and fruitless vision" (3.2.370–71). While a dream mistakes a likeness for something real, the lovers will mistake something real for a likeness. Rather than see a dream as unreal when they awake (cf. 2.2.144–49), they will see what is real as a dream. They will awake to think that they only dreamt what they saw. The lovers will then go back to Athens and live happily ever after: "And back to Athens shall the lovers wend, / With league whose date till death shall never end" (3.2.372–73). We must wonder whether Oberon is aware of Egeus's (and Theseus's) ban on Hermia's marrying Lysander, or whether he expects it to be waived. Whatever the case, the young Athenians will not be the only ones made happy. Oberon will go to Titania, he says,

> and beg her Indian boy;
> And then I will her charmed eye release
> From monster's view, and all things shall be peace.

> (3.2.375–77)

Puck warns that things must done quickly, "[f]or night's swift dragons cut the clouds full fast" (3.2.379). Perhaps not surprisingly, Puck, "that merry wanderer of the night" (2.1.43), treats the night not as the absence of daylight but as something existing in its own right. Drawn across the sky in a chariot pulled by dragons, it is a presence, not a privation.[28] Puck then speaks of dawn and the dead:

> And yonder shines Aurora's harbinger,
> At whose approach, ghosts wandering here and there
> Troop home to churchyards. Damned spirits all,
> That in cross-ways and floods have burial,
> Already to their wormy beds are gone,
> For fear lest day should look their shames upon:
> They wilfully themselves exil'd from light,
> And must for aye consort with black-brow'd night.
>
> (3.2.380–87)

Puck distinguishes between two kinds of ghosts or spirits: those who are buried in churchyards and those who are buried in unsanctified grounds. Both wander at night. But while the former troop home at the approach of the morning star, the latter are already in their beds by then. Driven by shame and damned because they are suicides,[29] they at once "wilfully" and "must" avoid daylight: they wish to do what they must do. Puck's second group of ghosts or spirits seems to be both Christian and pagan. On the one hand they are damned for killing themselves, but on the other they are governed by a sense of public shame. Although they are damned for what is a Christian but not a pagan offense, it is not God's judgment, but man's, that seems to matter most to them.

"But we are spirits of another sort" (3.2.388). Oberon's correction is equivocal and perhaps boastful. Oberon indicates that, unlike the ghosts of the damned, he does not have to flee the first light of day. But he also indicates that, much like the first group of ghosts, he must nevertheless flee the full light of day:

> I with the Morning's love have oft made sport;
> And like a forester the groves may tread
> Even till the eastern gate, all fiery-red,
> Opening on Neptune with fair blessed beams,
> Turns into yellow gold his salt green streams.
>
> (3.2.389–93)

Oberon may tread the grove "[e]ven till"—which is to say, "only till"—the sun has fully risen. We must wonder how he was able to sit "all day" with Phillida, while impersonating Corin (2.1.65–68). However that may be, Oberon says that he has often hunted in the early morning with Cephalus ("the Morning's love"), a mighty hunter loved by the pre-Olympian goddess Eos (Aurora), whose tragic tale Bottom and the other players will mention (in their way) in *Pyramus and Thisbe* (5.1.196–97; cf. Ovid, *Metamorphoses*, 7.661–865). This is the only time Oberon tells of his having spent time with a human and the only time he compares himself to one ("like a forester"). Just as Titania said that Hippolyta was "[his] buskin'd mistress and . . . warrior love" (2.1.71), so, when telling of spending time with a human, Oberon speaks in the same breath of hunting and love.

Notwithstanding his correction of Puck, Oberon wants to hurry and finish the business before day. He needs darkness for his plot. As soon as Oberon leaves, Puck delivers an incantation, presumably to produce the blinding fog:

> Up and down, up and down,
> I will lead them up and down;
> I am fear'd in field and town:
> Goblin, lead them up and down.

(3.2.396–99)

But before Puck needs to go further, Lysander enters ("Here comes one" [3.2.400]), looking for Demetrius.

## 7. Two of Both Kinds

Puck's illusive actions, while averting a dual between Lysander and Demetrius, bring out a major difference in the characters of the two men. When Lysander, who comes ready to fight, thinks Demetrius has slipped away, he generously praises his rival and blames himself for not being swift enough to keep up with him: "The villain is much lighter-heel'd than I: / I follow'd fast; but faster did he fly" (3.2.415–16; cf. 3.2.402). But when Lysander goes off to fight, Demetrius blames him for being too unmanly to face him: "Thou runaway, thou coward, art thou fled? / Speak! In some bush? Where dost thou hide thy head?" (3.2.405–6). Puck, accordingly, addresses each man differently. While he simply bids Lysander to follow him to more

level ground ("Follow me . . . / To plainer ground" [3.2.403–4]), he goads
Demetrius by answering him in kind:

> Thou coward, art thou bragging to the stars,
> Telling the bushes that thou look'st for wars,
> And wilt not come?
>
> (3.2.407–9)

Demetrius, pretending to be what he is not, is not just a "recreant" but "a
child" (3.2.409). He only pretends to be a man. A vain braggart, he is all
bravado (cf. 3.2.257–59, 267–68). Thus, whereas Puck challenges Lysander
with his (putative) sword ("Here, . . . drawn and ready" [3.2.402]), he denies
that Demetrius is worthy of a sword-fight. Threatening to "whip [him] with
a rod" instead, Puck declares, "[H]e is defil'd / That draws a sword on thee"
(3.2.410–11). Demetrius is to be treated like a slave or a beast; anyone who
treats him like a man only dishonors himself. While suggesting nothing of
the sort to Lysander, Puck thus describes the fight with Demetrius as a test of
"manhood" (3.2.412). Accordingly, when Demetrius and Puck return,
Demetrius, unable to find Lysander, accuses him, again, of lacking the daring
to stand and fight or even to look him in the face:

> Abide me if thou dar'st, for well I wot
> Thou runn'st before me, shifting every place,
> And dar'st not stand, nor look me in the face.
>
> (3.2.422–24)

And, while Lysander, who, lying down to sleep, vows to find Demetrius at the
first light of day and to revenge his own bad fortune of having gotten himself
into hilly ground underfoot, Demetrius, preparing to sleep, threatens that,
"[i]f ever" he sees his face again (3.2.427), he will make Lysander pay dearly
("buy this dear" [3.2.426; cf. 3.2.175, 335]) for mocking him. In brief, while
Lysander comes prepared to fight, generously praises his rival, and blames
himself for not being swift enough to keep up with him, Demetrius, needing
to be provoked to fight, blames Lysander for being too unmanly to face him
and is quick to feel a sense of bitter wrong (cf. 3.2.361).

While Lysander and Demetrius sleep, the one by choice (3.2.418) and the
other by constraint (3.2.428–29), Helena reenters. Like them, she wishes for
daylight. But, unlike them, she wants a quick end to the night—the "weary
night, . . . [the] long and tedious night" (3.2.431)—so she can return quickly
to Athens. Seeking "comforts" (3.2.432) from the light of day, she wishes to

get away from those whom she thinks detest her "poor company" (3.2.434). Helena also has a second wish. She wishes for sleep so she can also "[s]teal me awhile from mine own company" (3.2.436). If to be awake is to be with oneself, to be asleep is to be secluded from oneself—to be blind to "sorrow's eye" (3.2.435; cf. 1.1.7–8).

Earlier in the scene, Puck was delighted by the humorous prospect of three of the lovers—Helena and her two suitors—being together: "Then will two at once woo one" (3.2.114ff.). Now, silent about his own enjoyment, he awaits the fourth: "Yet but three? Come one more, / Two of both kinds makes up four" (3.2.437–38). Puck, as before, makes no distinction among lovers. They are just numbers or ciphers, to him. But having twice been chastised by Oberon, Puck now seems to care about a proper ending, not a foolish chase. "Here she comes," he says, referring to Hermia,

> curst and sad:
> Cupid is a knavish lad
> Thus to make poor females mad!
>
> (3.2.439–41)

Distancing himself from his former actions, Puck blames Cupid for doing what he himself said he most enjoys doing (3.2.120–21). And while repeating the word Oberon used to criticize him (3.2.346), he describes Cupid pejoratively with the very word ("knavish") which he had proudly claimed as his own (2.1.33). These are the first signs of change in Puck.

Hermia enters and, not realizing that Lysander is asleep nearby, declares that she can go no further and will await the break of day:

> Never so weary, never so in woe,
> Bedabbled with the dew, and torn with briars,
> I can no further crawl, no further go.
> My legs can keep no pace with my desires.
>
> (3.2.442–45)

Fairies may ornament themselves with dew and wander through briars (cf. 2.1.2–15), but Hermia, bedabbled with the one and torn by the other, is unable to go on. Her body exhausted and her soul in pain, her legs cannot keep up with her desires. We must wonder, though, where Hermia is going. Is she trying to return to Athens (like Helena) or trying to find Lysander? She does not say. Despite everything, however, Hermia evidently still loves Lysander and, falling asleep, prays for his protection: "Here I will rest me till the break of day. / Heavens shield Lysander, if they mean a fray!" (3.2.444–47).

With all four young Athenians asleep on the ground, Puck squeezes the antidote on Lysander's eyes. When he originally applied the love juice to his eyes, Puck thought Lysander was a "lack-love," a "kill-courtesy," a "[c]hurl" (2.2.76–77). Now, he calls him "[g]entle lover," while uttering for the first time a sweet-sounding chant:

> On the ground
> Sleep sound
> I'll apply
> To your eye
> Gentle lover, remedy
> When thou wak'st,
> Thou tak'st
> True delight
> In the sight
> Of thy former lady's eye.
>
> (3.2.448–57)

Puck, leaving the love juice on Demetrius's eyes, seems not to expect it ever to be removed. Demetrius's doting will receive no antidote.

Puck then closes with a pair of proverbs:

> And the country proverb known,
> That every man should take his own,
> In your waking shall be shown:
> Jack shall have Jill,
> Nought shall go ill;
> The man shall have his mare again, and all shall be well.
>
> (3.2.458–63)

Both proverbs mean that everything will end well, that everyone will be happy. The first substitutes a part for the whole, particular names for the general. The second also employs synecdoche, but a bawdy metaphor, as well: the woman shall bear her lover. Puck, still again, treats the lovers as mere ciphers: "Jack" and "Jill" mean "every man" and "every woman." But Puck speaks as though he now welcomes the lovers' happiness. In keeping with this change, his second proverb's metaphor, taken literally, reverses or retracts his first proudly boasted prank (cf. 2.1.44–46).

# Notes

1. Bottom, who says "more" (eleven times) and "most" (five times), uses no other adverb nearly so frequently and only one adjective ("good" and its variants [twenty times]) and one noun ("man" and its variants [fifteen times]) more often. No one says "more" or "most" more often than he.

2. "In Shakespearian dialogue (*dialogue*, be it observed) it is an inviolable rule that in alternate rhymes, when the second and fourth verses rhyme, the first and third rhyme likewise." Alexander Schmidt, quoted in Furness, 119 (his emphasis).

3. For a review of the textual difficulties, see Brooks, Appendix II.2, 155–58.

4. Marshall, 562.

5. Ronald Watkins and Jeremy Lemmon, *A Midsummer Night's Dream* (Totowa: Rowman & Littlefield, 1972), 74.

6. Mowat and Werstine, 74.

7. "A cue, in stage cant, is the last words of the proceeding speech, and serves as a hint to him who is to speak next." George Steevens in *The Johnson-Steevens Edition of the Plays of William Shakespeare*, ed. Samuel Johnson and George Steevens, 12 vols. (1773; London: Routledge/Thoemmes Press, 1995), 3:61.

8. Mowat and Werstine, 74.

9. Watkins and Lemmon, 75.

10. Malone, in Brooks, 57.

11. Wells, 142.

12. H. Staunton, in Furness, 126.

13. The play's only other mentions of "mortal" are the fairies' first greeting of Bottom, echoing Titania (3.1.168), and Puck's famous remark on human beings as fools (3.2.115).

14. See, e.g., the Quartos and Folios for 5.1.306.

15. Helge Kökeritz, *Shakespeare's Pronunciation* (New Haven: Yale University Press, 1953), 320.

16. For the tininess of a mote, see Matthew 7.3–5; Luke 6.41–42.

17. Cf., e.g., 2.1.1–7, 14–15, 43, 171–76, 247, 259–68; 2.1.1–7, 65–82; 3.1.151, 158; 3.2.94–101, 354–65, 396ff.; 5.1.377–82, 387–88, 401–8.

18. Humans "fly" only in the sense of "flee" (1.1.203; 2.1.246; 2.2.96; 3.1.100; 3.2.24, 416; cf. 2.1.156). The only human dancing is the players' Bergomask (5.1.339–48; cf. 5.1.32, where Theseus gets neither a masque nor a dance).

19. Alexander Schmidt, *Shakespeare Lexicon and Quotation Dictionary*, 2 vols. (1902; New York: Dover Publications, 1971), s.v. "Peascod."

20. For the ambiguity of "blood," similar to that of "heart," cf. 1.1.68, 74; 5.1.146 with 2.2.100; 3.2.48, 75, 97; 5.1.142, 145, 272.

21. Hence, perhaps, the similar root of their (real or putative) fathers' names, Nedar and Tyndarus; see Homer, *The Odyssey*, 24.199. Just as Helena is introduced as "Nedar's daughter, Helena" (1.1.107), Ovid, Virgil, and Lucretius, among others, call Helen "Tyndaris," "daughter of Tyndarus." See Ovid, *Metamorphoses*, 15.233; *Amores*,

2.12.18; *Heroides*, 5.91; 16.100, 308; 17.18; Virgil, *Aeneid*, 2.569, 601; *Catalepton*, 9.29; Lucretius, *On the Nature of Things*, 1.464.

22. Abbott, § 18.

23. Abbott, § 3.

24. No where else in the play are the words "one," "two," "both," and "all" mentioned so often as in Helena's speech: "one," ten times; "two," five times; "both," four times; and "all," four times. The closest is Lysander's "One heart, one bed" speech (2.2.40ff.).

25. The text here is probably corrupt. For a survey of attempts to remedy the difficulties, see Furness, 155–56.

26. "Puppet" derives from "poppet," meaning, originally, a small person; see *OED*, s.v. Puppet.

27. Kittredge, 194.

28. Cf. 3.2.53–55, on the one hand, and 2.2.69; 4.1.95, on the other. Likewise, for "day" as the opposite of night, cf., e.g., 2.2.37; 3.2.50, 385, 395, 418, 446; 5.1.169, 387, 408; for "day" including night, cf., e,g., 1.1.84, 86; 1.2.6–7; 2.1.139; 3.2.12; 4.1.134–35.

29. For the canon law's prohibition of Christian burial for suicides, see *Codex Juris Canonici* (1240), par. 2. See also *Hamlet*, 5.1.211–14, the Arden Edition, ed. Harold Jenkins (London: Routledge, 1995).

# ACT FOUR

~

## Act Four, Scene One

### 1. Beloved Bottom

Titania, who spoke of an angel waking her "from [her] flowery bed" (3.1.124), now invites that angel—"[her] gentle joy"—to sit down "upon this flowery bed" (4.1.1), while she caresses his amiable cheeks, crowns his bald head with musk-roses, and kisses his handsome large ears. Bottom, however, is oblivious to Titania's beauty and desire. Instead of paying her the slightest attention, he addresses the fairies whom she has ordered to be kind and courteous to him, and bids them to scratch his head and hunt a bumble bee's honey-bag for him. At once consort of the fairy queen and good democrat, Bottom attempts to be affable to the fairies. While giving them orders, he addresses Cobweb and Mustardseed as French or Italian nobles[1] and does not want them to bother too much in his behalf or to hurt themselves in any way. And, contradicting Titania's express order, he wants them to stop their bowing and scraping ("leave your courtesy" [4.1.20; cf. 3.1.167]) and to shake his hand, instead.

Although not normally taciturn, Bottom does not initially say much. While asking for Peaseblossom with just two words ("Where's Peaseblossom?" [4.1.5]), he orders him to scratch his head without giving him a title and using the fewest possible words: "Scratch my head, Peaseblossom" (4.1.7). But Bottom quickly proves equal to what he imagines to be the noble occasion. Originally he had spoken of using Cobweb to staunch bleeding (3.1.175–77). Now he orders "Mounsieur Cobweb, good moun-sieur," to get his "weapons in [his] hand, and kill [him] a red-hipped humble-bee on the top of a thistle; and . . . bring [him] the honey-bag" (4.1.10–13). The homely styptic is to become a brave hunter. Bottom then commands "Mounsieur Mustardseed" "to help Cavalery Cobweb to scratch" (4.1.19, 22–23). Despite his apparent attention to names both here and in his first meeting with the fairies (3.1.172–89), Bottom con-fuses Peaseblossom's and Cobweb's names: he ordered Peaseblossom to scratch and Cobweb to hunt. Yet, however difficult he may find learning the names of his fairy attendants, he appropriately if belatedly assigns Cobweb, the hunter, the title of a gentleman trained to arms: "Cavalery" is Bottom's bungled pronunciation of "Cavaleiro."

Titania, who woke up to the sound of his singing, offers Bottom, her "sweet love" (4.1.27), music. And Bottom, modestly praising his own ear ("I have a reasonable good ear in music" [4.1.28]), asks to hear not the harmo-nious music of the fairies, but the cacophonic striking of "the tongs and the bones" (4.1.29). Again calling him "sweet love" (4.1.30), Titania asks what he desires to eat. Bottom chooses oats and hay, and rejects nuts in favor of dried peas. "[G]ood hay, sweet hay, hath no fellow" (4.1.33). Bottom, who with unconscious literalness calls himself "such a tender ass" (4.1.25), chooses what would most satisfy an ass: "Asses would prefer hay to gold" (Heraclitus, frag. 9). But, most of all, Bottom wants to sleep. "I have an ex-position of sleep"—he means "a disposition to sleep"—"come upon me" (4.1.38). Telling him to sleep and dismissing all her fairies, Titania embraces Bottom:

> Sleep thou, and I will wind thee in my arms.
> So doth the woodbine the sweet honeysuckle
> Gently entwist; the female ivy so
> Enrings the barky fingers of the elm.
> O how I love thee! How I dote on thee!

$$(4.1.39–44)$$

Woodbine is another name for honeysuckle (cf. 2.1.251). Here, they are names of different vines. Lovers embraced, it seems, are neither simply one nor simply two (cf. 2.2.40–51). This is the only embrace in the play. The em-brace, however, is entirely one-sided. Bottom wishes only to sleep. He sleeps with Titania only in the literal sense. We might note that Bottom's insensi-bility to Titania's beauty and desire spares her the degradation of the women who sleep with asses in some of Shakespeare's sources.[2]

## 2. Reconciliation and Restoration

Oberon and Puck are spectators of the sight (4.1.45). Oberon, who has seen it from the start (s.d. 4.1.1), has changed, as he himself says. He has begun to "pity" (4.1.46) Titania for her dotage. Oberon explains that he recently saw Titania gathering flowers for "this hateful fool" (4.1.48) and criticized and quarreled with her again. Even the flowers, he says, bewailed "their own disgrace" (4.1.55) in serving as Bottom's crown. Rather than swell like pearls on the buds, the dew now stood within the flowers' eyes like tears (cf. 2.1.14–15). When Oberon taunted her, Titania mildly begged his patience. Her earlier anger had vanished. Oberon then, once more, asked for the Indian boy, and Titania yielded right away: "I then did ask of her her changeling child; / Which straight she gave me" (4.1.58–59). Unlike before, Titania put up no resistance at all. "And now I have the boy, I will undo / This hateful imperfection of her eyes" (4.1.61–62).

Why the changes in Oberon and Titania? Two things, with a single cause, have happened. Oberon and Titania, it seems, were initially jealous of each other's loves. Oberon was jealous of Titania's love of Theseus, and Titania of Oberon's love of Hippolyta and others (2.1.64ff.). The boy—a "changeling" in more than one sense—seems to have served as a substitute for the real objects of their jealousy. Bottom, however, has, by chance, ended the conflict. Consumed by her love for him, Titania is no longer jealous of Oberon's wanderings. Her new love quashes her jealousy. Only Bottom now matters to her. At the same time, the contemptible object of her dotage ("this hateful fool") arouses Oberon's "pity" rather than his jealousy. Bottom, unlike Theseus, is not a rival, and Oberon could never consider him one. What frees Titania also frees Oberon, but in opposite ways. Dotage, for her; pity, for him. Titania originally vowed that she would not trade the boy for all of fairyland; she would keep him for the sake of his mother (2.1.121–37, 144). But she now gives him up with no thought of his mother. And Oberon loses interest in the boy once he gets him. The boy is never mentioned again. Oberon's plan has worked, but not in the way or for the reason he seemed to expect. Its success rests on Puck's unauthorized and unexpected transformation of Bottom's head, which (if it actually happened), rested, in turn, on a series of accidents and chance events, including Quince's pointless alteration of the Pyramus and Thisbe plot. Chance permits Oberon's plan to succeed and reconciles the royal couple.

Playing on a word for both lover and lout ("swain" [4.1.64]), Oberon orders Puck to remove Bottom's transformed head, so

> That he awaking when the others do,
> May all to Athens back again repair,

> And think no more of this night's accidents
> But as the fierce vexation of a dream.

(4.1.65–68)

All the Athenians will think of the night's incidents as a mere image of what they experienced as real at the time. In doing so, they will reverse a dream. Instead of taking a resemblance for the reality, they will take the reality for its resemblance. They will, in effect, dream that they had been dreaming.

Squeezing his curative on Titania's eyes, Oberon delivers a brief incantation:

> Be as thou wast wont to be;
> See as thou wast wont to see:
> Dian's bud o'er Cupid's flower
> Hath such force and blessed power.

(4.1.70–73)

As may seem only fitting for a chant restoring Titania to herself, the first pair of lines—each strictly parallel to the other, each opening and closing with the same word, and each echoing both the other and itself—couple as well as rhyme "to be" and "to see": to be as one is wont to be means to see as one is wont to see. To be oneself means to see as oneself. The second pair of lines state how Oberon will accomplish this. While linking the love juice, once again, to Cupid, Oberon links its antidote to Diana. The antidote is not derived from Cupid's leaden arrow—the one with which Cupid shot Daphne when she was fleeing Apollo (Ovid, *Metamorphoses*, 1.468ff.; cf. 1.1.170; 2.1.159, 231). Unlike that arrow, Oberon's antidote does not prevent love, but simply does not interfere with it. At the same time, notwithstanding its great power (cf. 2.1.155ff.), Cupid's golden arrow or the wounded flower is not necessarily stronger than Diana's bud. Just as the moon's chaste beams could quench the fiery arrow (2.1.161–62), Diana's bud can subdue the flower.

Oberon for the first time speaks endearingly to Titania: "Now my Titania, wake you, my sweet queen" (4.1.75). Titania is "[his] Titania," "[his] sweet queen." And Titania answers in kind: "My Oberon!" (4.1.75; cf. 2.1.119). Love claims possession of its object. Although Oberon conceals from the Athenians the night's events by turning them into a dream, he confirms the reality of the "visions" that Titania has seen. When she, waking, exclaims, "What visions have I seen! / Methought I was enamour'd of an ass," Oberon points to the sleeping Bottom: "There lies your love" (4.1.75–77). Her vision was not a dream (cf. 3.2.371). Titania does not for a moment doubt that Bottom was her love: "O how mine eyes do loathe his visage now!" (4.1.78). Yet, for all that Oberon tells Titania, he does not explain how these things occurred. Oberon seems to promise that he will ("Silence awhile" [4.1.79]), but we never hear his explanation, and we might wonder what he would say.

Bottom's eyes, like Titania's, will return to their accustomed way of seeing: "Now when thou wak'st, with thine own fool's eyes peep" (4.1.83–84). Bottom will see as he was wont to see. It is hard to be sure whether he sees more foolishly with an ass's eyes or his own. In some respects, he never speaks more sensibly than when an ass (cf. 3.1.137–44).

After directing Puck to remove Bottom's bestial head, Oberon bids Titania to call for music which will put the five Athenians' senses into a deeper than ordinary sleep. And when Titania calls for "[m]usic ho, music, such as charmeth sleep!" (4.1.82), Oberon begins to dance with her: "Come my queen, take hands with me. / And rock the ground whereon these sleepers be" (4.1.84–85). While the music itself is to charm the mortals' sleep, the dancers are to rock the ground as a mother rocks a cradle. The dancing is to make sure that the mortals sleep well and awake fully refreshed.[3] Whereas earlier Oberon took advantage of people while they were asleep, now he seeks to produce sleep's restorative effects for them. Not only the Athenians, however, will benefit. The dancing has a second and indeed a third purpose. It is also to mark the reconciliation of Oberon and Titania and thus allow them to bless Theseus's house on his wedding night:

> Now thou and I are new in amity,
> And will to-morrow midnight, solemnly,
> Dance in Duke Theseus' house triumphantly,
> And bless it to all fair posterity.[4]

(4.1.86–89)

Oberon mentions Theseus by name in only two speeches. The speeches form a pair. Oberon mentioned Theseus in his first, angry encounter with Titania, when she accused him of having come to Athens to give "joy and prosperity" to Hippolyta and Theseus's wedding bed and he countered by accusing her of having led Theseus through the glimmering night (2.1.73–80). And he mentions him here. Where the first mention marked the initial appearance of their jealous quarrel, the second, in which Oberon echoes Titania's charge but in the spirit of reconciliation, marks its resolution. And where the first involved the charge of "break[ing] . . . faith" (2.1.79), the second speaks instead of faithful lovers: "There shall the pairs of faithful lovers be / Wedded, with Theseus, all in jollity" (4.1.90–91). Oberon, as earlier, ignores Athens's ancestral law or takes for granted that Theseus will overrule it (cf. 3.2.372–73).

When Puck alerts Oberon that he hears the morning lark, Oberon says that he and Titania must leave: "Then my queen, in sad silence, / Trip we after night's shade" (4.1.94–95). Previously, Oberon suggested that he does not have to flee the early morning's light (3.2.388–93). Now, he seems to concede that he does. Creatures of the night, he and Titania must follow the "night's shade." When Oberon, next, says that he and Titania will circle the globe swifter than the moon (cf. 2.1.7), Titania asks him to tell her in their flight

> how it came this night
> That I sleeping here was found
> With these mortals on the ground.

> (4.1.99–101)

Unlike when she first woke up (4.1.77), Titania now asks nothing about Bottom's appearing as an ass. In her eyes, Bottom is now merely one of five "mortals." Once more, however, for Titania, the principal difference between humans and fairies is that humans are mortal (cf. 2.1.101, 135; 3.1.132, 153–54).

### 3. The Foundation of Athens

As the fairy king and queen exit, Theseus and Hippolyta enter, with Egeus and the rest of Theseus's train. We have not seen any of them since the opening scene. The only Athenians have been the artisans and the lovesick lovers. And not until the married couples go to bed will we see the fairies again (5.1.357ff.). If the fairies are responsible for most of what happens in acts 2 and 3 and the first hundred lines of act 4, from this point on until midnight the Athenians, chiefly Theseus, are responsible for what occurs. As day succeeds night, the Athenian Duke supersedes the fairy king.

While A Midsummer Night's Dream as a whole is synchronic, beginning with Theseus's reappearance here Shakespeare poetically compresses Athens's development from barbaric to civilized into a few key steps. He does so by means of a series of substitutions. Act 4, scene 1—Theseus's central scene—links the ferocity of ancient heroism on the one end and the civility of Athenian democratic politics and intellectual life on the other.

One sign of the change from the fairy world to the human world is that the woods, which were at least part of fairyland (4.1.58–60), are now, as originally, Theseus's palace woods, with an officer to attend to them (cf. 1.2.94, 103). Where Oberon, boasting that he did not have to flee the first light of dawn, compared himself to a "forester" ("[a]nd like a forester the groves [I] may tread" [3.2.390]), Theseus, framing his opening words to his train, twice orders that someone go and "find out the forester" (4.1.102, 107). What is merely a boasted likeness for Oberon, is entirely real for Theseus.

Calling for the forester, Theseus explains that he and the others have finished observing the rite of May (4.1.103; cf. 4.1.132). Much earlier, Lysander and Hermia agreed to meet in the woods where he once met her with Helena "[t]o do observance to a morn of May" (1.1.167; 3.2.296). This, however, is the first time anyone indicates that the present day is May Day. Both the location and the occasion are the same as before. Theseus says that since the day is still early, "My love shall hear the music of my hounds" (4.1.105). We do not know what either Theseus or Hippolyta thinks of observing the rite of May, but we know that both of them love the music of hounds. Theseus tells Hippolyta that they will go up to the mountain's top "[a]nd mark the musical confusion / Of hounds and echo in conjunction" (4.1.109–10). They will hear not only the cry of his hunting hounds, but each cry's echo; and they will hear them "in conjunction." While the dogs themselves will be "[u]ncouple[d]" (4.1.106), each of their sounds will be doubled—the cry itself and its echo, sounded together.

Hippolyta's appreciative reply is the closest she ever comes to describing her life as an Amazon queen. It also contains her only explicit memory. "I was with Hercules and Cadmus once," she tells, "When in a wood of Crete they bay'd the bear / With hounds of Sparta" (4.1.112–14). As we have seen, Shakespeare, unlike his sources, largely ignores Theseus's role in ending Thebes's civil war between Oedipus's sons. At the beginning of the play, Egeus and Hermia replace the Argive suppliants. A dispute about marriage in Athens replaces a fratricidal war in Thebes. Theseus will mention his victory in Thebes only in passing and only after deposing Athens's patriarchal authority (5.1.50–51). Now, however, just before the overthrow of that authority, Shakespeare reminds us of Cadmus, the legendary founder of Thebes. That his mention of Cadmus, who lived some five generations before Theseus,[5] is wildly anachronistic serves only to heighten its significance. Cadmus is associated with the founding of Thebes as well as with the introduction of writing and other arts to Greece.[6] While Cadmus brought writing with him from Phoenicia, his founding of Thebes involved autochthonism in the strictest sense. After killing a dragon sacred to Mars, Cadmus sowed its teeth in the ground, as Athena had bid, and fully armed warriors (*spartoi* or "sown men") sprang from the earth and immediately began killing one another:

> [O]ne by one
> By mutual stroke of civil war dispatched everyone,
> This brood of brothers all behewn and weltered in the blood,
> Lay sprawling on their mother's womb, the ground where erst they stood,
> Save only five that did remain.
>
> (Ovid, *Metamorphoses*, 3.122–25; Golding, 3.139–43)

At Athena's bidding, one of the five survivors dropped his weapon and made peace with his surviving brothers, and all five then helped Cadmus find Thebes.[7] Born from their country's soil, the first Thebans were fratricidal. Thebes's autochthonism gave rise to its fratricide, which repeated itself five generations later with Oedipus's sons. In Thebes, it seems, there is no end to fratricide because there is nothing beyond the realm of one's own. One's own is everything, and the exclusive regard for one's own proves ultimately to destroy one's own, as Oedipus so plainly shows. Fittingly, a "Cadmean victory" is a victory involving one's own ruin.[8] Shakespeare's anachronism regarding Cadmus is thus of a piece with his substituting Theseus's role in resolving the question of Hermia's marriage for his role in ending Thebes's fratricidal civil war. Where the anachronism, emphasizing the self-perpetuation of the self-destruction, points to the power and the danger of the exclusive regard for one's own, the substitution, putting an end to the absolute authority over one's own, points to the mitigation of that power and danger. At least in respect to love, with Theseus's action Athens becomes Thebes's contrary.

Hippolyta's memory constitutes her fondest moment in the play, her only expression of deep pleasure. At no other time does she speak with nearly such ardor or at such length as in describing the Cretan hunt:

> [N]ever did I hear
> Such gallant chiding; for, besides the groves,
> The skies, the fountains, every region near
> Seem'd all one mutual cry; I never heard
> So musical a discord, such sweet thunder.
>
> (4.1.113–17)

Hippolyta praises the Spartan hounds for their supremely gallant sound, which filled the air, waters, and all the land nearby as well as the forest with a common cry. Some commentators suggest that Hippolyta, anticipating Theseus's remark on the players' oxymoronic description of their play ("How shall we find the concord of this discord?" [5.1.60]), refers to the creation of harmony out of disharmony, concord out of opposites.[9] But Hippolyta says nothing about harmony or concord. She praises the fierceness of the angry barking ("gallant chiding") and the encompassing ubiquity of its sound. The cry is common ("mutual") in more than one sense. It is of one kind, and it is everywhere. Hippolyta does of course appear to combine opposites. She speaks of "[s]o musical a discord, such sweet thunder." But everything she says suggests that she does not mean that the cry was musical despite being a discord or sweet despite being thunder, but rather the reverse: the cry was musical because it was so discordant, sweet because it was so thunderous. The opposition is merely apparent. To Hippolyta, war itself is musical, as thunder is sweet. Although she now lives in Athens, hers is still the taste of an Amazon queen.

Hippolyta suggests that the Spartan hounds in Crete were unequaled: "[N]ever did I hear / .... / I never heard." Theseus, however, claims that his hounds are better. "My hounds," he replies, "are bred out of the Spartan kind" (4.1.118). Theseus first describes in detail their appearance. His hounds, he says, are

> So flew'd, so sanded; and their heads are hung
> With ears that sweep away the morning dew;
> Crook-knee'd and dewlapp'd like Thessalian bulls.

> (4.1.119–21)

Theseus's description is Shakespeare's invention. Theseus's hounds may resemble Thessalian bulls, but they resemble no actual dogs, let alone the Spartan kind. At most, they partly resemble Ovid's description of two of Actaeon's hounds, which were sired by "a great / And large flewed hound," from a "Dam of Sparta" by "a Sire of Crete" (Ovid, *Metamorphoses*, 3.223–24; Golding, 3.267–69).[10] Theseus's hounds are bred out of a literary rather than an actual kind.[11] Whereas Spartan hounds were famous for their fierceness and speed,[12] Theseus says that his hounds are slow, and he praises them, instead, for their musical cry. The fast and the fierce are replaced by the slow and the musical:

> Slow in pursuit, but match'd in mouth like bells,
> Each under each; a cry more tuneable
> Was never holla'd to, nor cheer'd with horn,
> In Crete, in Sparta, nor in Thessaly.

> (4.1.122–25)

Hippolyta acclaimed the Spartan hounds for the force and fullness of their baying. Theseus, although initially praising his for their "musical confusion," now extolls them for their melodious ("tuneable") sound. Their cry is not a thunderous common chiding, but a well-tuned harmony of individual sounds (". . . match'd in mouth like bells, / Each under each").[13] The individual replaces the chorus, as the Athenian exceeds the Spartan. Furthermore, Theseus's hounds are superior to "the . . . kind" they "are bred out of." Owing to an art—the art of breeding—the descendants exceed their ancestors, the new exceeds the old. The excellence of art replaces the authority of age. Crete and Sparta, the oldest and most venerable cities of Greece, whose fundamental principle, moreover, is reverence for age, and whose laws are traceable to Zeus and Apollo,[14] are surpassed by Athens, whose principle is freedom and art. The best goes together with the arts, not with the ancestral.

Theseus urges Hippolyta to judge for herself the cry of his hounds when she hears it, but she never gets to hear it. The discovery of the young Athenians delays Theseus ("But soft . . ." [4.1.126]) and replaces the hunt and the cry (cf. 4.1.181–82). Once again, the marriage dispute between Hermia and her father interrupts Theseus's celebration of his own wedding (cf. 1.1.19ff.).[15]

Egeus's situation and behavior seem puzzling. Although this is the day that Hermia is to give her answer, Egeus is out with Theseus, evidently enjoying the observance of the rite of May. On the other hand, when Theseus does not recognize the sleepers ("[W]hat nymphs are these?" [4.1.126]), Egeus not only identifies each individually ("[T]his . . . / And this . . . ; this . . . / This . . ."), but emphasizes the paternity of the two women: "My lord, this is my daughter here asleep, / . . . / This, Helena, old Nedar's Helena" (4.1.127–29). His daughter seems to be, and not to be, on his mind. Egeus says he wonders about the four Athenians being "here together" (4.1.130). It is not clear whether he wonders at their being "here" or their being "together." Theseus will, pointedly, wonder about the latter, but not the former. Whatever the case, despite accusing Lysander of having cleverly stolen Hermia's heart and having made her a disobedient daughter (1.1.36–38), Egeus has evidently taken no precautions against their elopement. Nor does he seem to have noticed that Hermia has been missing.

Theseus, as though completely forgetting the lovers' rivalries and Hermia's plight, confidently surmises why they are here:

> No doubt they rose up early, to observe
> The rite of May; and hearing our intent,
> Came here in grace of our solemnity.

(4.1.131–33)

But then, seeming suddenly to remember ("But speak, Egeus" [4.1.134]), Theseus asks whether this is not the day when Hermia must make her choice known. And when Egeus, with uncharacteristic brevity, confirms that it is ("It is, my lord" [4.1.136]), Theseus orders that "the huntsmen wake [the four] with their horns" (4.1.137). The music of human art replaces the musical sound of beasts.

Without knowing Hermia's choice, Theseus describes the four lovers as coupling belatedly: "Good-morrow friends; Saint Valentine is past: / Begin these wood-birds but to couple now?" (4.1.138–39). If birds are to choose their mates on Saint Valentine's Day,[16] these lovers are late. They have waited until May Day. Theseus's good-natured tease, with its triple pun on "wood" (cf. 2.1.192; 3.1.143–44), stands in contrast not only to the tone of his last words to Hermia, warning that she must either die, marry a man she does not love, or live a celibate life (1.1.83–90). It stands in contrast also to the basis of that warning, by plainly if implicitly suggesting that it is not fathers but the lovers themselves who are to choose their mates. Wood-birds are free to couple as they wish.

The only real puzzle, for Theseus, is the apparent trust between the two men, who, so far as he knows, hate each other and therefore should not be found together, asleep:

> I know you two are rival enemies:
> How comes this gentle concord in the world,
> That hatred is so far from jealousy
> To sleep by hate, and fear no enmity?

> (4.1.141–44)

The coupling of the lovers is in accordance with nature. But the sleeping side by side of hated foes, without fear, is not. Since men can fight for love (2.2.241; 3.2.332–38), rivalry in love is tantamount to war. Theseus's perplexed question, containing his only mention of "hatred," "hate," "rival," "jealousy," "enemies," or "enmity," is the heroic warrior's most warlike speech.

Lysander tries to answer for all. Speaking with confusion about his confusion, he begins, "My lord, I shall reply amazedly, / Half sleep, half waking" (4.1.145–46). Lysander compares himself to someone in a maze (cf. 2.1.99, 113). And as a maze is characteristically double, full of ambiguities on all sides and constantly doubling back on itself, so Lysander, speaking here without coherent syntax, leaves uncertain whether the mixture of sleeping and waking will be the subject of his reply or will characterize it.[17]

Slowing collecting his thoughts, however, Lysander becomes sure of one thing:

> I came with Hermia hither; our intent
> Was to be gone from Athens, where we might,
> Without the peril of the Athenian law—

(4.1.150–52)

Lysander does not give the sort of innocent excuse which Theseus had offered with "[n]o doubt," when he came upon the lovers (4.1.131–33). Instead, he wishes to tell the truth ("—for truly I would speak—" [4.1.148; also 4.1.147]), and he tells the truth at his and Hermia's peril—"the peril of the Athenian law." Egeus may think that Lysander is artful and cunning (cf. 1.1.27–38), but Lysander seems to speak without the slightest guile or art. As noted earlier, no one talks of truth as often as he.

Egeus, crying "Enough, enough, . . . enough!" (4.1.153), angrily interrupts and begs "the law, the law upon his head!" (4.1.154). Egeus has, of course, invoked the law before. This time, however, there is a difference. Originally, it was Hermia who was to die (1.1.42–45). Now, it is Lysander. Egeus may wish to protect his daughter, despite his anger. But it seems more likely that he considers Lysander's confession as proof enough of his guilt and justification enough of his punishment. Initially, Egeus claimed (and Theseus confirmed) that his authority over his daughter rests on the fact that she is his (1.1.42; 1.1.47–51). Now, he seems to indicate that his authority rests on nothing so much as his anger. Anger seems to extend as it defends one's own. Thus, Egeus, who had seen Lysander's winning Hermia's heart as an act of theft (1.1.27–38), now sees their flight as one:

> They would have stol'n away, they would, Demetrius,
> Thereby to have defeated you and me:
> You of your wife, and me of my consent,
> Of my consent that she should be your wife.

(4.1.155–58)

The elopement would have been a double theft. Demetrius would have been defrauded of his wife and Egeus of his consent.[18]

Demetrius disappoints Egeus. Instead of arousing Demetrius's anger, as he intends, Egeus gets an answer he does not at all expect or want. Demetrius has been normally sparing of words. Until now, his longest speech was when he woke up with the love juice on his eyes and he fell in love with Helena—

some eight lines (3.2.137–44).[19] The present speech is more than twice as long. Demetrius says that he does not know "by what power— / But by some power it is—" his love for Hermia melted like snow (4.1.163–64). Unlike Lysander, Demetrius never claims that reason guides his love, though, in self-contradictory criticism, he has suggested that it should guide Helena's (cf. 2.1.188–94). Like Lysander, however, he blames his former love for Hermia on his youthfulness (cf. 2.2.110–121). His love for her, he says, now seems like the memory ("remembrance" [4.1.166]) of a foolish toy ("idle gaud" [4.1.166; cf. 1.1.33]) "[w]hich in my childhood I did dote upon" (4.1.176). The love, whose former existence seems greatly reduced in substance, seems no less removed in time. Now, however, Demetrius declares, he is fully devoted to his new love:

> And all the faith, the virtue of my heart,
> The object and the pleasure of mine eye,
> Is only Helena.

> (4.1.168–70)

With unintended irony, Demetrius describes "faith" as the virtue of his heart. And with no less irony, he pays unwitting tribute to the power of the love juice, by describing the unity of the object and the pleasure of his eye. What his eye sees and what gives it pleasure are, literally, one and the same. In seeing Helena, Demetrius sees all that he desires to see. She is indeed "[the] apple of his eye" (3.2.104).

Just as he is at a loss to explain how his love for Hermia melted away, Demetrius is at a loss to explain why he loved her in the first place. Acknowledging that he had been engaged to Helena before he "saw" Hermia, as Lysander had charged (4.1.171; cf. 1.1.104–10), he falls back upon a simile to explain what he does not understand:

> But like a sickness did I loathe this food:
> But as in health, come to my natural taste,
> Now I do wish it, love it, long for it,
> And will for evermore be true to it.

> (4.1.172–75)

Demetrius, who said that he was sick whenever he looked at Helena (2.1.212), thinks that he has now returned to his heathy state and his natural taste. Unable to explain his falling into or out of love, he appears to assume that one's first love is one's true love. Apart from this, Demetrius never attempts to say why he loves Helena. We, of course, know why he does and why he will be true to her. We might note that Oberon's leaving the love juice on Demetrius's eyes reflects not only on Demetrius's ability to love truly, but also on Egeus's ability to judge wisely.

Theseus, declaring that the lovers are "fortunately met" (4.1.176) and postponing further discussion of the events in the woods, summarily overrules Egeus's will: "Egeus, I will overbear your will" (4.1.178). Instead of preserving the law, Theseus overturns the law. He does what the lovers, not the father, wants. He liberates the daughter's desire from her duty. The two couples, Theseus says, will soon be married ("eternally . . . knit" [4.1.180]) when he and Hippolyta are married "in the temple" (4.1.179). The daughter's consent, not the father's, is what matters. Whereas Shakespeare's sources place Athens's founding in Theseus's unification of the villages of Attica, Shakespeare locates it in Theseus's liberation of love from patriarchal authority. Love is joined to marriage on the one hand and freed from patriarchal authority on the other. Shakespeare seems to understand Theseus's overthrow of patriarchal authority as equivalent to his unification of the villages. The former points up the significance of the latter, for it transforms Athens from a collection of sovereign fathers who, as in Rome, have absolute power over their family members to a union of families or households in which the city's power can reach family members.[20] The political equivalent of the union of reason and passion, love and art, Theseus's act democratizes Athens by replacing fathers with families as the fundamental component of the city.[21]

In Plutarch's account, Theseus's consolidation of the villages is preceded by his most famous and heroic act—his slaying the Minotaur in Crete (Plutarch, *Theseus*, 15–19). The same is true, in a certain sense, in *A Midsummer Night's Dream*. Although Shakespeare never refers to the act directly, Theseus's victory over the Minotaur exists in the form of a shadow— but only as a shadow—in the scenes in the woods. Titania and Bottom substitute for Pasiphae and the Minotaur (with Bottom combining the bull and its offspring). The woods—easy to enter but hard to leave, with entangling paths, bewildering reversals, and continual errors—substitute for the murderous Cretan maze. And while Oberon explicitly mentions Ariadne (2.1.80), who aided Theseus with a mixture of art and love (Plutarch, *Theseus*, 19.1), the young "amazed" lovers (3.2.220, 344; 4.1.145) replace the Athenian youth. As Theseus in the legend frees Athens and the Athenian youth from the tyranny of Minos and the Minotaur, Theseus in the play frees Athens and the Athenian youth from the tyranny of Egeus and the patriarchy. Athens becomes civilized through its greatest hero, whose heroic act remains an absence-presence.

With Theseus's action, the love of the beautiful is liberated and overcomes the love of one's own in Athens ("[W]hat is mine my love shall render him; / And she is mine" [1.1.96–97]). Unlike in Crete, Sparta, and Thebes, the claims of erotic love defeat those of generation, the claims of excellence defeat those of birth. Shakespeare, accordingly, gives Hermia's father the name which Plutarch gives to Theseus's father, for whose death Theseus was at least indirectly responsible.[22] While A Midsummer Night's Dream begins with a father invoking "the ancient privilege of Athens" (1.1.41) to marry his daughter to the man he wishes, it ends with the father absent from his daughter's wedding. Indeed, from the present moment on, Egeus remains completely silent and is mentioned just once (4.1.195). He disappears with his power. And what is true of him (and Helena's father, Nedar), is true of Pyramus and Thisbe's parents as well. Although their parts have been cast (1.2.56–59), they do not appear in Pyramus and Thisbe and are only briefly mentioned (5.1.173, 338).

Theseus's overthrow of the Athenian fathers' authority amounts to the overthrow of the ancestral gods in Athens ("To you your father should be as a god" [1.1.47]).[23] The act mirrors the early strife among the Greek gods, in which Zeus overthrows the power of his father, Cronos, and banishes him and the other Titans to Tartarus.[24] Titania's name—"daughter of Titans"— signifies the strife and its result. But although Theseus deposes the ancestral gods, he does not simply replace them by the Olympian gods or gods of the city. Where the Romans are always thinking of, turning to, and thanking the gods for everything,[25] the Athenians treat the sacred as largely irrelevant. Theseus does not invoke any god when overruling Egeus's will, and his only hint of the gods in connection with the marriages is to say that the weddings will take place "in the temple" (4.1.179). But even that slim hint of the sacred seems overstated, for we, in fact, do not see the wedding ceremonies, but only their celebration, which takes place after the newlyweds have "com[e] from the temple" (4.2.15). Once Theseus overturns the patriarchal authority, Athenians mention Olympian or pre-Olympian gods only in the descriptions or the dialogue of the artisans' poetry or in profane, mock oaths (5.1.48, 52, 176, 273–74, 307–8, 323–28).[26] The gods, now existing chiefly in fiction, seem to be driven out of Athens by love and replaced by art. Only fairies are said to follow a god (5.1.369–70).

The sweeping aside of religion in Athens may account for one of the play's more puzzling doubles. Although the play's title suggests that the events take place around the time of the summer solstice, the weddings occur on the first of May (4.1.131–33).[27] There seem to be two calendars in Shakespeare's Athens, a solar calendar saying one thing, a lunar calendar saying something else. Now, historically, Athens used two calendars simultaneously. In Rome, where every activity of the city, and most of those of its citizens, involved the gods in some fashion, there was just one calendar, a lunar calendar, at once sacred and civil, which was governed by priests.[28] But, in Athens, there were two calendars, one lunar and one solar. And while the lunar was the sacred and the solar was the civil calendar, the lunar calendar was adjusted to the solar (or the prytany) calendar, so that religious festivals, while dated according to the lunar calendar ("To do observance to a morn of May" [1.1.167]), were, in fact, reckoned according to the civil calendar. And, most importantly, neither calendar was governed by priests.[29] Where the single Roman calendar points to the power and authority of gods and priests in Rome, the double Athenian calendar, with the civil governing the sacred, points to the absence or irrelevance of the sacred in Athens.[30] Athena is never mentioned in the play.

Finally, "the morning . . . now something worn" (4.1.181), Theseus expressly "sets aside" the "purpos'd hunting" (4.1.182), so that the three couples can return to Athens for "a feast in great solemnity" (4.1.184)—a celebration which takes the form of a dramatic presentation. As the barbaric passes into the civilized, Theseus's presence in the scene is followed by the lovers' discussion of thinking's natural double vision.

## 4. Double Vision

While the others leave, the four young lovers (and a sleeping Bottom) remain. To all of them, the night's events are to "seem a dream and fruitless vision" (3.2.371; also 4.1.65–68). Demetrius, no longer laconic, leads the discussion of whether the events were in fact a dream. He begins, in confusion, describing how what has happened appears to him (4.1.186–87); then, he doubts that the four are now awake (4.1.191–92) and soon concludes that they are (4.1.197); and he ends the discussion by saying that they will recount their dreams on their way back to Athens (4.1.197–98). With as many lines as the other three combined, he has the first, last, and virtually the central speech in the exchange. One might wonder whether the love juice is affecting Demetrius in ways other than simply causing him to love Helena. Previously, as he loved Hermia because she loved someone else and someone else loved her, so he also spoke largely in response to what others said or did. Now, his love may depend on the love juice, but, for that very reason, it no longer depends on his jealousy or rivalry. And as his passion is direct, so too, it seems, is his speech. In another sense, as well, Demetrius's new garrulousness may reflect his love. The most laconic of the four lovers, he has fallen in love with the most loquaciousness, and, as he himself suggested earlier and

Titania seemed to demonstrate with Bottom, a lover should take after his beloved (3.1.191–93; 3.2.58–59).

Demetrius, expressly confused, offers a comparison to describe how he regards what has occurred: "These things seem small and undistinguishable, / Like far-off mountains turned into clouds" (4.1.186–87). As though affected by great distance, things that had appeared large to him now seem small; what had appeared distinct now seems undistinguishable. Like solid mountains transformed into soft clouds, the appearance of things seems "turned" or altered.

Hermia, in reply, says something different: "Methinks I see these things with parted eye, / When everything seems double" (4.1.188–89). Where Demetrius speaks of things seeming to turn into their opposites, Hermia speaks of things seeming double. Duplication replaces transformation. By seeing things as double, Hermia means, most particularly, waking from a dream and recognizing it as a dream—that is, distinguishing a likeness from that of which it is a likeness and at the same time recognizing that she had previously failed to make the distinction. As we saw when she awoke from her dream in the woods (2.2.144–49), the doubleness involves the recognition of the literalness of a dream. More generally, Hermia signifies the double vision natural to human thinking. With our body's eye, we see what is before us. And with our mind's eye, we see what it means. Our natural "parted eye" permits us to recognize a likeness as a likeness, an image as an image. It allows us to see that there is more than meets the eye and thus to separate the significance of a sight from the sight itself, the meaning or the reality from the appearance. Further, in so doing, it allows us to step back from ourselves and reflect on our sensing: "Methinks I see. . . ." Ironically, Demetrius just demonstrated what Hermia indicates. With his mind's eye he looked at what his body's eye saw. He perceived that he perceived, understanding what he saw by likening it to something else, which itself turned into still something else.

Helena, agreeing with Hermia (and not with Demetrius), speaks of desire rather than of knowing: "So methinks," she begins; "And I have found Demetrius, like a jewel, / Mine own, and not mine own" (4.1.189–91). Using both a simile and antithesis, Helena describes the doubleness of desire. Like a precious jewel which is found and therefore of uncertain ownership, an object of desire is at once present and absent. Desired but not yet possessed, it is present in the imagination but absent as a reality (cf. 1.1.1–6). The counterpart of an image, which is and is not what it is, the desired object is and is not one's own. Demetrius's sudden and inexplicable reversal only heightens the uncertainty of Helena's possession.[31]

Demetrius, in contrast to the women, doubts that they are awake. With the love juice still in his eyes, he has the hardest time of the four lovers distinguishing reality from a dream:

> Are you sure
> That we are awake? It seems to me
> That yet we sleep, we dream.
>
> (4.1.191–93)

As before, Demetrius's confident conclusion is self-contradictory (cf. 2.1.188–94). We do not distinguish between being awake and dreaming when we are asleep. We do that only when awake. When asleep, we dream that we are awake, but do not know that we are dreaming. Only after waking does the dream seem to us ("It seems to me . . .") a dream.[32] To wonder whether one is dreaming, then, is necessarily to be awake, not asleep. Demetrius contradicts himself in a second way as well. Dreams are single not only in lacking the double vision of awakeness, but also in being radically private. "There is one world in common for those who are awake, but everyone when asleep turns away to a private world of his own" (Heraclitus, frag. 89). Demetrius, however, says "we dream." The dream, he seems to think, is public, not private. It is shared directly by all the lovers while asleep. Demetrius then asks whether the others think that the Duke was there and bid them to follow him. And when they confirm that he was, that Egeus and Hippolyta were with him, and that Theseus told them to follow him to the temple, Demetrius quickly reverses himself and concludes, "Why then, we are awake" (4.1.197). Once more, he seems to get things backwards. He concludes from the context and consequences of events that they are awake, when, on the contrary, it is from being awake that he is able to understand the context and to expect consequences.[33] Dreams make no distinction between true and false. Demetrius then urges that they follow Theseus, "[a]nd by the way let us recount our dreams" (4.1.198). Reversing what he suggested a moment ago, Demetrius now seems to recognize that dreamers can have access to one another's dreams only indirectly and in their common awakeness. Their dreams have to be translated into stories. Yet, as Oberon arranged, Demetrius, though now convinced that they are awake, still thinks that all that happened to them was a dream or a collection of dreams. None of the other lovers contradicts him. All of them seem to think that the night in the woods was a dream. So does Bottom.

## 5. Bottom's Dream

Bottom wakes up thinking or perhaps dreaming that he is rehearsing his part in the play. Returning to the moment immediately preceding his transformation, he picks up just after where he left off, determined now, however, not to miss his cue (cf. 3.1.96ff.). Finding himself alone, Bottom calls out his fellow actors' names and concludes from their silence that they have run away. But whereas he originally imagined that the others were trying to make an ass of him by frightening him (3.1.115ff.), he now supposes that they have merely "[s]tolen hence, and left [him] asleep" (4.1.202–3). He thinks, in other words, that he fell asleep before they fled and that what happened afterwards—his transformation and his time with Titania—was not real but only a dream, though "a most rare vision" (4.1.203). He may be right.

Bottom, who at the time seemed to find nothing extraordinary in the fairy queen's falling in love with him, now, looking back, does. The only human in the play to have seen the fairies, he says that his dream was beyond the power of human intelligence to describe: "I have had a dream, past the wit of man to say what dream it was" (4.1.204–5). Then, in his next breath, he says that a man would be "but an ass" if he undertook to explain or interpret ("expound" [4.1.205–6]) the dream. Bottom, however, at least twice starts, but stops, to say what he thought he dreamt:

> Methought I was—there is no man can tell what. Methought I
> was—and methought I had—but man is but a patched fool if he
> will offer to say what methought I had.
>
> (4.1.206–9)

Much as he collapses the distinction between being a fool and wearing the costume of a professional fool ("is but a patched fool"), the literal-minded Bottom fails to distinguish between reciting his dream ("to say what dream it was") and "expound[ing]" its meaning. Everything to be said about the dream, he seems to think, would be told in its retelling.

Like Quince, directing his play (3.1.85–87), Bottom, elevating his dream, confuses the senses. "The eye of man hath not heard," he says;

> the ear of man hath not seen, man's hand is not able to taste, his
> tongue to conceive, nor his heart to report, what my dream was.
>
> (4.1.209–12)

Bottom's confusion of man's sensory functions goes together with his literalness. To Bottom (and Quince), each of the senses is isolated from the others, with no power behind them able to discriminate between the objects of different senses (such as a sight, a sound, or a taste), allow us to perceive that we are sensing, or interpret what we are sensing. There is nothing beyond the sensation itself. Even as he describes (or mis-describes) his sensing, Bottom implicitly denies that man can sense his own sensing. In his view, nothing mediates either among the senses themselves or between them and reason. The senses, for Bottom, are a plurality without a unity, which, paradoxically, makes them at the same time a unity without a plurality. They are at once unconnected to and interchangeable with one another. Any sense can sense anything, leaving man not a whole but a heap of disjointed faculties or parts (cf. 3.2.177–82).[34]

Now all the artisans (except Snug, who has only a last name) have Christian first names—Peter, Nick (Nicholas), Francis, Tom (Thomas), and Robin (Robert).[35] All but Snug and Starveling, the two least talkative, utter Christian oaths (1.2.11; 3.1.12, 29; 4.1.202; 4.2.13–14), and none of them mentions a Greek divinity, except when reciting a poem or performing a play (1.2.31; 5.1.176, 273–74, 323). Commentators often suggest that Bottom, here, is garbling the words of Paul:[36]

> The eye hath not seen, and the ear hath not heard, neither have entered into the heart of man, the things which God hath prepared for them that love him (1 Corinthians 2.9: Bishops' Bible).

Paul is describing the life that God has prepared for those who love him. Bottom wishes to describe what could fairly be called his only spiritual experience. Where Theseus's Athens combines art and love, and minimizes the sacred, Bottom's epiphany is that of a literal-minded, unerotic man. It is a parody of the Christian alternative to classical Athens.

Although his dream was indescribable and unfathomable, Bottom will get Quince to write a ballad of it. What is past the wit of man to say, Quince will write (and Bottom will sing). Indeed, "it shall be called 'Bottom's Dream,' because it hath no bottom" (4.1.214–15). Named for what it is and is not, "Bottom's Dream" is the dream of Bottom that has no bottom: it is either a dream with no foundation at all or one with bottomless profundity. Once again relishing the prospect of his theatrical triumph (cf. 1.2.21–35, 66–69), Bottom says that he will sing the ballad at the end of the play before the Duke. "Peradventure, to make it the more gracious, I shall sing it at her death" (4.1.216–17). However extraordinary his "most rare vision" might have been, the dream seems overshadowed in Bottom's mind by the part (or now two parts) he is to perform in the play. Returning to where his soliloquy began, Bottom either forgets that as Pyramus he is to die before Thisbe or else imagines that he will come back from the dead to sing his song, his dead love lying at his feet.[37]

## Act Four, Scene Two

### 1. Praise of Bottom

The scene shifts back to the city. The artisans are distressed that Bottom is still missing. Starveling, at least, has no doubt that Bottom is "transported" (4.2.3–4). What he means, though, is uncertain. He might mean what Quince meant when he said that Bottom was "translated" (3.1.113–14), that is, that he has been transformed. Or he might mean that Bottom has been carried away by madness, murder, or whoever transformed him, perhaps to a different realm or world. Or he might mean all these things. The artisans are concerned both for Bottom and for themselves. Bottom—"bully Bottom," "sweet bully Bottom," "sweet Bottom" (3.1.7; 4.2.19, 31)—is, in fact, the only player the others ever speak of with appreciation or affection. Quince may be their author, director, producer, and fellow-actor, but Bottom, who seems to have their love and esteem, appears to be their natural leader.[38] At the same time, the artisans' own fortunes are tied to Bottom's well-being. "If he come not, then the play is marred: it goes not forward, doth it?" (4.2.5–6). Bottom is indispensable to the play's performance. Explaining why, Quince, who thought that Bottom should play Pyramus "for Pyramus is a sweet-faced man" (1.2.79–80), praises him for having the best personal appearance and a sweet voice as well as the best wit among the artisans: "Yea, and the best person too; and he is a very paramour for a sweet voice" (4.2.11–12). Quince utters a malapropism which is more nearly accurate than he or any of the other artisans realizes. Oddly, it is the young Flute (cf. 1.2.43–44) who catches the more worldly Quince's malapropism, though in admonishing Quince he only adds to the obscenity: "You must say paragon. A paramour is, God bless us, a thing of naught" (4.2.13–14). "Naught" not only means something shameful or evil; it is a naughty word for illicit sex.[39] Despite—or perhaps because—they are unerotic, the artisans often inadvertently speak of sex (e.g., 1.2.9–10; 3.1.179–80; 5.1.188–89; cf. 1.2.90–91; 3.1.126–31).

### 2. Pericles' Democratic Politics of Art

Snug arrives with the news that the Duke is coming "from the temple" (4.2.15) and two or three other couples have also been married. As already noted, we never see the weddings in the temple, only their celebration afterwards. Theatrical art takes the place of the temple ceremony. Just before, in discussing their need of Bottom, Quince and Flute tacitly identified Athens with their own class:

> Quince: You have not a man in all Athens able to discharge Pyramus but he.
> Flute:  No, he hath simply the best wit of any handicraft man in Athens.
>
> (4.2.7–10)

"[A]ll Athens" is made up of the "handicraft m[e]n in Athens." Snug, however, refers to the other married couples as "two or three lords and ladies" (4.2.16). If Quince and Flute identify the artisans with all of Athens, Snug distinguishes the upper Athenian class, who are, after all, the players' audience (cf. 1.2.70–76; 3.1.10–11, 26–44). Quince is certain that all the acting crew would have made their fortunes if they had performed their play ("[W]e had all been made men" [4.2.17–18]). And Flute, thinking specifically of Bottom, says no fewer than four times in six lines that if Bottom had played Pyramus, the Duke would have paid him six pence a day for life (4.2.19–24). The artisans' reason for wanting to perform their play before the Duke and Duchess on their wedding night becomes clear. The art of acting has become more lucrative in Athens than the mechanical arts. The deep disappointment of Quince and Flute, especially combined with their democratic description of Athens, points far ahead to Pericles' consolidation of democracy in Athens at the expense of the nobles and the Council of the Areopagus. According to Plutarch, notwithstanding Thucydides's characterizing Pericles' administration as aristocratic—"a democracy in speech but in deed rule by the first citizen,"[40]

> Pericles at his first coming, sought to win the favour of the people . . .
> [by the] distribution of the common money. . . . And having won
> in a short time the favour and good will of the common people, by
> distribution of the common treasure, which he caused to be divided
> among them, as well as to have place to see these plays, as for that
> they had reward to be present at the judgements, and by other such
> like corruptions: he with the people's help, did inveigh against the
> court of the Areopagus (Plutarch, Pericles, 9.1–3; North, 2:11–12).

Pericles won the favor of the people by distributing public money through grants for public plays as well as fees for jury service, and then he used the people to restrict the Areopagus, thus initiating, as Aristotle puts it, "the manner [in which] each of the popular leaders proceeded by increasing [the power of the people] until it became the present democracy" (Aristotle, *Politics*, 1274a7–10).[41] Continuing the kind of compression we saw in the previous scene, scene 2 telescopes the development of the people's rising power in Athens. Where scene 1 dealt with the overthrow of patriarchal authority and the transition from the ferocity of heroism to the civility of freedom and art, scene 2 portrays public support for the arts, particularly for the theater, as a means to democratic power in Athens. If the previous scene ends by parodying the post-Athenian antithesis of Athens, the present scene parodies the political development of Athens's Periclean peak.

### 3. Bottom's Return
Bottom, ebullient, bursts in upon the gloomy scene with wonders to tell, but is both willing and unwilling (or perhaps unable) to tell them:

> Masters, I am to discourse wonders: but ask me not what; for if I
> tell you, I am not true Athenian. I will tell you everything, right as
> it fell out.

> (4.2.28–30)

When Quince asks him to tell, Bottom, reversing himself again, refuses ("Not a word of me" [4.2.32]). And instead of providing Quince with the material for his ballad, he tells the players that the Duke has dined and urges them to get their costumes ready, meet right away at the palace, and look over their parts, "for the short and the long is, our play is preferred" (4.2.36–37). Although Bottom is confident of their success, their play has, in fact, not been chosen. It not only is merely on the short list, but is frowned upon by Philostrate (cf. 5.1.42ff.). Then, exhorting the players, Bottom, forgetting his fear of bringing in a frightening lion (3.1.26–44), confounds the actors and their roles:

> In any case, let Thisbe have clean linen; and let not him that plays
> the lion pare his nails, for they shall hang out for the lion's claws.

> (4.2.37–39)

Finally, echoing his original confusion of a piece of paper and a piece of writing (1.2.3), Bottom conflates two senses of "breath"—the air exhaled from one's lungs and the words spoken in a play:

> And most dear actors, eat no onions nor garlic, for we are to utter
> sweet breath; and I do not doubt but to hear them say, it is a sweet
> comedy.

> (4.2.39–42)

Oberon described hearing a mermaid on a dolphin's back "[u]ttering such dulcet and harmonious breath" that the rough sea grew civil and stars shot madly from their spheres (2.1.151). Bottom literalizes and materializes the conceit: a pleasing comedy is one in which the actors have a pleasing odor (cf. 3.1.78–80). Unlike Snug and Flute, Bottom says nothing about likely monetary rewards (cf. 4.2.15–24).[42] Significantly enough, just as Athens's "handicraft m[e]n" think they can practice an art of the mind, so at least Bottom, always confident of his excellence, is able to ignore mere utility and, like Athens itself, show (in his way) a love of beauty and art.

## Notes

1. "Mounsieur Cobweb" (4.1.7–8, 10 [twice], 12–13, 14–15 [twice]), "Cavalery Cobweb" (4.1.22–23), "Mounsieur Mustardseed" (4.1.17, 19, 20, 22, 23–24), and "signior" (4.1.17) .

2. For example, Lucian, *Lucius or the Ass*, 50ff.; Apuleius, *The Golden Ass*, 10.19ff.

3. Alan Brissenden, *Shakespeare and the Dance* (London: Macmillan Press, 1981), 44.

4. The First Quarto reads "prosperity"; the Second Quarto and Folio, "posterity." The former would point back to 2.1.73; the latter, ahead to 5.1.391–400.

5. Sophocles, *Oedipus Tyrannus*, 266–68; Herodotus, 5.59.

6. For his introduction of writing and other arts, see Herodotus, 5.58; Diodorus Siculus, 3.67.1.

7. Euripides, *The Phoenician Women*, 638–89; Ovid, *Metamorphoses*, 3.1–130. We might note that, notwithstanding Hippolyta's memory, Cadmus, famously, was never in Crete. When Zeus carried off Europa, Cadmus's sister, to Crete, Agenor, their father, dispatched him to find her and threatened him with exile if he failed. But Cadmus, caught between impiety toward a god and impiety toward his father, wandered the world in search of his sister but would not go to Crete. Instead of finding her or returning to his father, he founded Thebes (Ovid, *Metamorphoses*, 2.833–3.130).

8. Herodotus, 1.166. For a "Cadmean victory" being the most shameful and worst of victories, see Plutarch, *On Brotherly Love*, 488.

9. For example, *A Midsummer Night's Dream*, ed. Peter Holland (Oxford: Oxford University Press, 1994), 222; Wells, 153; Foakes, 109; Harold C. Goddard, *The Meaning of Shakespeare* (Chicago: University of Chicago Press, 1951), 75–76.

10. For Actaeon's being the first in Cadmus's family to bring him grief, see Ovid, *Metamorphoses*, 3.138ff.

11. See, esp., T. W. Baldwin, "The Pedigree of Theseus' Pups," *Shakespeare Jahrbuch* (1968), 109–20.

12. See, for example, Pindar, frag. 106; Sophocles, *Ajax*, 8; Xenophon, *Cynegeticus*, 3.1ff., 10.1, 4; Virgil, *Georgics*, 3.405; Seneca, *Hippolytus*, 36–38; Oppian, *Cynegetica*, 1.372, 396; Pollux, *Onomasticon*, 5.37–40.

13. "If you would have your kennel for sweetness of cry, then you must compound it of some large dogs, that have deep solemn mouths, and are swift in spending, which must, as it were, bear the base in the consort, then a double number of roaring, and loud ringing mouths, which must bear the counter-tenor; then some hollow, plain, sweet mouths, which must bear the mean or middle part; and so with these three parts of music you shall make your cry perfect." Gervase Markham, *Countrey Contentments* (London, 1615; New York: Da Capo Press, 1973), 7. For Cretan and Spartan music as choral music, see Plato, *Laws*, 666d9–e9.

14. See, e.g., Plato, *Laws*, 624a1–6, 634a1–2, 662c7, d7–e7; *Minos*, 318c1–3.

15. The two scenes have parallel structures. In both, there are three speeches before the interruption, the first and last by Theseus, the second by Hippolyta. And as the earlier scene stresses Hippolyta's simile of a bow (1.1.9–10), the later scene centers on her memory of hunting.

16. Chaucer, *The Parlement of Foules*, 309ff.; Tilley, S66.

17. "[S]leep" and "waking" could be either nouns, objects of "reply," or else adjectives, equivalent to "sleeping and waking"; see Furness, 189.

18. Echoing his original complaint, Egeus speaks in doubles, implicitly or explicitly, in every line, including repetition (4.1.153–58; cf. 1.1.24–29), antithesis (4.1.154–58; cf. 1.1.43–44), anaphora (4.1.153–58; cf. 1.1.25, 27, 28, 30, 31, 33, 36), varying words slightly for the same thing (4.1.156–58; cf. 1.1.23–36), twice mentioning his "consent" (4.1.15–58; cf. 1.1.25, 40), and charging a double theft (4.1.156–57; cf. 1.1.36–38).

19. Half of his previous thirty speeches have been no more than two lines.

20. See Introduction, n. 20, in this volume.

21. For Theseus as the founder of democratic Athens, see Euripides, *Suppliant Women*, 352–54, 404–5; Isocrates, *Helen*, 35–37; *Panathenaic*, 128–29, 148; Plutarch, *Theseus*, 25.1–2, 36.2; Pausanias, 1.3.3.

22. For example, Plutarch, *Theseus*, 3.3ff., 22.1; *Comparison of Theseus and Romulus*, 5.2; Ovid, *Metamorphoses*, 7.404ff.; Apollodorus, *Library*, 3.16.1.

23. Cf. Plutarch, *Theseus*, 24.3–5.

24. Hesiod, *Theogony*, 453–506, 617–726; Apollodorus, *Library*, 2.1.

25. Cicero, *De Natura Deorum*, 2.8; Varro, *The Latin Language*, 6.16; Virgil, *Georgics*, 1.340–50; Plutarch, *Numa*, 14; Pliny, *Natural History*, 18.2. See *Coriolanus*, 1.1.22–23, 71–73; 1.4.10–12; 1.5.20–22; 1.6.6–9; 1.8.6; 1.9.8–9; 2.1.1, 100, 104, 120–21, 139, 169–70, 178, 217; 2.3.56, 110, 133–35, 155; 3.1.85, 140–41, 231, 287–91; 3.3.32–37, 72–74, 143; 4.2.11–12, 45–48; 4.1.136; 4.6.20–25, 36–37, 154; 5.2.75–77; 5.3.46–48, 70–75, 104–9, 166–68, 183–85; 5.4.31–35, 56; 5.5.2. For augurs, divines, and priests, see *Coriolanus*, 1.10.21; 2.1.1; 2.1.83; 2.3.60; 5.1.56.

26. The word "god" occurs four times after Theseus's action, always in the form of profane swearing, once each by Bottom (4.1.202) and Flute (4.2.13–14), uttering

Christian oaths, and twice, with deliberate irony, by Demetrius, calling attention to the absurdity of the artisans' performance (5.1.307, 308).

27. "I know not why Shakespeare calls this play *A Midsummer Night's Dream*, when he so carefully informs us that it happened on the night preceding *May* day." Johnson, 3:95 (his emphasis). Cf. also 3.1.147–48.

28. See, for example, Macrobius, *The Saturnalia*, 1.14–15.

29. See, for example, Thucydides, 5.20; Geminus, *Elementa Astronomiae*, 6, in Sir Thomas Heath, *Greek Astronomy* (London: J. M. Dent & Sons, 1932), 136ff. Theseus, in his opening speech, uses the verbal form of the technical term ("wan[ing]") for the last decade of the Athenian month; cf. 1.1.4 and Plutarch, *Solon*, 25.3.

30. For Pericles's denigration of Athenian fathers and his silence regarding the gods, see Thucydides, 2.36–45; also Leo Strauss, *The City and Man* (Chicago: Rand McNally, 1964), 161.

31. Interestingly enough, while, to Hermia, Lysander is "my Lysander" (1.1.168, 217; 3.2.62), and, to both Lysander and Demetrius, Hermia is "my Hermia" (1.1.224; 2.1.193), no one ever calls Helena "my Helena," nor does she ever call anyone her own (cf. 1.1.221).

32. Erwin Straus, "Awakeness," in *Phenomenological Psychology* (New York: Basic Books, 1966), 103.

33. Straus, 112.

34. Cf. Aristotle, *De Anima*, 425b12–25, 426b12–27a14; *De Sensu*, 447b17–48a19, 448b17–49a20.

35. Cox, 173.

36. For example, Kittredge, 197; Brooks, 99; Foakes, 113; Mowat and Werstine, 134.

37. Kittredge, 197.

38. Lowenthal, 84–85.

39. Gordon Williams, *A Glossary of Shakespeare's Sexual Language* (London: Athlone, 1997), s.v. Naught.

40. Thucydides, 2.65.

41. See also Aristotle, *Constitution of Athens*, 27.3–4. On Pericles's generosity in funding frequent theatrical performances and festivals, see Plutarch, *Pericles*, 11.4; Xenophon, *Athenian Constitution*, 2.9.

42. Lowenthal, 85.

# ACT FIVE

~

## Act Five, Scene One

In a sense, *A Midsummer Night's Dream* might have ended with Bottom's return to Athens. The obstacles to a happy marriage have been removed for all the couples, including the fairy king and queen. Jack shall have Jill, nought shall go ill. And, we are told, the artisans' sport will go forward; all the artisans will become made men. Except for Egeus, whose wishes no longer seem to matter, everyone has or is about to receive what he desires. Shakespeare, nonetheless, presents act 5, whose explicit theme is imagination and whose action is the performance of a play about love—a play which itself closely mimics *A Midsummer Night's Dream*. While the main plot of *A Midsummer Night's Dream* largely mirrors the Pyramus and Thisbe story, the play's final act focuses on the artisans' farcically incompetent enactment of that tragic tale. *Pyramus and Thisbe* is at once a subplot of *A Midsummer Night's Dream* and the model for its main plot. It is at once copy and original.

### 1. Imagination

Act 5 begins like act 1, with Theseus and Hippolyta. Then, they were awaiting their wedding. Now, they are married. Previously, Hippolyta never referred to Theseus by any term of endearment or even by his name. Now that they are married, he is "my Theseus" (5.1.1). In this and other respects, between her appearance in the woods in the morning (4.1.111–17) and the celebration of her wedding at night, Hippolyta seems to have passed from

Amazon to Athenian. If lawful marriage is not a cause of her becoming civilized, it is a sign of it.

Theseus and Hippolyta are discussing what the lovers have told them. Neither is sure what to think. Hippolyta begins by commenting on the strangeness of what the lovers have said: "'Tis strange, my Theseus, that these lovers speak of" (5.1.1). The last we heard was that the lovers were going to recount their "dreams" on their return to Athens (4.1.198). It is not clear what they have said or concluded, or how they now understand what happened during the night in the woods. We are never told. Instead, we hear Theseus's famous speech on—or against—imagination, in which he reduces imagination to, or dismisses it as, mere madness.

Theseus, rejecting the lovers' words as "[m]ore strange than true" (5.1.2), refuses to believe such accounts: "I never may believe / These antique fables, nor these fairy toys" (5.1.2–3). Theseus's words are themselves strange. The legendary founder of Athens, Theseus is himself an "antique fable"—a "fabulous antiquity," as Plutarch calls him (Plutarch, *Theseus*, 1.3; North, 1:29). Nevertheless, to him, the "antique" is at once the old fashioned and the grotesque: the ancient is the antic.[1] We also must wonder why Theseus describes the lovers' accounts as "fairy toys." The lovers know nothing of the fairies. Their ignorance of the fairies, in fact, only adds to their puzzlement about the events in the woods. Theseus thus speaks more wisely than he knows. His phrase—a figure of his own imagination—is literally true, but he seems to mean it only figuratively, the particular used for the general. "[F]airy toys" are fairy tales— unreal or incredible tales, not necessarily ones about fairies. Whether or not Titania led Theseus through the glimmering night (2.1.76–80), Theseus is entirely unaware of her. To him, fairies are nothing but fairy tales.

Theseus, generalizing, as he does for the rest of the speech, launches into the main body of the speech by linking lovers and madmen. "Lovers and madmen have such seething brains," he says with a rich quibble,

> Such shaping fantasies, that apprehend
> More than cool reason ever comprehends.
>
> (5.1.4–6)

Lovers, like lunatics, claim to see what, in fact, exists only in their imagination. Instead of mediating between sense perception and reason, their imagination forms its own fantasies which it then presents to the mind as though the fantasies came from the senses. Having thus set imagination against sense perception and reason in lovers and lunatics, Theseus, going further, says that the same is true of poets:

> The lunatic, the lover, and the poet
> Are of imagination all compact.

> > (5.1.7–8)

Not only lovers are like lunatics. Poets resemble madmen, too. All three consist of nothing but imagination. All three "see" what they merely imagine:

> One sees more devils than vast hell can hold;
> That is the madman.

> > (5.1.9–10)

The madman sees more evils ("devils") than could ever exist. Led by fear, he invents countless things to fear in order to have things to fear. The lover is no less crazy:

> [T]he lover, all as frantic,
> Sees Helen's beauty in a brow of Egypt.

> > (5.1.10–11)

The lover sees great beauty even in an ugly face (cf. 1.2.232–34). Where fear leads the madman to see untold devils in the world, love leads the lover to see only beauty in his beloved. Theseus then describes the poet:

> The poet's eye, in a fine frenzy rolling,
> Doth glance from heaven to earth, from earth to heaven.

> > (5.1.12–13)

Unlike the lunatic and the lover, the poet starts with his bodily "eye." But, like them, he does not really see. The poet looks ("glance[s]") from heaven to earth and back again. But, in a disorder of the mind akin to madness, in which his eye turns around as on an axis ("in a fine frenzy rolling"), instead of taking in what he sees in the world, he lets his imagination project unto heaven and earth what he has never seen and does not know:

> And as imagination bodies forth
> The forms of things unknown, the poet's pen
> Turns them into shapes, and gives to airy nothing
> A local habitation and a name.

> > (5.1.14–17)

The poet's imagination gives bodily shape to things unknown. It gives reality to things which exist only in the imagination of the poet himself. Then, the poet's pen, following his imagination, turns those forms into particular beings and gives them a specific place and name. It makes them seem real by localizing and particularizing them. Theseus then moves from the imagination of the lover, the lunatic, and the poet to strong imagination in anyone:

> Such tricks hath strong imagination,
> That if it would but apprehend some joy,
> It comprehends some bringer of that joy.

> (5.1.18–20)

If imagination sees ("apprehend[s]") some joy, it also includes ("comprehends") someone who brings that joy. It does not simply wish; it imagines its wishes fulfilled. And as with joy, so with fear:

> Or, in the night, imagining some fear,
> How easy is a bush suppos'd a bear!

> (5.1.21–22)

Because being in the dark makes us afraid of what we do not know, we easily imagine what is unknown to be something that we know to fear. Unable to resolve a fear whose object we cannot identify, our fear of the unknown transforms the unknown into a specific, identifiable fear (cf. 3.2.27–30). As with the lover, the lunatic, and the poet, strong imagination, in general, "sees" what it only imagines that it sees. What it calls seeing is—in the contemporary antiphrastic slang term—simply "seeing things."

Theseus, the founder of the city renowned for the love of beauty and the highest accomplishments in art, disparages both love and art. Their dependence on the imagination lowers both to the level of a lunatic. In a most important way, Athens's founder does not fit into the city that he founds. If heroic ambition places Coriolanus outside of Rome, heroic taste places Theseus outside of Athens. The hero whose actions make Athens possible, and who is himself the subject of much of the city's great art, has no taste for art. The subject of poetry is himself antipoetic. A heroic warrior, Theseus appreciates deeds, not poems, action, not imitation. What is tactile is real; what exists in the imagination is unreal. Imagination deals only with the imaginary. Theseus implicitly distinguishes between comedy ("joy") and tragedy ("fear"). But rather than understand either as an imitation of men or actions, he understands both—and imagination as such—as projections of one's wishes or fears onto the stage and the world. Unreal in every sense, the objects of poetry, referring to no original, are nothing more than tricks of our feverish brains—fantasies which, much like our dreams, we fabricate and then deceive ourselves into thinking are real. "Creativity" may be the mantra of Romantic poetry,[2] but on Theseus's lips the term would be one of patronizing disparagement and derision.

The deepest irony, however, is not that Theseus fails to fit into the city that he founds. A deeper irony lies in his failure to see the connection between imagination, even dreams, and action. First we dream of what we will do, then we do it. Theseus himself exemplifies this perfectly. Describing Theseus's emulation of Hercules, Plutarch writes:

> [T]he fame and glory of Hercules' noble deeds had long before
> secretly set [Theseus's] heart on fire, so that he made reckoning of
> none other but of him, and lovingly hearkened unto those which
> would seem to describe him what manner of man he was, but
> chiefly unto those which had seen him, and been in his company,
> when he had said or done anything worthy of memory. For then he
> did manifestly open himself that he felt the like passion in his heart
> which Themistocles long time afterwards endured when he said
> that the victory and triumph of Miltiades would not let him sleep.
> For even so, the wonderful admiration which Theseus had of
> Hercules' courage made him in the night that he never dreamed but
> of his noble acts and doings, and in the daytime, pricked forward
> with emulation and envy of his glory, he determined with himself
> one day to do the like.
>
> (Plutarch, *Theseus*, 6.6–7; North, 1:34–35)

If poetry imitates men's deeds, men's deeds, in turn, imitate poetry. Contrary to what Theseus thinks, his own actions show that heroism is not the opposite but rather an imitation of "antique fables." It is an imitation of an imitation of deeds.

Hippolyta tries to answer Theseus:

> But all the story of the night told over,
> And all their minds transfigur'd so together,
> More witnesseth than fancy's images,
> And grows to something of great constancy;
> But howsoever, strange and admirable.
>
> (5.1.23–27)

Hippolyta qualifies what Theseus said. She does not dispute his dismissing mere imagination ("fancy's images"). Nor does she deny that all the lovers' minds were altered ("transfigur'd") and that what they say is strange. But she places importance on the fact that all their minds were changed in the same way, at the same time. The consistency of the lovers' story attests to the story's substance. Where the strange is unreal or merely imaginary for Theseus, for Hippolyta it could be an object of wonder ("strange and admirable"). Remarkably enough, the Amazon—or former Amazon—seems more open to the effects of dramatic poetry than does the Athenian.[3]

This is the last time anyone refers to the lovers' night in the woods. For a reason we shall see, no one in the onstage audience ever even hints at the resemblance between the actions of Pyramus and Thisbe and those of Lysander and Hermia.

## 2. Art and Life

Theseus greets the newlyweds, who are "full of joy and mirth," with wishes of more days of joy and love: "Joy, gentle friends, joy and fresh days of love / Accompany your hearts!" (5.1.28–30). Notwithstanding the lunacy of lovers, Theseus seems to think that the joy of love is real (cf. 1.1.76). Lysander, who, unlike before, uses no formal terms of address (cf. 1.1.99; 4.1.140, 145), returns a saltier salutation: "More [joy] than to us / Wait in your royal walks, your board, your bed!" (5.1.30–31). Previously, Lysander and Demetrius were always deferential to Theseus. Now, following Theseus's overthrow of patriarchal authority, they speak to him much more as equals.[4] On the other hand, neither Hermia nor Helena says a word in act 5. Both remain completely silent even as their husbands banter. The Athenian family becomes democratic in that it comes to be based on the wife's consent rather than on the father's authority. But it remains nondemocratic insofar as the husband rules the wife. As Hermia herself put it, the husband is a "lordship" possessing "sovereignty," but a sovereignty based on the wife's wishes or "consent" (1.1.81–82). The Athenian replacement of fathers by families implies not the full democratization of the family, but hierarchy based on consent.

The three couples, now married, must wait three hours before going to bed. For Theseus, the wait is torture. "[W]hat masques, what dances shall we have, / To wear away this long age of three hours . . . ?" (5.1.33; cf. 1.1.11–15). Calling upon Philostrate, "our usual manager of mirth" (5.1.35), Theseus painfully asks, "Is there no play / To ease the anguish of a torturing hour?" (5.1.36–37). As poetry, for Theseus, is mere madness, plays, for him, are nothing more than entertainment. They are simply a diversion or "delight" to "beguile / The lazy time" (5.1.40–41).[5] There may now be only three hours, not four days, until "bed-time" (5.1.34), but time still lingers Theseus's desires.

Theseus chooses from a list of possible entertainments. First on the list is "'The battle with the Centaurs, to be sung / By an Athenian eunuch to the harp'" (5.1.44–45). According to the legend, Hercules, on his way to perform one of his labors, visited the Centaur Pholoe, one of only two Centaurs distinguished for goodness and wisdom. While they were eating, Hercules urged Pholoe to open a bottle of wine, which Dionysus was thought to have left for him. The other Centaurs soon smelled the wine and, driven mad by it, rushed into Pholoe's cave and, armed with rocks, tree trunks, and flaming logs, began plundering the wine. While Pholoe hid himself in terror, Hercules fearlessly fought the attackers, killing most and forcing the rest to flee.[6] The proposed entertainment epitomizes Theseus's pejorative view of poetry: Hercules's heroic deed is to be sung by a eunuch to the music of a harp. Poetry, divorced from what is tactile or real, involves the effeminate presentation of manly deeds. Poetic Athens—where eunuchs sing the works of madmen—is an emasculated Athens. Accordingly, Theseus rejects the presentation out of hand, explaining that he has already told Hippolyta "[i]n glory of my kinsman Hercules" (5.1.47).[7] Glory comes from heroes, not poets, telling of heroic deeds, whose glory poets can obliterate even as they intend to celebrate (cf. 1.2.24–37).

Theseus cites Hercules as the hero of "The battle with the Centaurs." He might have mentioned himself. According to another version of the legend, it was Theseus who fought and defeated the drunken Centaurs.[8] Theseus, expressly guarding the glory that he emulated, preserves Hercules as his heroic example.

The second choice is "'The riot of the tipsy Bacchanals, / Tearing the Thracian singer in their rage'" (5.1.48–49). This is the story of the death of Orpheus, Greece's greatest poet, who was himself mythical. According to the myth, Orpheus's music was so sweet that birds flew over his head, fish leapt straight out of the sea, ravenous animals became tame, violent seas became calm, rivers stopped, rocks followed him, and trees ceased to rustle. When Orpheus's wife, Eurydice, died, the beauty of his music persuaded the Furies to let him bring her back from the Underworld to Earth. They did so, however, on the condition that Orpheus not look back at her before reaching the land of the living. Just as they reached the gates of the Underworld, Orpheus turned to see whether Eurydice was behind him, and she disappeared forever right before his eyes. When Orpheus, wholly despondent, retreated into the wilds and spurned the company of women, the Thracian women, chagrined, became drunk, attacked him and, unaffected by his music, tore him to pieces in a mad fury.[9] The Orpheus myth is the mirror image of the Hercules legend. Both involve Dionysus (Bacchus). Where the Hercules myth involves the drunken, attempted rape of women, the Orpheus myth involves the drunken, murderous revenge of women. Instead of heroism defeating drunken madness, drunken madness defeats art. Art is destroyed by wild passion. Orpheus's music may be able to persuade the Furies, but it cannot tame an angry Dionysus.

Theseus rejects the second choice because the work is trite and was recently performed: "This is an old device, and it was play'd / When I from Thebes came last a conqueror" (5.1.50–51). This is Theseus's sole reference to his ending the Theban civil war. It is significant that Theseus refers to his Theban victory only after resolving the problem of patriarchal authority in Athens, which was initially raised in its place (1.1.20ff.). As we have seen, while Thebes represents the claims of birth or generation, Athens represents the defeat of those claims, in the name of love and art.

While the first selection involved a song and the second a poet-singer, the third concerns the Muses themselves. "'The thrice three Muses mourning for the death / Of learning, late deceas'd in beggary'" (5.1.52–53). Theseus rejects the third selection as inappropriate for a wedding celebration. One might wonder whether the themes of rape and murder would be better suited to the occasion. Theseus, however, seems not to mean the theme of the death of learning so much as its manner of treatment: "That is some satire, keen and critical, / Not sorting with a nuptial ceremony" (5.1.54–55). The selection seems out of place not only for a wedding, however, but for early Athens, as a whole. Not unlike the names Lysander and Demetrius, it deals with the end of what has only just begun.[10] The selection is the only one of the first three that Theseus seems to praise. He praises it for its satiric quality. Given his condescending dismissal of poetry, it seems that, for Theseus, the important difference between poetry, in general, and satire, in particular, is that satire, "keen and critical," is essentially political in its subject and purpose. Although using the language of poetry, it seeks to criticize and correct a corruption of the time—in this case, the impoverishment and death of learning. Like rhetoric rather than poetry, its purpose is practical, not theoretical. Its aim is action, not understanding.[11]

The fourth choice is "'A tedious brief scene of young Pyramus / And his love Thisbe, very tragical mirth'" (5.1.56–57). Theseus is intrigued by the title or description:

> Merry and tragical? Tedious and brief?
> That is hot ice, and wondrous strange snow!
> How shall we find the concord of this discord?
>
> (5.1.58–60)

Theseus says nothing about the inappropriateness of the Pyramus and Thisbe story for a wedding, especially that of Hermia and Lysander, as he might well have. Instead, he wonders, humorously, how to reconcile the title's oxymora. Philostrate, pressing the joke, addresses the self-contradictions, explaining, first, how the play is at once tedious and brief. Although just some ten words long, which is as brief as any play he has known, it is too long, he says, which makes it tedious; "for in all the play / There is not one word apt, one player fitted" (5.1.64–65). And as neither the script nor the actors are suitable, so the performance turns the tragedy into a comedy:

> And tragical, my lord, it is,
> For Pyramus therein doth kill himself;
> Which, when I saw rehears'd, I must confess
> Made mine eyes water; but more merry tears
> The passion of loud laughter never shed.
>
> (5.1.66–70)

The play is at once a tragedy and a comedy. A tragedy because of its plot, it is a comedy because of the players' performance. Their ludicrous ineptitude transforms the intended tragedy into an unintended farce. The tragedy becomes a comic parody of itself.

Although we saw Puck interrupt the players after just ten lines (3.1.73ff.), Philostrate thrice claims to have witnessed the entire play's rehearsal, including its conclusion: "[I]n all the play, / There is not one word apt, one player fitted"; "For Pyramus therein doth kill himself, / Which when I saw rehearsed . . ."; "It is not for you; I have heard it over, . . ." (5.1.64–65, 67–68, 77). In a play in which there are many strange twists and numerous discrepancies between the fairies and the surrounding play, none seems more curious—and unnecessary to the plot in any ordinary sense—than Philostrate's repeated insistence that he saw the full play rehearsed. Philostrate's apparently needless claim, which Shakespeare stresses, seems to suggest that the literal-minded Bottom may, for once, have spoken correctly when he called what he saw his dream. It may indeed have had "no bottom" (4.1.215). Titania, in her first narrative, described Oberon's pursuit of Phillida in the guise of Corin—an imitation of a poetic imitation of a lover, who is himself a poet, pursuing a poetic imitation of a beloved (2.1.64–68). Oberon, as the amorous Phillida's lover, was imaginary. So, too, at least on some level, Shakespeare suggests, was Bottom's encounter with Titania. Despite what we have seen for ourselves, Bottom's spending all night with her may have been as imaginary as Oberon's sitting all day with Phillida. Theseus's criticism of lovers, lunatics, and poets draws a sharp line between imagination and reason, poetry and reality. But the fairies, in general, and Puck, in particular, seem to point up the ambiguous unity of the pairs. Puck, able to mimic whatever he wishes, not only is at once audience, actor, playwright and stage manager. He also characteristically turns life into drama and drama into life. Obscuring while nevertheless maintaining the distinction between art and life, he seems to be Shakespeare's playful, comic exaggeration of the fundamental twin truths that a reality is unintelligible apart from its image and that life imitates art even while art imitates life. Leading (or misleading) people to believe in the reality of his images, while at the same time turning people's lives into theater for himself, Puck embodies the ambiguous "union in partition" of an image and its reality, of dramatic acting and real action. They are the same and not the same. The imitation is and is not the imitated.

When Theseus, partly shifting the focus of discussion, asks who the players are, Philostrate, still joking at their expense, answers by contrasting their hands and their minds:

> Hard-handed men that work in Athens here,
> Which never labour'd in their minds till now;
> And now have toil'd their unbreath'd memories
> With this same play, against your nuptial.
>
> (5.1.72–75)

Theseus's wedding—or what it represents—marks a turning point for Athens's artisan class, as Shakespeare underlines here with the anadiplosic, antithetical "now": "never . . . till now; / And now have. . . ." As we saw in the previous scene, the artisans, for the first time, at least make the claim to work with their minds and not merely with their hands. They are actors as well as artisans, as Philostrate reports with ridicule and scorn.

Theseus chooses the artisans' play. "And we will hear it" (5.1.76), he announces, where "And" means "Yes, you are right, and. . . ."[12] Theseus chooses the play not in spite of but because of Philostrate's appraisal. Philostrate, however, warns again, this time without jest: "No, my noble lord, / It is not for you" (5.1.76–77). Philostrate says that he has heard the whole play and there is nothing in it to enjoy unless Theseus can find amusement "in [the players'] intents" (5.1.79) to do him service, exerted beyond their abilities and requiring an agony of effort on their part. Where the players feared that the audience would see them only as their characters, Philostrate suggests that Theseus might enjoy seeing them only as actors. Not the plot or the characters but the actors themselves would be the show.

Theseus repeats his choice. But, rather than wanting to laugh at the arti-sans' overreaching, he says that he will hear the play out of respect for the sincerity and duty of the players in offering it: "For never anything can be amiss / When simplicity and duty tender it" (5.1.82–83). "[I]ntents" are everything. Theseus will watch the play in the spirit of noble condescension. The harder the players try, the less fault he will find. He will graciously over-look their merit and judge only their intention to serve him.

### 3. Noble Respect

While Philostrate goes to bring in the players and the women take their seats, Theseus and Hippolyta have their only private exchange. It concerns the proper treatment of people whose efforts exceed their ability in doing their duty. It seems to be Theseus's best moment.

Hippolyta expresses her concern: "I love not to see wretchedness o'er-charg'd, / And duty in his service perishing" (5.1.85–86).[13] It is not immedi-ately clear whether she doubts the effectiveness of Theseus's distinction be-tween merit and intent or simply fails to understand it. When Theseus tries to reassure her that she will not see what she fears, Hippolyta only repeats her concern: "He [Philostrate] says they can do nothing in this kind" (5.1.88). Theseus, then, as though Hippolyta's teacher, explains his distinction.

Echoing, with a chiasmus and a pun, her final phrase ("nothing in this kind"), by which Hippolyta meant the sort of thing the players can do, Theseus speaks of their own kindness in thanking the players for nothing: "The kinder we, to give them thanks for nothing" (5.1.89; cf. 5.1.78). The more the players reach beyond their abilities, the greater his kindness in giving them thanks. Thus, punning on the antithesis of "take" and "mistake," Theseus describes how they should accept ("take") what the actors get wrong ("mistake"):

> Our sport shall be to take what they mistake:
> And what poor duty cannot do, noble respect
> Takes it in might, not merit.
>
> (5.1.90–92)

The noble way of judging futile attempts of incapable people to perform their duty is to judge their performance in the light of their power, not their achievement. One should judge their effort, not their effect. Theseus then remembers other examples. The examples are of great scholars ("great clerks" [5.1.93]) who had intended to greet him with rehearsed welcomes, but instead Theseus has

> seen them shiver and look pale,
> Make periods in the midst of sentences,
> Throttle their practis'd accent in fears,
> And, in conclusion, dumbly have broke off,
> Not paying me a welcome.
>
> (5.1.95–99)

Unlike the players, these are men of considerable knowledge and intelligence, whose fears choked their speech. Theseus saw in their inability a devotion that made them speechless:

> Out of this silence yet I pick'd a welcome,
> And in the modesty of fearful duty
> I read as much as from the rattling tongue
> Of saucy and audacious eloquence.
>
> (5.1.100–3)

Their silence bespoke their deference better than their eloquence might have done. And as with fear, "[l]ove . . . and tongue-tied simplicity / In least speak most" (5.1.104–5). Tongue-tied inability tells of intention. It remains to be seen whether—or in what way—Theseus lives up to his words.

## 4. The Play within the Play

Theseus just described great scholars who "[m]ake periods in the midst of sentences" in their rehearsed speeches, out of fear. Prologue (Quince), as though on cue, makes periods in the midst of sentences in his rehearsed prologue, out of nervousness. Stage-fright does to him what deference does to the scholars. Theseus also just said that he could pick a welcome out of the scholars' garbled words, for he would judge their intent rather than their merit. Prologue garbles a speech which explicitly asks that the players be judged by their intent and not their merit. His nervous mispunctuation turns a declaration of goodwill into a declaration of the opposite:

| Intended | Actual |
|---|---|
| If we offend, it is with our good will [that is, it is our wish] | If we offend, it is with our good will [that is, that is our wish]. |
| That you should think we come, not to offend, | That you should think, we come not to offend, |
| But [that is, on the contrary] with good will to show our simple skill: | But [that is, except] with good will. To show our simple skill, |
| That is the true beginning of our end [that is, our purpose]. | That is the true beginning of our end [that is, our purpose]. |
| Consider then, [that] we come—but in despite | Consider then, [that] we come but in despite |
| [that is, in ill will, to vex you] | [that is, in contempt]. |
| We do not come—as minding to content you | We do not come, as minding to content you |
| [that is, to please you]; | [that is, to please you], |
| Our true intent is all for your delight: | Our true intent is. All for your delight, |
| We are not here that you should here repent you; | We are not here. That you should here repent you, |
| The actors are at hand. . . . | The actors are at hand. . . . |

(5.1.108–16)

Inverting what he intends to say and what the players intend to do, Prologue declares just what he means to deny and denies just what he means to declare. We might note that Prologue's meter is neither "eight and six," as Quince wanted, nor "eight and eight," as Bottom insisted (3.1.23–25), but, more expansively, ten and ten.

When Theseus, quibbling, suggests to the others in the onstage audience that Prologue is not punctilious about either punctuation or details ("This fellow doth not stand upon points" [5.1.118]), Lysander quickly echoes him with his own wordplay, punning on "stop" as a technical equestrian term and a punctuation mark: "He hath rid his prologue like a rough colt; he knows not the stop" (5.1.119–20). Lysander then adds and twists a moral lesson, shifting the sense from "speak truthfully" to "speak truly": "A good moral, my lord: it is not enough to speak, but to speak true" (5.1.120–21). Hippolyta, agreeing, says that Prologue has played on his prologue "like a child on a recorder; a sound, but not in government" (5.1.122–23): the material was there, but the form was missing. Theseus, concluding the exchange, offers a third simile: "His speech was like a tangled chain; nothing impaired, but all disordered" (5.1.124–25): the parts were not damaged, but everything was out of order. Lysander, Hippolyta, and Theseus largely repeat one another, each emphasizing his or her own mocking simile, while adding a negative antithesis to explain it: "not enough to speak, but to speak true"; "a sound, but not in government"; "nothing impaired, but all disordered." Prologue's mispunctuated speech is a heap of parts which do not constitute a whole. The words, misdivided, lack proper meaning. The relation of whole and parts will be a recurring theme of the audience's jibes.

Just before Prologue spoke, Theseus reassured Hippolyta that his pleasure would be not in ridiculing the bungling actors, but in taking kindly what they mistake. Yet, at the first opportunity he mocks the players, and he and the others, including Hippolyta, will continue to do so throughout the artisans' performance. Some commentators suggest that Quince leaves the stage momentarily and is unable to hear the audience's unkind comments.[14] But nothing in Shakespeare's stage directions indicates that he leaves after his first speech or reenters now with the other players (s.d. 5.1.125). Moreover, Bottom and Moonshine, stepping out of character, will soon confirm that the players can hear the audience just as well as the audience can hear the players (5.1.180–85, 231–49). It seems that Hippolyta and Theseus's concern for kindness does not survive the players' first speech.

The audience's behavior, no doubt, partly reflects the fact that the "noble respect" of the few is tantamount to their contempt for the many. The ungracious conduct brings out what is hidden in the noble kindness. Democratic politics does not so much remove as disguise the contempt (cf. 5.1.341–48).[15] But the audience's behavior also comically reflects the players' misunderstanding of dramatic art. The players, fearing that the audience would see them only as their characters, added prologues to their play. Now a prologue, by its nature, breaks through the basic form of a drama, which separates the actors and the audience. In a drama, the actors' actions take place in a world discrete from the audience's. The illusion that the action on the stage is real action rests, paradoxically, on the audience's recognition that it is not. The audience must at once believe and disbelieve the action's reality. The actors must allow the audience both to keep together and to keep apart the dual senses of acting—to do and to simulate. Unlike a narrator, the actors must not, therefore, talk directly to their audience, for to acknowledge the audience is to announce that the action on stage is entirely unreal. A prologue, however, addresses the audience directly. It, literally, announces that the play is just a play and the actors are just actors, as not only Prologue but all the characters (except Thisbe) will soon do. Afraid of creating too much dramatic illusion, the artisans destroy what little they might have had. Theseus and the others in the audience, in fact, see the players as actors—as men in costume rather than as the characters they are presenting. They mock Starveling, for example, for his unmanliness, Snug for his lack of intelligence, and Bottom for being an ass. But even while seeing the players as actors, they treat them as their characters. While usually speaking *of* the players as actors (though as actors having the names and some of the attributes of their characters), they always speak *in front of* them as though they were only the characters they play and not the actors they are. Mimicking the artisans' misunderstanding of their art, they sever the double vision of dramatic illusion. Just as the players break up the wholeness of dramatic illusion into its parts, the members of the audience keep the imitators and their imitations apart. This explains the two biggest puzzles in act 5—the failure of anyone in the onstage audience to note the resemblance of the artisans' play to the actions of Hermia and Lysander and the audience's unkind treatment of the players, contrary to Hippolyta's concern and Theseus's assurance. On the one hand, seeing the actors and not the characters, the audience's members ignore or fail to see the resemblance of Pyramus and Thisbe to Lysander and Hermia. And, on the other hand, treating the actors as their characters, they speak as though the actors were not there and therefore cannot hear what is said about them. We might note that just as the audience begins its unkind bantering as soon as the players begin, it ends it as soon as they finish (5.1.341–48). If the players (unwittingly) parody their own play, their audience (deliberately) parodies the players' grasp of their new art. It imitates their failure to grasp imitation.

Notwithstanding the artisans' efforts, however, Shakespeare preserves some of the necessary discontinuity between the players and their audience. Until now, the nobles have spoken only in verse, while the artisans have spoken only in prose, except when attempting to act (1.2.27–24; 3.1.78–98). Now that the players are performing the play and therefore speaking in verse, the nobles switch to prose. Beginning with their comments on Prologue's performance, the nobles speak only in prose until the players' final exit (5.1.349).

Prologues, traditionally, greet the audience in a few words, often asking for an indulgent hearing. They also sometimes tell the audience what it needs to know in order to understand the plot. Prologue's first speech attempted the former; his second attempts the latter. It introduces the actors and the characters, and describes the plot. Prologue begins, however, with a two-line preface: "Gentles, perchance you wonder at this show; / But wonder on, till truth make all things plain" (5.1.126–27). Prologue twice mentions wonder and will mention it again in just a moment. According to Aristotle, the unfolding of a tragedy's plot should produce wonder. Wonder—the cause of philosophy—is the proper effect of tragedy.[16] As we might expect, Prologue confounds Aristotle's thought. Instead of producing wonder, the unfolding of the players' plot will remove it: "At the which, let no man wonder" (5.1.133).

When introducing the characters and their actors, Prologue treats human and inanimate characters differently. For the two human characters, he uses the verb "is": "This man is Pyramus . . . / This beauteous lady Thisbe is certain" [5.1.128–29]). For the two inanimate characters, he uses the verb "present": "This man . . . doth present / Wall"; "This man . . . / Presenteth Moonshine" (5.1.130–31, 134–35). Where the actor is playing the part of a human, Prologue identifies the actor with his character. Where the actor is playing the part of the scenery, he distinguishes between them. What is true of all the parts Prologue states accurately only where the representation is obviously symbolic. Surprisingly, Prologue treats Lion much the way he treats the human characters. Snug will later deliver the sort of prologue that Quince agreed to write to prevent the ladies from fearing the lion—one that tells Snug's name and reassures them that he is not a real lion (5.1.214–21; cf. 3.1.35–45). But Prologue makes no distinction between the character and the actor playing Lion. In fact, he identifies them more closely than he does with Pyramus and Thisbe. Instead of saying "this man" is Lion, he speaks of Lion as though it were really a lion:

> This grisly beast, which Lion hight by name,
> . . . . . . . . . . . . . . . . . . . . . . . . . . . . . .
> Did scare away, or rather did affright [Thisbe].
>
> (5.1.138–40)

The lion's only "name" is Lion (as Prologue redundantly states), in effect forgetting the reason for Lion's own prologue.

Besides lengthening its meter, Quince fills his prologue with archaic diction to make it seem more dignified or lofty. "Certain" is archaically accented on the second syllable,[17] "hight" is an archaism,[18] and "Lion" (5.1.142), "blade" (5.1.145 [twice]), and "mulburry" (5.1.147) appear, archaically, without an article.[19] To make the prologue seem more learned, Quince includes verbatim translations of some of Ovid's Latin phrases and lines: for example, "To meet at Ninus' tomb"; "conveniant as busta Nini" (5.1.137; Ovid, *Metamorphoses*, 4.88); "And as she fled, her mantle did she fall"; "dumque fugit, tergo velamina lapsa reliquit" (5.1.141; Ovid, *Metamorphoses*, 4.101); and ". . . with bloody mouth"; "cruentato ore" (5.1.142; Ovid, *Metamorphoses*, 4.104).[20] He also includes numerous echoes, some far from exact, of Golding's translation.[21] And, to make the speech seem more poetic, Quince not only lades it with alliteration throughout, but does so with particular excess in describing Pyramus's suicide—an excess unmatched even by Bottom's impromptu poetry (1.2.27–34): "Whereat with blade, with bloody blameful blade, / He bravely broach'd his boiling bloody breast" (5.1.144–45).

Alliteration is not Quince's only sort of repetition. There are redundancy and revision,[22] and frequent echoing of words and phrases.[23] There are also assonance in place of rhyme[24] and monotonous rhythm from start to finish. Nor is the repetition limited to the diction. By narrating all the play's action, Prologue, who speaks far more than any character other than Pyramus, makes the enactment of the play largely superfluous. As a result, the actors, who deliver declamatory speeches instead of performing their parts, mostly repeat, in oratorical tone, what the audience has already been told. They narrate what has just been narrated.

Prologue also seems to miss the principal point of his story. He tells of the wall separating the lovers ("Wall, that vile wall which did these lovers sunder" [5.1.131]), but not of the fathers (cf. 5.1.173, 338). By personifying the wall and imputing moral qualities to it, he eliminates the need for the forbidding fathers.[25]

After Theseus, mocking Prologue, "wonder[s]" (5.1.151) whether the lion will speak, Demetrius, not fully appreciating his own wisecrack, and quibbling on the word "wonder,"[26] says that "one lion may when many asses do" (5.1.151–53). Wall then delivers his own prologue. We can only guess why Quince (or anyone) thinks the prologue is needed. It was not originally planned (cf. 3.1.63–67). In addition to containing its own repetitions[27] and redundancies,[28] the speech itself is repetitious or redundant. While repeating what Prologue just said about "[t]his man" presenting the wall and that the lovers whisper through a chink in it, Wall adds only that his actor's name is Snout (5.1.155) and that the wall contains stone in addition to loam and rough-cast (cf. 5.1.160 with 5.1.130). Wall does, however, expand Prologue's remarks on his dramatic function:

> . . . I, one Snout by name, present a wall;
> And such a wall as I would have you think
> That had in it a crannied hole, or chink. . . .
>
> (5.1.155–57)

Stepping out of character to say who he really is and what he wants the audience to think he is, Wall breaks the very illusion he explicitly intends to create.

As Wall's speech was preceded by a brief exchange between Theseus and Demetrius, it is followed by another, parallel to the first. Both concern speaking. The first, quibbling on "wonder," wondered whether the lion would speak—the same lion (Snug) who is reluctant to speak (cf. 1.2.62–65). The second, quibbling on "partition," praises the wall's ability to speak—the same wall (Snout) who frequently repeats what others say (cf. 3.1.12, 26, 33–34): "It is the wittiest partition that ever I heard discourse, my lord" (5.1.165–66). A "partition" could be either a wall or the division of a formal speech into parts (*partitio*). Here, each meaning is a pun on the other.[29] Where the first exchange settled on Demetrius's quip concerning "one lion" and "many asses," the second settles on the division of a whole into parts.

Bottom, who thought he could move storms playing the part of Pyramus (1.2.21–23), begins with a dozen lines of nearly nothing but exclamations. The lines, shifting quickly from fear, to hope, to gratitude, and to anger, are divided into three pairs of alternately rhymed couplets. The first pair (5.1.168–71) is addressed fearfully to the "grim-look'd," "black" night. With five cries of "O" and three of "alack," Pyramus fears that Thisbe has forgotten her promise. The second pair (5.1.172–75) is addressed hopefully to the "sweet and lovely" wall. With five cries of "O," Pyramus asks to see its chink so he can look through it. The last pair (5.1.176–79) is addressed at first gratefully to the wall, with an invocation to Jove to reward the "courteous" wall, but then, with a cry of "O," angrily to the "wicked" wall, with a curse upon its stones for deception. Pyramus is grateful to the wall for providing a chink, but angry at it for not showing Thisbe on the other side. Pyramus's running, tragic hyperbole is coupled with almost unbroken privation or negativity in the first and last—the fearful and angry—parts. Not only does Pyramus not see Thisbe: "No Thisbe do I see. / . . . I see no bliss" (5.1.177, 178). He also expressly describes night as the absence of day ("O night, which are ever when day is not" [5.1.169]). And underscoring his calls upon the night (which he mentions five times in the first four lines), he thrice utters an exclamation of surprise and woe which (no doubt unwittingly) puns on the word "lack": "O night, O night, alack, alack, alack" (5.1.170). Tragedy goes together with loss.

Pyramus's speech differs altogether from the one he rehearsed in the woods. Originally, Pyramus addressed Thisbe through the wall and, hearing a voice, left her with the promise to return soon (3.1.78–82). His exit allowed for Puck's mischief. Now, his script adheres to the traditional Pyramus and Thisbe story. The lovers agree to flee their fathers and meet in the woods.[30] Pyramus also implicitly corrects Prologue. While Prologue was silent about the lovers' fathers and gave no hint that anything other than "[w]all, that vile wall . . . did these lovers sunder" (5.1.131), Pyramus, though personifying the wall, explains that it "stand'st between her father's ground and mine" (5.1.173). This is the sole mention of the fathers in Quince's final script and one of only two mentions of them in act 5. The other, also out of Bottom's mouth, will make a pair with the first.

Theseus, joking, suggests that the wall, having human senses and intelligence, should curse Pyramus in return: "The wall, methinks, being sensible, should curse again" (5.1.180–81). But Bottom, stepping out of character, rejects Theseus's suggestion, explaining that it goes against the script:

> No, in truth, he should not. "Deceiving me" is Thisbe's cue: she is
> to enter now, and I am to spy her through the wall. You shall see it
> will fall pat as I told you: yonder she comes.
>
> (5.1.182–85)

Bottom has misunderstood Theseus's "should." Theseus meant what the wall ought to do. Bottom thinks he meant what comes next in the play.[31] Seeming intent on making up for his and Flute's (Thisbe's) missed cues in rehearsal (3.1.93–96), Bottom confuses sequence for consequence. What "should" happen is what is to happen.

Thisbe enters and addresses the wall. Accusing it of parting the lovers, she unwittingly gives her complaint an obscene meaning. While all the players are unerotic, and Thisbe is intended to be their play's most virginal character (as Flute is in life), her words are, ironically, the bawdiest in Shakespeare's play. Pyramus, for his part, hearing Thisbe, again confuses the senses: "I see a voice; now will I to the chink, / To spy and I can hear my Thisbe's face" (5.1.190–91). Once they recognize each other, Pyramus and Thisbe begin a lovers' exchange. The exchange, the play's only dialogue, mimics that of Hermia and Lysander (1.1.132ff.), whose situation mirrored theirs. Like Hermia and Lysander, Pyramus and Thisbe, speaking in stichomythia, understand their love in the light of literature. Pyramus and Thisbe, however, mangle their stories in affirming their fidelity. First, they confuse Limander and Helen for Leander and Hero. Leander, separated from his lover by a stretch of water, swam the Hellespont at night to see Hero, until a storm put out the light she used to guide him, and he was drowned. When his body washed up on the shore, Hero threw herself from a tower to die on his corpse.[32] Pyramus thus earnestly declares, "And like Limander am I trusty still." And Thisbe answers in kind, "And I like Helen, till the Fates me kill" (5.1.194–95). Pyramus and Thisbe's mistaken names for the lovers, however, invert their story. While Helen of Troy was notorious for infidelity, "Limander" suggests "Alexander," another—and, in the *Iliad*, the more common—name for Paris, Helen's lover. As stated by Pyramus and Thisbe, the model of faithfulness becomes the model of unfaithfulness.

Pyramus and Thisbe then confuse the names of Cephalus and Procris:

> *Pyr.*: Not Shafalus to Procrus was so true.
> *This.*: As Shafalus to Procrus, I to you.

(5.1.196–97)

The story of Cephalus and Procris is one of fidelity and jealousy, in which jealousy aroused by one goddess (Aurora) and gifts from another (Diana) lead a loving husband to kill his faithful wife inadvertently.[33] Unlike Helen and Paris, Cephalus and Procris were faithful, but they falsely and, finally, fatally distrusted each other. Pyramus and Thisbe mean them as a model of trustiness ("Not Shafalus to Procrus was so true"), but their story is, above all, a cautionary tale of lovers' distrust.

When Pyramus and Thisbe exit to meet "at Ninny's tomb" (5.1.200), Wall breaks out of character again and, as when he first spoke, comments on his character, though this time not distinguishing between himself and his role: "Thus have I, Wall, my part discharged so; / And, being done, thus Wall away doth go" (5.1.202–3; cf. 5.1.154–63). Following Wall's departure, Theseus has two brief exchanges. The first is with Demetrius. Theseus begins by speaking, ironically, with the lovers' hope, as though Prologue had not already told the audience the outcome of the lovers' flight: "Now is the moon used between the two neighbors" (5.1.204).[34] Although the wall parted the lovers, the moon will now unite them. Demetrius, at once personifying the wall and alluding to a proverb ("Walls have ears"[35]), disagrees: "No remedy my lord, when walls are so willful to hear without warning" (5.1.205–6). If walls are so willful as to hear everything without warning, this one will be willful enough to resist its removal. Where Theseus speaks of the moon as a dramatic contrivance, Demetrius speaks of it as the literalization of its personification. The one sees the imitation as an imitation, the other appears to take it at face value.

Theseus's second exchange is with Hippolyta. It explicitly concerns dramatic poetry. Unlike Theseus and Demetrius, who just pretended to take *Pyramus and Thisbe* seriously, though in opposite ways, Hippolyta dismisses it as pure foolishness: "This is the silliest stuff that ever I heard" (5.1.207). Theseus defends the artisans' play, but only by disparaging plays and players as such. "The best in this kind are but images or shadows; and the worst are no worse, if imagination amend them" (5.1.208–9). Because plays and players are nothing but shadows of reality, the best and the worst are the same. Their illusory quality levels them. The worst are no worse than the best, "if imagination amend them." Imagination must improve upon—make up for—the defects of imagination. "It must be your imagination then, and not theirs,"

Hippolyta adds (5.1.210). The spectator's imagination must correct the play-wright's and players'. It must amend the play's images and shadows. The spectator must translate the play's shadowy images back into things that are real. He must make the insubstantial and fabricated real. The spectator must, in effect, use his imagination to cancel the poet's imagination. As in Theseus's speech on imagination (5.1.2–22), realism is everything.

Theseus does not challenge Hippolyta's interpretation of his thought. Instead, he changes the topic and speaks of how the actors imagine themselves—what they think of themselves: "If we imagine no worse of them than they of themselves, they may pass for excellent men" (5.1.211–12). Not surprisingly, for Theseus, the topic of imagination leads directly to the topic of vanity. There is no more substance to the best work of drama than to the high opinion the foolish players have of themselves. Both playwrights and players think that they are excellent, but both, in fact, are poor and empty. What they consider their excellence is nothing but a reflection of their vain imaginations. Thus, seeing two players approach, Moonshine and Lion, Theseus remarks, "Here come two noble beasts, in a man and a lion" (5.1.212–13).[36] Theseus is no doubt playing on the characters' names, Man-in-the-Moon and Lion. But whether he is referring to the characters, the actors, or a combination of the two, at least one actor becomes a beast. Such men may imagine themselves "excellent men," but to Theseus, at best, they are more akin to "noble beasts."

Lion (Snug), as planned, addresses the ladies in the audience, to prevent them from mistaking him for a real lion (cf. 3.1.35–44). First, he describes to them their general tendency to fear and their consequent likely fear, now, of the roaring lion. They whose "gentle hearts" fear even the "smallest. . . mouse," which they consider "monstrous," may now "both quake and tremble here, / When lion rough in wildest rage doth roar" (5.1.214–17). Evidently not realizing that his speaking (if nothing else) belies their fear, Snug, then, tries to disabuse the women of their fear by naming himself and distinguishing between himself and his part, as Bottom counseled (3.1.35–44):

> Then know that I as Snug the joiner am
> A lion fell, nor else no lion's dam;
> For if I should as lion come in strife
> Into this place, 'twere pity on my life.
>
> (5.1.218–21)[37]

The men in the audience, disregarding Snug's attempted distinction, discuss his virtues and vices as a "beast" (5.1.222, 223). They assimilate the actor to his role.[38] "A very gentle beast, and of good conscience," Theseus remarks, referring to Lion's reassurance of the ladies (5.1.222). "The very best at a beast" that he ever saw, Demetrius puns (5.1.223). Lysander, then, using metonymy, begins to substitute the names of other beasts for this one's qualities: "This lion is a very fox for his valour" (5.1.224). This lion is not a lion but a fox: afraid to frighten anyone for fear for his own life, the lion lacks valor. Theseus, extending the joke, pretends to agree. "True, and a goose for his discretion" (5.1.225). Just as he is a fox, not a lion, for valor, so Lion is a goose, not a fox, for discretion: he announces his own selfish concerns in serving others. Lacking both courage and prudence, Snug is neither a lion nor a fox.[39] He knows nothing of war or wisdom. Demetrius ostensibly contradicts Theseus: "Not so, my lord, for his valour cannot carry his discretion; and the fox carries the goose" (5.1.226–27). Demetrius, as though catching Theseus in a self-contradiction, quibbles on the word "carry," using it first to mean support and then to mean carry off or away: Lion's valor (fox) cannot support his discretion (goose), yet the fox carries off the goose. Theseus, concluding the jibe, reverses the terms, while continuing the confusion between supporting and seizing something: "His discretion, I am sure, cannot carry his valour; for the goose carries not the fox" (5.1.228–29). If Snug is "[a] very gentle beast, and of a good conscience," as Theseus initially said, that beast is a stupid, cowardly goose.

Moonshine has the most difficult time of all the players. "This lanthorn doth the horned moon present—," he begins (5.1.231). Moonshine means that the lantern ("lanthorn"[40]) symbolizes the crescent ("horned") moon. Demetrius, resorting to a hackneyed joke,[41] takes the timorous Starveling's slenderness as a sign of his unmanliness and accuses him of being a cuckold: "He should have worn the horns on his head" (5.1.232). Theseus shifts the joke: "He is no crescent, and his horns are invisible within the circumference" (5.1.233–34). Starveling is too thin to be not only a growing ("crescent") moon, but anything other than a new ("invisible") moon. Moonshine, interrupted once, tries again: "This lanthorn doth the horned moon present; / Myself the Man i'th'Moon do seem to be" (5.1.235–36). Again, Moonshine is interrupted. "This is the greatest error of all the rest," Theseus declares, with a confusion of two superlatives; "the man should be put into the lanthorn. How is it else the Man i'the Moon?" (5.1.237–39). Theseus's quip rests on a double literalism, first, regarding the term "Man in the Moon" and, then, taking a symbol for the thing itself. The Man in the Moon should be in the moon; and since the lantern presents the moon, the Man in the Moon should be in the lantern, not carrying it. The part should be in the whole, not the whole in the part. Demetrius, trying to keep up, resumes poking fun at Moonshine's unmanliness. Answering Theseus, he triply puns on the word "snuff": "He dares not come there for [fear of] the candle; for you see he is already in snuff" (5.1.240–41). Already faint and feeble ("in snuff"), Moonshine needs to have the burnt out part of himself ("snuff") removed; and even before that is tried, he is taking offense ("in snuff").

Hippolyta, sounding much like Theseus at the beginning of the play (1.1.3–4), says she is "aweary of this moon. Would he would change!" (5.1.242). And Theseus, sounding much like her in reply to him (1.1.7–8), urges patience. "It appears by the small light of his discretion that he is in the wane," he says, combining ridicule of both Starveling's slender body and his slender wisdom in the slender moon's small light. Showing such little light, the moon will quickly vanish. "[B]ut yet in courtesy," Theseus continues, "in all reason, we must stay the time" (5.1.243–45). The insult is not lost on Starveling. When Lysander orders, "Proceed, Moon" (5.1.246), Moonshine, giving up verse for prose and his dramatic character for his own person, hurriedly sums up what he would have said:

> All that I have to say is, to tell you that the lantern is the moon; I the Man i'th'Moon; this thorn-bush my thorn-bush; and this dog my dog.

> (5.1.247–49)

Exasperated, Moonshine drops not only verse and his role, but the distinction between a likeness and that of which it is a likeness. Instead of the lantern "present[ing]" the moon and Starveling "seem[ing] to be" the Man in the Moon (5.1.235–36), "the lantern is the moon; I the Man i'th'Moon; this thorn-bush my thorn-bush; and this dog my dog."[42] Demetrius concludes the heckling of Moonshine, which he began, by returning to Theseus's joke concerning the incorporation of parts into a whole and to his doubly literal understanding of Moonshine's words: "Why, all these should be in the lanthorn, for all these are in the moon" (5.1.250–51). Whatever is in the moon should be in the lantern, for the lantern is the moon. And the word "thorn" is in the word "lanthorn," and the word "horn" ("the horned moon") is in both words "thorn" and "lanthorn." Hence, the moon ("horn") should be in the bush ("thorn") and the bush ("thorn") in the moon ("lanthorn"). What is true of the words themselves should be true of what they name: the whole should be in the part, and the part should be in the whole. It was Starveling, in particular, who failed to recognize a play as more than the sum of its parts (3.1.13–14).

While nearly all *Pyramus and Thisbe* is narrative, Thisbe's frightened flight is the play's most extended action. Thisbe enters, announces that she is at "old Ninny's tomb" (5.1.252) and looks for Pyramus. But then, frightened away by the roaring lion, she drops her scarf, which the lion tears and bloodies before dropping[43] and running off himself as Pyramus enters. Interestingly, the onstage audience provides Shakespeare's audience with a narrative for the action, addressing the characters directly, while describing, partly with mock praise and partly with direct description, every step, including the moon's shining brightly (5.1.254–60). The onstage audience, in effect, takes on the role of a chorus.

Bottom finally gets to "condole in some measure" (1.2.23). His grand speech contains two parts of equal length (5.1.261–76, 280–95) and largely similar form, each overloaded with nearly continual alliteration, apostrophes, exclamation, repetition, and tortured rhyme. Pyramus begins in confusion— and with a mistranslation of Ovid's "lunae radios" (Ovid, *Metamorphoses*, 4.99)[44]—as he graciously thanks the moon "for thy sunny beams" (5.1.261). Evidently determined to speak in hyperbole, he enhances the moon by substituting the direct light of the sun for the indirect light of the moon, mistaking a reflection for what it reflects. Pyramus thanks the moon, "[f]or by thy gracious, golden, glittering, beams, / I trust to take of truest Thisbe sight" (5.1.263–64). But, his hope quickly turning to fear, he no sooner expresses his trust in seeing Thisbe than he laments what he sees. Seeing her scarf, stained with blood, he concludes the worst:

> But stay! O spite!
> But mark, poor knight,
> What dreadful dole is here?
> Eyes, do you see?
> How can it be?
> O dainty duck! O dear!
> Thy mantle good,
> What stain'd with blood?
>
> (5.1.265–72)

Pyramus's error, constituting the play's tragic "recognition" and "reversal" (Aristotle, *Poetics*, 1452a22–b9), is the opposite of the players' literalness. Where the latter fails to see an image as an image, the former sees what is not a sign as a sign. It sees significance where there is none. Pyramus then cries out:

> Approach, ye Furies fell!
> O Fates, come, come!
> Cut thread and thrum:
> Quail, crush, conclude, and quell.

> (5.1.273–76)

While combining or confusing the Fates and the Furies, Pyramus, piling up passion in a paroxysm of grief, also manages to confuse the Fates with Bottom's own trade. Calling for them to "[c]ut thread and thrum," he implores them to end his life. While the Fates spin, draw out, and cut the thread of life (Hesiod, *Theogony*, 217–22), "thread and thrum" are a weaver's terms referring to his warp ("thread") and its tufted end ("thrum"), which is left attached to the loom when the finished piece of cloth is cut and removed. Unlike the thread, the thrum is unwoven and worth little.

The second part of Pyramus's speech is separated from the first by a brief exchange between Theseus and Hippolyta. Remarking on the very thing that Bottom relished, Theseus says that Pyramus's passion counts for nothing—or even less: "This passion, and the death of a dear friend, would go near to make a man look sad" (5.1.277–78). Hippolyta, however, contrary to her wishes, pities the man: "Beshrew my heart, but I pity the man" (5.1.279). Tragedy is of course intended to arose pity (Aristotle, *Poetics*, 1449b24–28), but Hippolyta seems to mean that she pities the actor, Bottom, rather than his character, Pyramus.

Where the first part of Pyramus's speech began by thanking the moon for its sunny beams, the second part begins by blaming nature for forming lions: "O wherefore, Nature, didst thou lions frame, / Since lion vile hath here deflower'd my dear?" (5.1.280–81). Having misunderstood what he sees, and misstating what he fears, Pyramus tries to describe Thisbe: "Which is—no, no— which was the fairest dame / That liv'd, that lov'd, that lik'd, that look'd with cheer" (5.1.282–83). Besides repeating the apostrophe used lavishly in the first part, Pyramus uses other pompous rhetorical tropes, here, to suit the tragic occasion. He asks Nature a rhetorical question and, then, attempts to demonstrate both his passion and his scrupulousness by interrupting and correcting himself: only the living can be spoken of in the present tense; one must speak of the dead in the past tense. Pyramus also attempts to heighten the dramatic effect with a combination of ploche and alliteration, repeating the same word after intervening words that repeat the same sound. This is the last time Pyramus mentions Thisbe. The rest of his speech is devoted to stabbing himself and dying. Invoking his tears and sword ("Come tears, confound! / Out sword . . ."), and directing his sword to his chest (". . . and wound / The pap of Pyramus, / Ay, the left pap, / Where heart doth hop"), Pyramus, playing to the audience with all he has, stabs himself four times ("Thus die I, thus, thus, thus!") and then only slowly dies:

<blockquote>
Now am I dead,<br>
Now am I fled<br>
My soul is in the sky.
</blockquote>

(5.1.284–92)

Although he could not speak of dead Thisbe in the present tense, Pyramus speaks of himself in the present tense as "dead" and "fled." Able to announce his own death, he is both present and gone. Finally, confusing the organ of speech with the organ of sight ("Tongue, lose thy light" [5.1.293; cf. 4.1.209–12; 5.1.190–91]), and dismissing the moon, whose light he thanked to begin the speech, Pyramus, despite having already declared himself dead, dies at least once again: "Now, die, die, die, die, die" (5.1.295). Unlike Ovid's Pyramus, Quince's never blames himself for Thisbe's imagined death (cf. Ovid, *Metamorphoses*, 4.108ff.).

Demetrius quibbles on Pyramus's reechoed dying word and thought: "No die, but an ace for him, for he is but one" (5.1.296). Whereas a die is one of a pair of dice, an ace is a die marked with one spot. The lowest or worst number with the throw of a die, it is "but one"—a single point. Pyramus is one, not two, for, while a living person is both a body and a soul, the dead are bodies without souls ("My soul is in the sky"). He is "but one" because he is but a body. Lysander, continuing the joke, tries to correct or top Demetrius. "Less than an ace, man; for he is dead, he is nothing" (5.1.297). To be something means to be alive, as Pyramus's rejection of the present tense for the deceased Thisbe suggested. Taking him at his word, Lysander suggests, in order for Pyramus to be one, he must, paradoxically, be two. Unless he is both a body and a soul, he is nothing. No one can ever be simply one; a whole human being is two. Theseus, ostensibly contradicting Lysander, in fact, seconds him. Jesting about Pyramus's repeated deaths (and, like Demetrius earlier, not fully appreciating his own joke [cf. 5.1.152–53]), he puns on the word "ass"/ "ace"[45]: "With the help of a surgeon he might yet recover, and prove an ass" (5.1.298–99). If alive, Pyramus would be an ass and hence be one (an "ace"). Like Snug (Lion) and perhaps Starveling (Moon), Bottom would not be human (cf. 5.1.212–13, 222–29).

When Pyramus, close to dying the final time, bid the moon to "take thy flight" (5.1.294), Moonshine obediently exited. It seems safe to suppose that

Bottom was averse to sharing the audience's attention with anyone, even Moonshine, when Pyramus died. It was his lofty moment. Hippolyta, however, now wonders how it chances that Moonshine is gone before Thisbe returns and finds her lover. And Theseus tells her that Thisbe will find him "by starlight" (5.1.302). The short exchange points to the striking fact that during the scenes in the woods the fairies had the benefit of moonlight, but the lovers did not. There was moonlight for the one ("Ill met by moonlight, proud Titania" [2.1.60; also, e.g., 2.1.141; 3.1.166]), but, notwithstanding Lysander's saying that Hermia and he would flee Athens when "Phoebe doth behold / Her silver visage in the wat'ry glass" (1.1.209–10), only starlight and darkness for the others ("O wilt thou darkling leave me? [2.2.85; also, e.g., 3.2.60–61, 177–82, 187–88, 356, 417–19, 431–33]).[46] "Dark night [may] . . . from the eye his function take" (3.2.177), but a lover's imagination is not blinded by darkness (cf. 1.1.222–23). A lover can see his beloved without light.

Before Thisbe speaks, Theseus says that her "passion" will end the play (5.1.302). He means, by "passion," what he meant when he spoke disparagingly of Pyramus's "passion" (5.1.277). A "passion" is at once the suffering and its expression in words, particularly in a literary composition. It is analogous to what Demetrius will suggest, in a moment, by the word "means" when he says, "And thus [Thisbe] means, videlict—" (5.1.310; cf. 1.1.91–92; 3.2.84–87). The verb "mean," like the noun "passion," signifies at once moaning or lamenting (especially for the dead) and presenting a formal complaint[47]—hence Demetrius's legal term "videlict." Both words combine the soul's passion and its utterance in speech.

When Theseus remarks that Thisbe's passion ends the play, Hippolyta, who has already shown impatience (5.1.242), first responds that Thisbe should not use a long lamentation ("passion") for such a Pyramus, and then she adds, "I hope she will be brief" (5.1.305). These are Hippolyta's final words. Her change seems complete. While in her opening speech Hippolyta thought that the four days until her nuptial hour would pass quickly enough (1.1.7–11), in her closing speech she is eager for the final minutes until midnight to pass quickly.

Demetrius, in his last words on Pyramus, denigrates his manliness, as he had Starveling's or Moonshine's (and Lysander's):

A mote will turn the balance, which Pyramus, which Thisbe, is the better; he for a man, God warrant us; she for a woman, God bless us!

(5.1.306–8)[48]

But while no one else tends to disparage the manliness of others so much as Demetrius does, Thisbe, whom Demetrius, here, chivalrously defends as a woman, inadvertently supports his reproach of the man she loves. Finding Pyramus on the ground, Thisbe first wonders whether he is asleep, but, seeing that he can neither rise nor speak, she concludes that he is dead (cf. 2.2.99–101). Then she describes his face—the colors of his lips, nose, and cheeks. In each instance, she gives a feature of his face an epithet that would seem better suited to a woman than a man: "sweet eyes / . . . lily lips, / . . . cherry nose, / . . . yellow cowslip cheeks" (5.1.317–19; cf., e.g., 2.1.10, 15; 5.1.188, 309).[49] At the same time, Thisbe muddles whether Pyramus—or, more exactly, his face—is present or absent. She first refers to "These . . . lips, / This . . . nose, / These cheeks," using demonstrative adjectives indicating something present or near. But, then, echoing Pyramus (cf. 5.1.282), she concludes, "Are gone, are gone!" (5.1.317–20). What is present is gone.

Like Pyramus, Thisbe calls upon the Fates. She invokes the "Sisters Three" (5.1.323) to come and do to her what she says they did to Pyramus. The Fates should come to her

> With hands as pale as milk;
> Lay them in gore,
> Since you have shore
> With shears his thread of silk.
>
> (5.1.325–28)

Pyramus's "thread and thrum" (5.1.275) have become "his thread of silk." Perhaps especially in death, love idealizes its object. Then, calling upon her tongue not to say a word (5.1.329; cf. 5.1.293), Thisbe takes Pyramus's sword, stabs herself, and dies in five lines and seventeen words (5.1.330–34), in contrast to his eleven lines and fifty words (5.1.285–95). Unlike him, she mentions others ("And farewell, friends" [5.1.332]), not just herself. Yet, Thisbe fails to recognize the tragic crux of her love story. She wants to be killed by Fate, as Pyramus was, and to die by the same sword. But she does not seem to realize that Pyramus died for love of her ("A lover, that kills himself most gallant for love" [1.2.20]). His silence regarding his own responsibility for her imagined death is matched by her silence regarding her responsibility for his death. In Ovid, Pyramus and Thisbe each takes blame for the other's death (Ovid, Metamorphoses, 4.108ff., 151–52). And, telling the dead Pyramus that "of thy death I was the only cause and blame, / So am I thy companion eke and partner in the same," Thisbe asks their apostrophized parents for a common burial:

[W]e whom chaste and steadfast love
And whom even death hath joined in one, may as it doth behoove
In one grave be together laid.

(Ovid, *Metamorphoses*, 4.151–52, 156–57;
Golding, 4.183–84, 189–91)

In Quince's play, however, as Thisbe never recognizes why Pyramus killed himself, she never seeks the union in death that their parents denied them in life. Rather than be buried together, Pyramus is to be buried alone: "A tomb / Must cover thy sweet eyes" (5.1.315–16). Just as their deaths, though a double suicide, are not said to be reciprocal acts of love, so their burials are to be separate.

Theseus, surveying the survivors, says, "Moonshine and Lion are left to bury the dead" (5.1.335). But when Demetrius adds that Wall, too, is left, Bottom, at once rising from the dead and stepping out of character, confidently corrects him: "No, I assure you; the wall is down that parted their fathers" (5.1.337–38). Bottom is the only one to mention fathers in act 5, and, as already suggested, his two references are paired. As Pyramus, Bottom told of the wall "[t]hat stand'st between [Thisbe's] father's ground and mine" (5.1.173). As himself, he now insists that that wall is down. Where the movement of *A Midsummer Night's Dream*, a comedy, is from the authority of fathers to the freedom of their children in marriage, the movement of *Pyramus and Thisbe*, a tragedy, is from the quarreling of fathers to the reconciliation of fathers in the deaths of their children. The authority of fathers in Athens and the wall parting fathers in the artisans' play are both down. "[F]athers" is Bottom's last word on the plot of the artisans' play.[50]

Bottom, however, is not through. Confusing the senses once more, he concludes by offering the onstage audience the choice of "see[ing] the epilogue, or . . . hear[ing] a Bergomask dance" (5.1.339). He has evidently forgotten the ballad he wanted to sing at Thisbe's death (cf. 4.1.212–17). In contrast to the fairies' dances, although perhaps not to the tongs and the bones, a Bergomask dance is a clownish dance mimicking the clumsy movements of the peasants of Bergamo. Here, it amounts to the inept imitating the inept.[51] Theseus, nevertheless, chooses it rather than the epilogue. Offering an excuse for not hearing the epilogue, he tells Bottom and the others that their play "needs no excuse" (5.1.341–42). Epilogues, like prologues, traditionally ask for the audience's indulgence (as Puck's epilogue soon will). Theseus, however, now dropping his open ridicule of the artisans' performance, conceals his criticism in the guise of warm praise and helpful advise:

> Never excuse; for when the players are all dead, there need none to be blamed. Marry, if he that writ it had played Pyramus, and hanged himself in Thisbe's garter, it would have been a fine tragedy—and so it is, truly, and very notably discharged.

(5.1.342–47)

Notwithstanding that his ironic praise confirms that there is indeed blame to be removed, now that the play is over, Theseus, addressing the players as actors and playwright rather than as characters, finally takes what the artisans mistake in might and not in merit.

After the artisans complete their dance and leave, Theseus, hearing a bell strike midnight (and resuming verse), sends all the lovers to bed: "Lovers, to bed; 'tis almost fairy time" (5.1.350). Fairy time, for Theseus, is simply the hours between midnight and dawn. If there is magic then, it is not that of fairies, but of love. Saying that the onstage audience has perhaps stayed awake too long, Theseus offers his summary assessment of the artisans' play: "This palpable-gross play hath well beguil'd / The heavy gait of night" (5.1.353–54). Though conspicuously crude and stupid, the play did indeed "beguile / The lazy time" (5.1.40–41), as Theseus had sought. Just as Theseus initially described his desire and its satisfaction in temporal terms, he does so, again, at the end. Times, however, have changed. Theseus may still find the night's pace to be painfully slow ("[a] heavy gait" [cf. 1.1.3–4]), but, now that it is midnight of his wedding day, "not yet" has become "almost now." Where Theseus began impatient for his nuptial hour and eager for merriments and mirth to distract him (1.1.1–6, 10–15), now he concludes by announcing that there will be two weeks of celebration "[i]n nightly revels and new jollity" (5.1.355). The revels and jollity will accompany the lovers' pleasure, not divert them from their pain.

## 5. Death and Birth

The fairies appear in Athens for the first time. What Theseus meant only figuratively turns out to be literally true. When we initially saw Puck, we heard that he laughs at the harm his pranks cause, though he also helps those who conciliate him with a kind name (2.1.34–42). At the end of act 3, we saw the first signs of a change. Chastised by Oberon, Puck began to care about the happiness of lovers, whose confusions had been mere comedy or "sport" to him (3.2.118–21, 352–53). Now, in Athens, we see the completion of his change. Beneficence replaces sport, kindness replaces comedy, happiness replaces humor. Puck now benefits lovers who know nothing of him, let alone call him Hobgoblin or sweet Puck.

Puck starts by describing three sorts of evils of the night. The first has to do with predatory beasts, the second with screeching owls, and the third with ghosts. Puck will associate the fairies with "triple Hecate's team" (5.1.370). "[T]riple Hecate" refers to the moon goddess's three names: Diana on earth, Phoebe in the sky, and Hecate or Proserpine in the underworld.[52] Each of the night's three sorts of evils—on earth, in the air, from the underworld—corresponds to one of Hecate's names or aspects. Puck's beneficence appears against the background of the night's evils, all of which have to do with death.

The first evil concerns the danger of death:

> Now the hungry lion roars,
> And the wolf behowls the moon;
> Whilst the heavy ploughman snores,
> All with weary task fordone.

> (5.1.356–60)

Much earlier, when narrating the natural disorder caused by their quarreling, Titania described how "[t]he ploughman lost his sweat" (2.1.94), just as the ox labored in vain and the corn rotted while still green. Now the ploughman, exhausted from his work, snores in his sleep. Yet, as Puck seems to emphasize by rhyming "snores" and "roars," although the ploughman does not work in vain, he is nonetheless threatened in his sleep by hungry beasts. He may be "fordone," in a second sense as well.

The second evil concerns imagining one's own death:

> Now the wasted brands do glow,
> Whilst the screech-owl, screeching loud,
> Puts the wretch that lies in woe
> In remembrance of a shroud.

> (5.1.361–64)

Where the first evil pertained to the sleeping, the second pertains to the sleepless. The owl's shrill screech, which is thought to foretell death, forces the ill, sleepless man not only to think of his own death, but to imagine himself as a corpse laid out for burial.

While the first evil concerned the danger of death and the second the thought of dying or of being dead, the third concerns the dead themselves—or, more exactly, their ghosts:

> Now it is the time of night
> That the graves, all gaping wide,
> Every one lets forth his sprite
> In the church-way paths to glide.
>
> (5.1.365–68)

Not just some graves release their ghosts. All of them do, as Puck stresses with redundancy: ". . . the graves, all gaping wide, / Every one lets forth his sprite." At this time of the night, all the dead return to walk ("glide") in churchyards.

With an ambiguous "And," at once connecting and distinguishing them from the nocturnal evils, Puck describes the fairies as being at home in the night's darkness and yet frolicsome and wishing to protect Theseus's house:

> And we fairies, that do run
> By the triple Hecate's team
> From the presence of the sun,
> Following darkness like a dream,
> Now are frolic; not a mouse
> Shall disturb this hallow'd house.
>
> (5.1.369–74)

Echoing Oberon's concession that they have to flee the early morning light (4.1.94–95), Puck confirms that the fairies run from the presence of the sun and follow darkness. They are creatures of the night. At the same time, though, Puck confirms that the fairies are "spirits of another sort" (3.2.388). They are not only playful and well disposed; they even perform good deeds: "I am sent with broom before / To sweep the dust behind the door" (5.1.375–76).[53] If Puck initially caused people to labor in vain, in the end he does their drudgery. His final transformation is his domestication.

Oberon and Titania enter, followed by their royal train. Their final appearance is paired with their first (cf. 2.1.59 s.d.). This time, however, they have come to sing and dance. Instead of quarreling over a young boy, they will bless the newly married couples and their offspring. Oberon orders the fairies to give "glimmering light" through the house near the now-dim fires (5.1.377). The "glimmering night" (2.1.77) through which Oberon had said

Titania led Theseus to desert numerous women has become the "glimmering light" with which Oberon orders the fairies to bless his marriage. The taming of the fairies goes together with the moderating or the civilizing of Athens's founder.

Titania has also changed. Oberon, using the word "light" to denote both the illumination of the house and the weightlessness of their hops (5.1.377, 380), urges the fairies to "[s]ing, and dance" their song nimbly ("trippingly") (5.1.382). Titania, at least partly correcting him, instructs the fairies to learn, first, to sing the song well:

> First rehearse your song by rote,
> To each word a warbling note;
> Hand in hand, with fairy grace,
> Will we sing, and bless this place.

(5.1.383–86)

Titania had emphasized that Oberon's disruption of her dances with her fairies caused their quarrel and its consequences (2.1.82ff., 140–42). And when they finally reconciled, Oberon, asking her to call for music, bid Titania to dance with him, saying that tomorrow they will "[d]ance in Duke Theseus's house triumphantly, / And bless it to all fair posterity" (4.1.88–89). Titania has almost always stressed dancing at least as much as singing.[54] As indicated by the double meaning of "roundel" (2.2.1), songs and dancing have gone together, for her. Now, however, preparing to bless the married couples and their posterity, Titania emphasizes song rather than dance. And just as the song is prior to the dance ("[f]irst rehearse your song by rote"), so, too, its words are prior to the music ("[t]o each word a warbling note"). Music is to be added to the words, as the dance is to be added to the song. For Titania, now in Athens, "word[s]" are the core of a "bless[ing]."[55]

Oberon begins by ordering each fairy to "stray" through the house "until the break of day" (5.1.388–89). As is their wont, the fairies are to wander, and do so until dawn. Oberon and Titania, however, will bless Theseus and Hippolyta's bed:

> To the best bride-bed will we,
> Which by us shall blessed be;
> And the issue there create
> Ever shall be fortunate.

(5.1.389–92)

The king and queen of the fairies are to bless the Duke and Duchess, in particular. Yet, all three couples will receive the same benefits:

> So shall all the couples three
> Ever true in loving be;
> And the blots of Nature's hand
> Shall not in their issue stand.
>
> (5.1.393–96)

The fairies are to protect or protect against two things especially subject to chance: true love and birth defects. And both benefits will be continuous. The couples' true love is to be for "[e]ver," while their children's birth deformities are to be "[n]ever" (5.1.397).[56] While Shakespeare's play has shown dangers to true love, Oberon lists dangers of birth defects:

> Never mole, hare-lip, nor scar,
> Nor mark prodigious, such as are
> Despised in nativity,
> Shall upon their children be.
>
> (5.1.397–400)

Oberon speaks only of visible defects. The defects to be averted are ugly as distinguished from harmful. They cause a person not to be ill, but to be despised. They work against being loved (cf. 2.2.89ff.). Oberon then adds a third blessing. He instructs every fairy to take some consecrated field dew and bless separately the rooms in the palace "with sweet peace" (5.1.404). It should come as no surprise that Oberon would appreciate the need for peace in marriage. Oberon then concludes the song by ordering the fairies to meet him before dawn. As he began the song by rhyming "break of day" with "stray" (5.1.387, 388), he ends it, and the play proper, by rhyming "stay" with "break of day" (5.1.407–8). The fairies have a role in Athens only after everyone has gone to bed and only in the beds of married lovers.

Oberon's final song speaks of the newly married couples as future parents. No one has spoken of them that way before. Lysander once spoke of the "nativity" of what is his, but he meant the word metaphorically. He spoke of his "vows . . . born" in tears, in whose "nativity all truth appears" (3.2.124–25). The nativity of vows has been replaced by the nativity of children. Natural generation returns to Athens with the marriages of the lovers.

Puck's speech regarding night and the prospect of death prepared the way for Oberon and Titania's speeches regarding night and the blessing of birth.

Death and birth imply each other. Mortality is an essential precondition for generation, and night seems as much associated with the one as with the other. The fairies' blessing requires the recognition of death's inevitability.

We must wonder, though, how effective the royal fairies' blessing will be. *A Midsummer Night's Dream* is a comedy. Unlike *Pyramus and Thisbe*, it ends happily. Oberon and Titania's blessing might lead us to believe that the three couples live happily ever after. Yet, Shakespeare places at the heart of a comedy of love an ancient hero whom earlier playwrights placed at the heart of tragedies of love. Although Shakespeare's ancient sources usually identify Theseus's bride as Antiopa,[57] Shakespeare calls her Hippolyta, while relegating Antiopa to ranks of the many women Theseus deserted in the glimmering night (2.1.80). Shakespeare gives to Theseus's bride a name which is the feminine form of Hippolytus. He thus calls attention to the tragic story of Theseus's son, Hippolytus. Hippolytus was devoted to the hunt and the virgin Diana, spurning Aphrodite, who punished him by afflicting his stepmother, Phaedra, with an overwhelming passion for him. When Hippolytus rejected Phaedra, she accused him to Theseus of having raped her. Theseus believed her and prayed to Poseidon, who, granting Theseus's prayer for his son's destruction, caused Hippolytus's death.[58] Just as Theseus was responsible for his father's death, he was also responsible for his son's. Phaedra, the last of four stepmothers in *A Midsummer Night's Dream*, is paired with Medea, the first, whose presence is also only implied. Both women attempt to kill their stepsons, one of whom is Theseus himself and the other his son. If comedy draws upon tragedy in *A Midsummer Night's Dream*, in general, and in *Pyramus and Thisbe*, in particular, Oberon's final song points up that tragedy may never be far beneath the surface. Like so much else in *A Midsummer Night's Dream*, it seems present in its absence—present as a shadow. The fairies' magical power may avert ugly birth defects in Theseus's children, but just as their charm did not protect Titania (2.2.1–33), their blessing will not prevent Theseus's family's tragic end. It is perhaps no accident that Neptune (Poseidon) is the only god Titania ever mentions and the only Olympian Oberon ever mentions other than Cupid, Venus, and Diana (2.1.126; 3.2.392). For all the difference between the two cities, Theban self-slaughter is not altogether foreign to Athens. Thebes, as we have seen, stands for the love of one's own and hence ancestry and birth, while Athens stands for the love of the beautiful and hence reason and freedom. Theseus's founding act amounts to the overthrow of Thebes's fundamental principle. Yet, unlike Lysander's aunt's placeless place (1.1.156–63), no real city can exist without generation. No real city can fully replace birth by choice. And, hence, no real city can exist without at least the potential for the fundamental conflicts or tensions that gives rise to tragedy. Even the city that frees love from the authority of fathers—that frees the love of the beautiful from the love of one's own—cannot ignore or escape the effects of generation and succession, birth and death. Only by pointing beyond the family and the city—only by pointing away from the subpolitical and the political to the transpolitical—can Athens, or any city, escape the shadow of tragedy. Within the city or the family, the requirements of the soul's double nature can never be wholly satisfied.

## 6. Comedy and Tragedy

A *Midsummer Night's Dream* might have been expected to end several times—after the resolution of the love stories and the Athenians' return to Athens, after the *Pyramus and Thisbe* performance, or, certainly, after Oberon's song. But Shakespeare has Puck deliver an epilogue. Quince, beginning his prologue, said—or meant to say—that "[i]f we offend," we came "not to offend" (5.1.108–9). And Theseus, wanting to hear "[n]o epilogue" (5.1.341), admonished the players, "Never excuse" (5.1.242). But Puck, addressing Shakespeare's audience directly, says, "If we shadows have offended . . ." (5.1.409), and then offers an apology or excuse—or at least promises to make amends—for the offense. Puck's epilogue, which is and is not part of the play, mirrors part of the play. It also mocks both the play and its audience.

Like the players, Puck steps out of his role and addresses the audience not as a character but as an actor playing a character. He breaks the dramatic illusion by talking about the play and the players rather than performing in the play. Yet, he retains his character's name: "I am an honest Puck" (5.1.417), "Else the Puck a liar call" (5.1.421), "And Robin shall restore amends" (5.1.424). Thus, Puck, who called Oberon "king of shadows" (3.2.347), now calls the actors "shadows" (5.1.409), just as Theseus called even the best plays and players "shadows" (5.1.208). The difference between the actors and their characters virtually vanishes. So, too, does the difference between the characters and the audience. Puck, who as a character was himself both "auditor" and "actor" (3.1.75–76), tells the audience what to think if they have been offended by what might appear to them a trifling play. They are to do what the lovers did after their night in the woods. Just as Oberon said that when the lovers awake "all this derision / Shall seem a dream and fruitless vision" (3.2.370–71; also 4.1.67–68), Puck tells Shakespeare's audience to

> Think but this. . . .
> That you have but slumber'd here
> Whiles these visions did appear.
> And this weak and idle theme,
> No more yielding but a dream,
> Gentles, do not reprehend.

$$(5.1.410\text{--}15)$$

The spectators are to think that what they saw was a dream, not a drama. They are to take the lovers' "dream"—and Shakespeare's *Dream*—for their own dream. Puck's addressing the audience directly breaks the dramatic illusion in one way; his suggesting that they think of the play as a dream breaks it in the opposite way. The former does so by distinguishing the actor from his role; the latter, by suppressing the distinction between a resemblance and what it resembles. No one seems less like the players than does Puck. Yet, his suggestion ironically mimics them. By turning the drama into a dream, Puck would transform Shakespeare's play into the artisans' literal understanding of a play, while his addressing the audience directly reproduces their device for avoiding blame. As we saw in the central section of the central scene of the play (3.1.73–123), an excess of the literal and an excess of imagination appear together just where one might most expect them to remain apart.

Yet, Puck's apology is highly qualified. It is addressed not to all of Shakespeare's audience, but only to those who have been "offended"—those who think the play is a "weak and idle theme." Tragedy, not comedy, might suit most people (Plato, *Laws*, 658d3–5, 817b1–c1). Puck's apology is thus no apology, at all. Instead of apologizing for the play, it pointedly if implicitly blames those who think it needs an apology. It tells those who find the play trivial to think that they "have but slumber'd here / While these visions did appear." In an important sense, they have. At least in this respect, Puck is indeed "an honest Puck."

Puck promises to make amends if the audience will pardon the actors: "Gentles, do not reprehend. / If you pardon, we will mend" (5.1.415–16). "Mend" and "amends" (5.1.410, 416, 420, 424) are the major theme of Puck's speech, as they are of the artisans' proper crafts:

> And, as I am an honest Puck,
> If we have unearned luck
> Now to 'scape the serpent's tongue,
> We will make amends ere long;
> Else the Puck a liar call.

$$(5.1.417\text{--}21)$$

Yet, both as character and as actor, Puck is of course a liar. As a character, he is a mischievous sprite who deliberately leads people astray, by making them mistake the false for the true and the true for the false. And as an actor, he, like any actor, is always pretending to be what he is not. He is, in fact, more than doubly dishonest. He is an actor playing a deceiver, and he only compounds his lying by claiming to be "an honest Puck," which he claims, furthermore, just when he is being most ironical.

Puck, bidding the audience goodnight, concludes his excuse by offering amends as Puck the actor. Punning with his final word on "ends," he promises that in return for the audience's applause "Robin shall restore amends" (5.1.424). He shall make up for the play's defects by providing something better in the future than a "weak and idle" play. If Theseus spoke down to the players in declining their epilogue, Puck speaks down to part of Shakespeare's audience in delivering his own. He speaks to those who think of A Midsummer Night's Dream as Hippolyta thinks of Pyramus and Thisbe ("This is the silliest stuff that ever I heard" (5.1.207; cf. 5.1.210) and Theseus thinks of plays, in general ("shapes . . . give[n] to airy nothing" [5.1.16]). The seriousness of tragedy seems to speak for itself. One could easily believe that tragedy is the truth of life. It would be hard to think that of comedy. Socrates suggests that a tragic poet could also be a comic poet, but not the converse (Plato, Symposium, 223d3–6). Shakespeare seems to parody the implication of Socrates's suggestion by having the artisans inadvertently transform their tragedy into a comedy— into a parody of a tragedy. But he also seems to ratify the suggestion by having A Midsummer Night's Dream mirror the Pyramus and Thisbe story, while, furthermore, framing the play with Medea and Phaedra, and suffusing it with numerous shadows of Athens's defeated and victorious enemies. In an untoward way Starveling is correct when he says, "I believe we must leave the killing out, when all is done" (3.1.13–14). Literally, from beginning to end, the comedy of A Midsummer Night's Dream rests on tragedy averted.

## Notes

1. For the pun on "antique," see Kökertiz, 334.

2. See, e.g., William Wordsworth, Prelude, 12.201–7 (Text of 1805); Preface to Lyrical Ballads (text of 1802), ed. W. J. B. Owen (London: Oxford University Press, 1969), 165; William Blake, A Vision of the Last Judgment, 69–70, in The Complete Writings of William Blake, ed. Geoffrey Keynes (London: Nonesuch Books, 1957),

60506. *The Marriage of Heaven and Hell*, 12–13, Keynes 173; *Annotations to Berkeley's "Siris,"* Keynes 773; *The Laocoön*, Keynes 776.

3. Cf. Aristotle, *Poetics*, 1452a1–11; 1460a11–18.

4. They resume addressing Theseus as "my lord" at 5.1.120 but cease, again, after 5.1.226.

5. Hence, the double meaning of "abridgement" (5.1.39), a shortening of time and of text; see *OED*, s.v. Abridgement.

6. Diodorus Siculus, 4.12.1–6; Apollodorus, *Library*, 2.5.4; Virgil, *Aeneid*, 8.293–95.

7. For Theseus's kinship with Hercules, see Plutarch, *Theseus*, 7.1.

8. Ovid, *Metamorphoses*, 12.210–44; cf. 12.536ff.; Plutarch, *Theseus*, 30.3; Apollodorus, *Epitome*, 1.21.

9. Ovid, *Metamorphoses*, 10.1–85; 11.1–43.

10. In fact, the actual literary work to which it most likely alludes is not classical at all, but Renaissance in origin; see Edmund Spenser, "The Teares of the Muses," in *Complaints* (1591), *The Yale Edition of the Shorter Poems of Edmund Spenser*, ed. William A. Oram, et al. (New Haven: Yale University Press, 1989).

11. See, e.g., Juvenal, *Satire One*, 79. See, further, Blits, *Deadly Thought*, 144–45.

12. Abbott, § 97.

13. While Hippolyta twice speaks of "lover[s]," referring to the young Athenians and Pyramus (5.1.1, 301), the phrase "I love not to see" is the only time she speaks of her own love. For the Amazons' declared war on love itself and not just on men, see Boccaccio, 1.24.

14. E.g., Watkins and Lemmon, 125; Anne Barton, "*A Midsummer Night's Dream*," in *The Riverside Shakespeare*, ed. G. Blakemore Evans (Boston: Houghton Mifflin Co., 1974), 219–20.

15. For the Greek contempt for artisans, see, e.g., Herodotus, 2.167.

16. Aristotle, *Poetics*, 1452a1–11, 1460a11–18; *Metaphysics*, 982b12–17.

17. Kittredge, 199.

18. Schmidt, s.v. Hight.

19. Abbott, § 82.

20. Anthony Brian Taylor, "Golding's Ovid, Shakespeare's 'Small Latin,' and the Real Object of Mockery in 'Pyramus and Thisbe,'" *Shakespeare Survey*, 42 (1990), 61.

21. See Brooks, 149–53.

22. E.g., "hight by name" (5.1.138); "Did scare away, or rather did affright" (5.1.140).

23. E.g., "this show," "This man," "This . . . lady," "This man," "This man," "This beast" (5.1.126, 128, 129, 130, 138); "Wall, that . . . wall" (5.1.131); "there, there" (5.1.137); "did . . . sunder," "did . . . think," "Did scare," "did affright," "did fall," "did stain" (5.1.131, 136, 140 [twice], 141, 142); "if you would know," "if you will know" (5.1.128, 135); "trusty Thisbe," "trusty Thisbe's" (5.1.139, 144); "with blade, with . . . blade" (5.1.145); "bloody . . . blade," "bloody breast" (5.1.145–46); "let no man," "Let

Lion" (5.1.133, 149); "perchance you wonder," "wonder on," "Let no man wonder" (5.1.126, 127, 133).

24. E.g., "plain" and "certain" (5.1.127, 129).

25. As though to underscore the elimination, Snout, who plays Wall, was originally cast as Pyramus's father (1.2.58–59).

26. Switching the sense from "I would like to know" to "Do not be surprised."

27. E.g., "I, one Snout by name, present a wall"; "I am that same wall" (5.1.155, 161); "Through which the lovers," "Through which the . . . lovers" (5.1.158, 163); "That I," "That I" (5.1.155, 161); "this . . . interlude," "This loam, this rough-cast, . . . this stone," "this . . . cranny" (5.1.154, 160, 162) .

28. E.g., "a crannied hole, or chink" (5.1.157); "the lovers, Pyramus and Thisbe" (5.1.158).

29. For the pun, see, e.g., Cicero, *Topics*, 27.

30. The only resemblance between the artisans' original version and Ovid's is the reference to Ninus's tomb, which Bottom, of course, botches: cf. 3.1.92 and Ovid, *Metamorphoses*, 4.88; 4.108, Golding.

31. Kittredge, 199.

32. Virgil, *Georgics*, 3.258–63; Ovid, *Heroides*, 18–19; Musaeus, *Hero and Leander*.

33. Ovid, *Metamorphoses*, 7.661–865.

34. Here, I follow the Quartos. The Folios read, "Now is the moral down. . . ." Many contemporary editors follow Pope's conjecture: "Now is the mural down . . ."; see Furness, 221. For "Now is the mure rased . . . ," see Brooks, Appendix II, 159–62.

35. Tilley, W19.

36. The Folios and Quartos place the comma after "beasts." Rowe (1709), who is followed by most modern editors, moves it to follow "in."

37. On the grammatical difficulties in the second line, see Furness, 224–25.

38. It is perhaps worth noting that, although his disclaimer closely follows Bottom's original formulation, Snug omits stating explicitly that "'I am a man, as other men are'" (cf. 5.1.218–21 with 3.1.40–44).

39. Cf. Machiavelli, *The Prince*, ch. 18.

40. The modernized spelling obscures the pun on "horn." "The form *lanthorn* is prob. due to popular etymology, lanterns having formerly been almost always made of horn." *OED*, s.v. Lantern.

41. Tilley, H625.

42. The thorn bush and the dog are associated with the moon and the Man in the Moon only symbolically and only by moldy legends. See Ben Jonson, *News from the New World Discovered in the Moon*, in *The Works of Ben Jonson*, ed. W. Gifford, 9 vols. (London: Bickers and Son, 1875), 7:339. Quince mentions the bush of thorns but not the dog at the players' rehearsal (3.1.55–56). Caliban mentions both; see *The Tempest*, 2.2.141, Arden Edition, ed. Frank Kermode (London: Methuen, 1962). Dante describes Cain with his bush of thorns appearing in the moon (Dante, *Inferno*,

20.124–26; also *Paradise*, 2.51). According to another legend, the man in the moon is one who stole a bundle of thorns and was banished to the moon forever; see Jacob Grimm, *Teutonic Mythology*, 4 vols. (London: George Bell and Sons, 1883; rpt. New York: Dover Books, 1966), 2:717–19.

43. In Ovid's account, the lion's jaws are dripping with the blood of fresh-slain cattle (Ovid, *Metamorphoses*, 4.96–98). Quince's script does not explain the blood.

44. Taylor, 61.

45. On their similar pronunciation, see Kökeritz, 89.

46. "The young couples, so long as they are in the wood, at no time make the slightest reference to the moon as actually shining. There is merely a rhetorical image referring to the moon in one of Hermia's speeches [3.2.52–55]. But they do complain of darkness." Smidt, 131. Similarly, the artisans speak of the moon as shining before they enter in the wood (1.2.95), but, once there, they speak of it as shining only when they consult a calendar, and only in regard to the night of the play. Even then, they substitute an impersonation of the moon for the moon itself (3.1.46–58). The shining moon becomes Moonshine.

47. See *OED*, s.v. Mean, v². Thisbe uses the similarly ambiguous cognate "moan" (5.1.186, 321).

48. If Demetrius's words are addressed to Hippolyta, this is the only time anyone but Theseus speaks to her.

49. Note Pyramus's own implicit confusion in stabbing himself in the "pap" (5.1.286, 287).

50. "[F]ather" is also Hermia's final word (4.1.195).

51. Brissenden, 45.

52. Hesiod, *Theogony*, 411ff.; Ovid, *Metamorphoses*, 7.94, 194.

53. For the ambiguity of Hecate, at once terrible and benign, cf., e.g., Sophocles, frag. 534–35, Euripides, *Medea*, 397, Theocritus, 2.12–16, Horace, *Satires*, 1.8.33, and Apollonius Rhodius, *Argonautica*, 3.1035ff., on the one hand, and Hesiod, 450, and Aeschylus, *The Suppliant Maidens*, 676, on the other.

54. The only exceptions are in connection with Bottom (3.1.132–33, 152; 4.1.27) and when she accuses Oberon of playing on pipes of corn for Phillida (2.1.66).

55. Notwithstanding what modern editors often indicate in their stage directions (e.g., Brooks, s.d. 5.1.387; Holland, s.d. 5.1.392; Wells, s.d. 5.1.390), it is not certain that anyone dances to what follows (5.1.387–408). Stage directions in neither the Quarto nor the Folio call for a dance. Nor is it clear whether the lines are the "ditty" that Oberon mentions (5.1.381) or the "song" (5.1.383) that Titania wants the fairies to sing—or even whether they are a song. While the Folio marks them as "The Song," and indents and italicizes them as a song (without assigning them to any character), the First Quarto prints the lines in roman as a speech and gives them to Oberon. Although Shakespeare usually differentiates his songs metrically (e.g., 2.2.9ff.), these lines have the same meter as the previous part of the

fairies' dialogue (5.1.357ff.). Despite these difficulties, however, for persuasive reasons to consider them a song, with Oberon in the lead and the other fairies joining in, see Richmond Noble, *Shakespeare's Use of Song* (Oxford: Oxford University Press, 1923), 55–56.

56. Five of Oberon's twenty-two lines begin with "[e]ver," "[n]ever," or "[e]very" (5.1.392, 394, 397, 402, 406).

57. E.g., Plutarch, *Theseus*, 26, 28; Ovid, *Metamorphoses*, 15.552; also Pausanius, 1.2.1. Plutarch reports only one writer who says that the Amazon Theseus married was Hippolyta; Plutarch, *Theseus*, 27.4.

58. Euripides, *Hippolytus*; Plutarch, *Parallel Stories*, 34; Ovid, *Metamorphoses*, 15.497; Apollodorus, *Epitome*, 1.17–19.

~

# Index

Actaeon, 145, 160n10
Aegeus (Theseus's father), 9, 151, 197
Aeschylus, 203n53
Alexander (Paris), 181, 182
Amazon taste, 21, 30, 144–45
anger, 120, 127, 148
Antiopa, 197
Aphrodite. *See* gods
Apollo. *See* gods
Apollonius Rhodius, 203n53
Ariadne, 150
Arion, 65
Aristotle, 34, 158–59, 177, 186, 187
art: defeated by madness, 169–70;
    excellence of vs. authority of age,
    146; and life, 6, 34–35, 82, 95, 112,
    121–22, 167, 172; replaces the gods,
    151; of love, 23, 37–38; vs. love, 41;
    vs. nature, 82. *See also* Athens,
    comedy, dramatic illusion,
    imagination, love, poetry, tragedy
Athena. *See* gods
Athens: and art, 2, 10, 13, 43, 145–46,
    151, 158, 172; core of, 2; vs. Crete
    and Sparta, 146, 151; and democracy,

27, 150, 158–59, 168, 176;
development of, 142, 143–46;
enemies of, 12, 200; and productive
arts, 10–11, 15n26, 43; two calendars
of, 151–52; union of families, 150;
and fathers, 22–26, 45, 150–51, 191;
foundation of, 22, 24, 150–51; and
founder of, 166; and generation,
196–98; metonymy for the soul, 4;
and Pericles, 1, 158–59; piety largely
irrelevant in, 151; and the private
realm, 1–2, 24–25; vs. Rome, 2, 150,
151, 152; Shakespeare's equivocal
presentation of, 10–14; vs. Thebes,
22, 144, 170, 197; and tragedy, 10,
197–98; universalism of, 13–14; and
"utopia," 34, 197–98. *See also* choice,
Duke, gods, heroes, love
Aurora (Eos), 131, 182
autochthonism, and fratricide, 12, 22,
143–44. *See also* Thebes

beauty: comparisons of, 81, 125; of the
beloved's eyes, 7, 42, 80–81, 84. *See
also* love

205

~

# About the Author

Jan H. Blits is professor, University Honors Faculty, at the University of Delaware. He received his B.A. from St. John's College, Annapolis, Maryland, and his Ph.D. from the New School for Social Research in New York City. He has served as Secretary of the Navy Distinguished Fellow at the U.S. Naval Academy and has won the University of Delaware's Excellence in Teaching Award. He is the author of *The End of the Ancient Republic: Shakespeare's "Julius Caesar,"* and *The Insufficiency of Virtue: "Macbeth" and the Natural Order*, both published by Rowman & Littlefield. His book *Deadly Thought: "Hamlet" and the Human Soul* was published by Lexington Books, an imprint of the Rowman & Littlefield Publishing Group. His articles have appeared in *Political Theory, The Journal of Politics, Interpretation, Educational Theory, The Southern Journal of Philosophy, Apeiron,* and other journals.